Art
In
Black & White

Les Kaluza

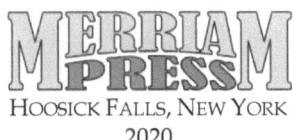

MERRIAM PRESS
HOOSICK FALLS, NEW YORK
2020

Les Kaluza

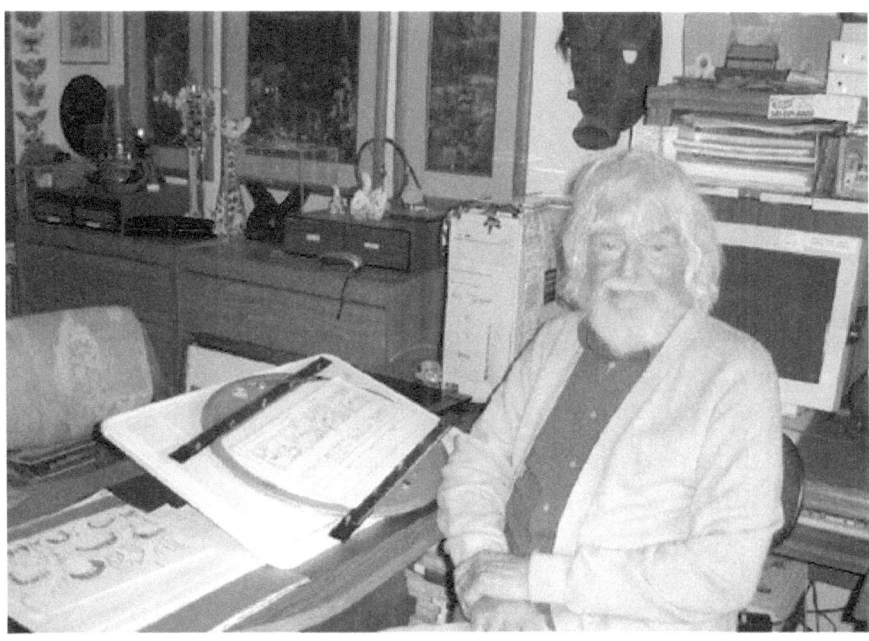

My dear husband, Les, was born in Poland and from an early age he enjoyed drawing; he fell in love with animated films and became an accomplished animator/layout artist.

In 1960 he and I moved to the USA. First to New York, where we found work at the Paramount animation studios, working on "Popeye", "Beetle Bailey" and others.

Four years later we moved to Hollywood and were hired by Hanna-Barbera. We worked on "The Flintstones", "The Jetsons" and many others. Les was in the animation department, and I in ink and paint.

We also worked for Filmation on such shows as "The Archies", "Sabrina and the Groovey Ghoolies" and the features "Flash Gordon", "Back to Oz", etc. Again Les was in the Animation Department and he also was a layout supervisor.

He also produced several animated shorts on his own, which were shown at Intern. Film Festivals all over the world.

Later on he was asked by Bill Hanna if he wanted to supervise the production of "The Flintstone Kids" and "The Snorks" in Poland. He accepted. The work was done in the same studio in which he had worked before we moved to the USA. It was a joyous reunion with his former colleagues.

When this work was finished, we supervised the production of animated shows and features in Seoul, South Korea.

In 2002 we retired and Les spent his time painting and writing his memoirs *Once Upon A Time There Was A War* (also published by Merriam Press.) We also have an art book published.

Unfortunately in late 2017 Les became very ill and, after several months in and out of hospitals, he passed away in June of 2018.

I miss him terribly!

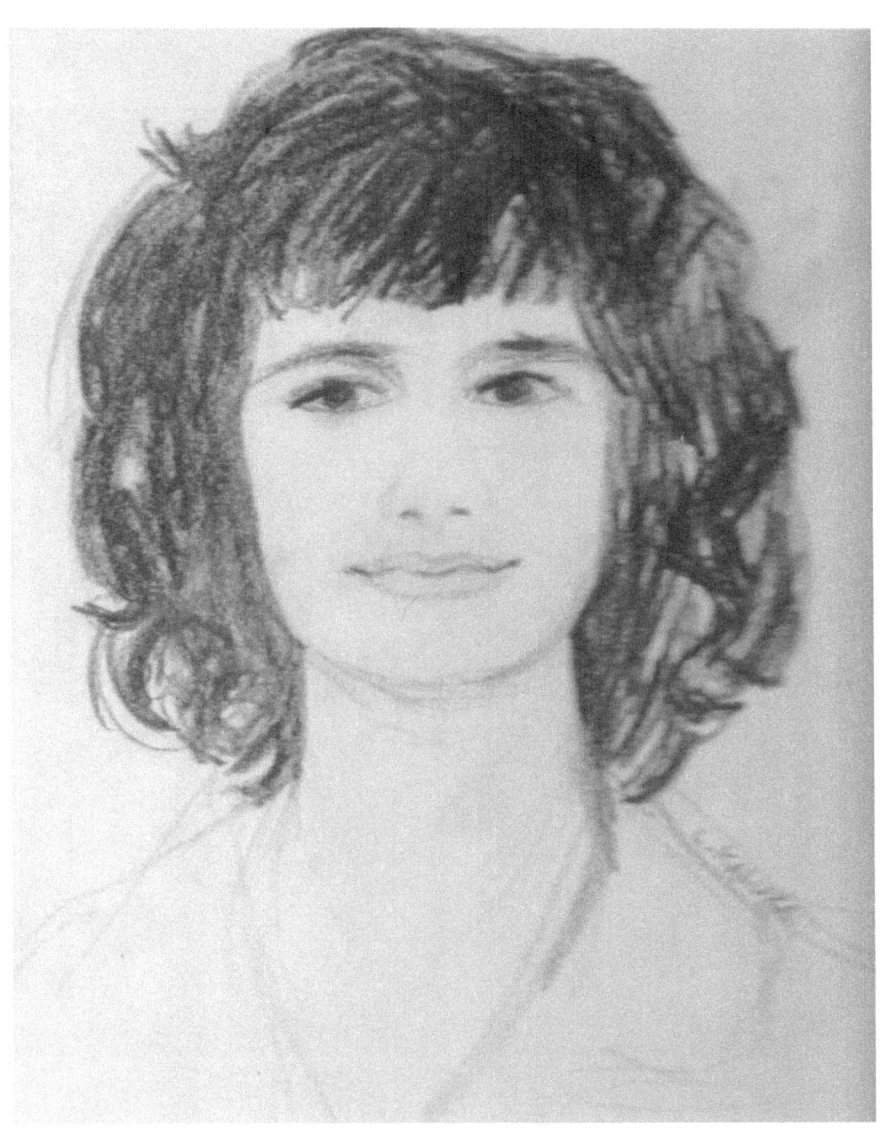

Erna Kaluza portrait by Les Kaluza.

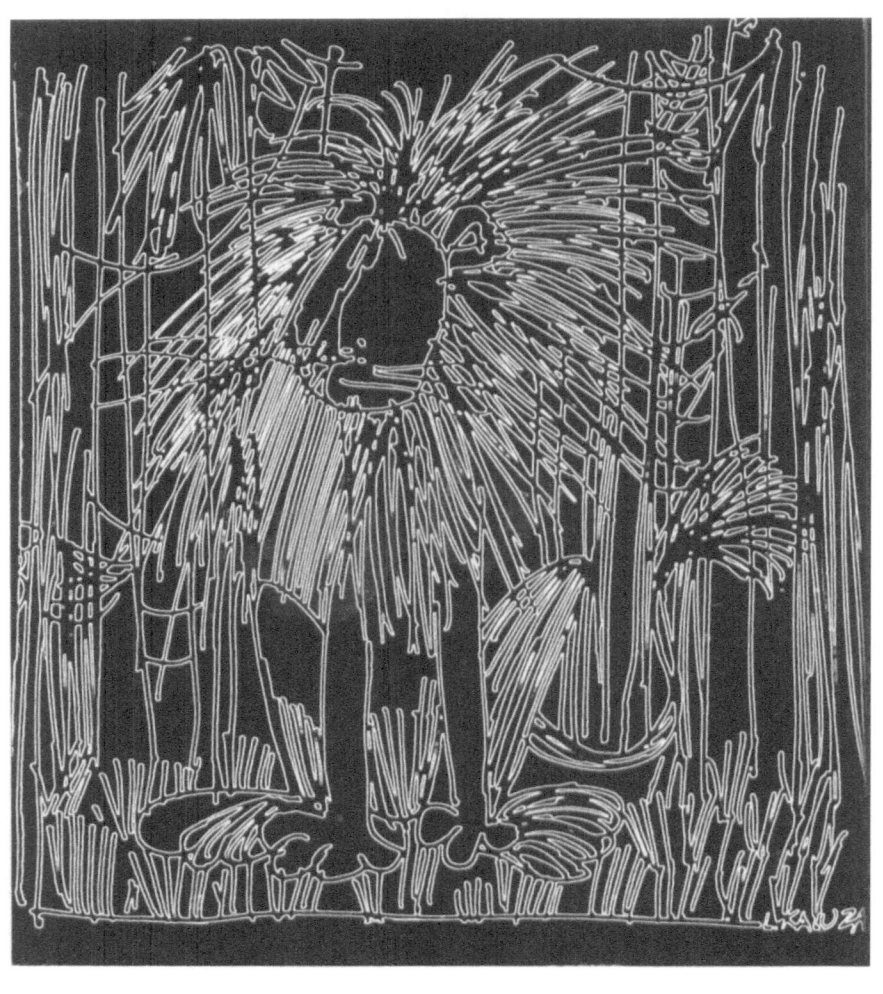

Lion

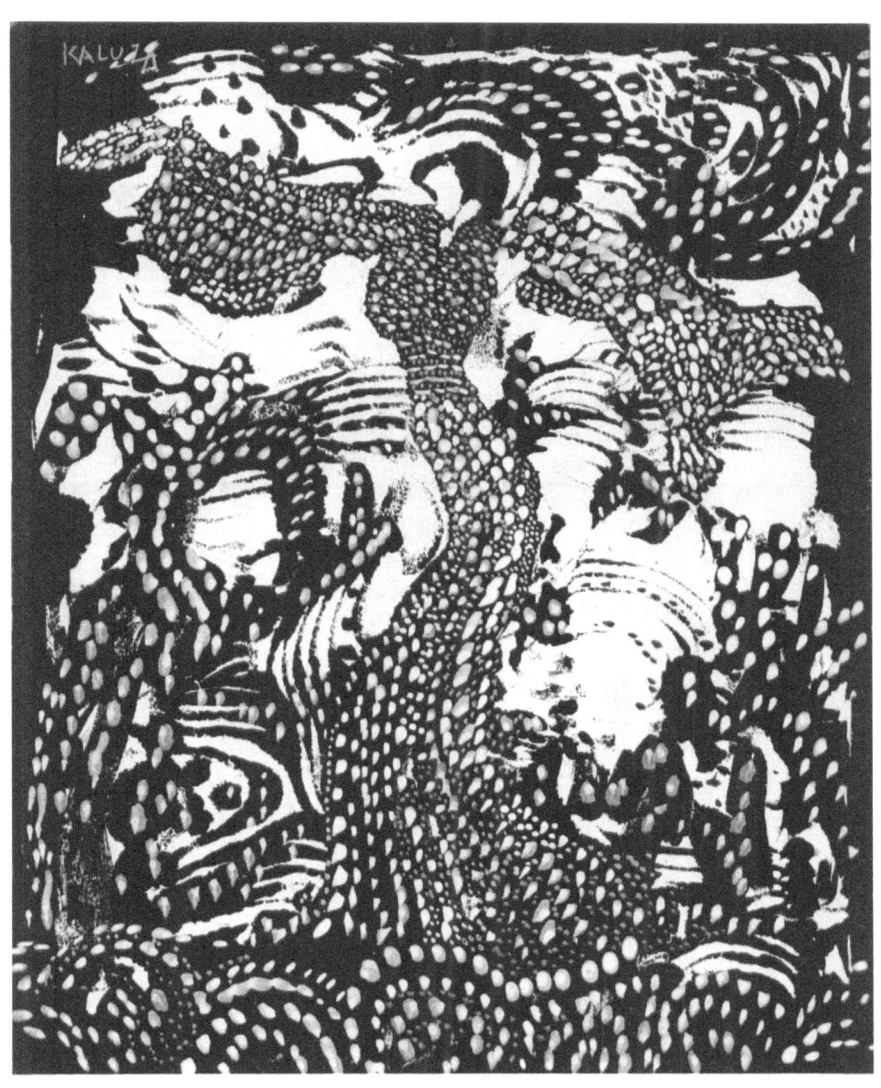

Dancer

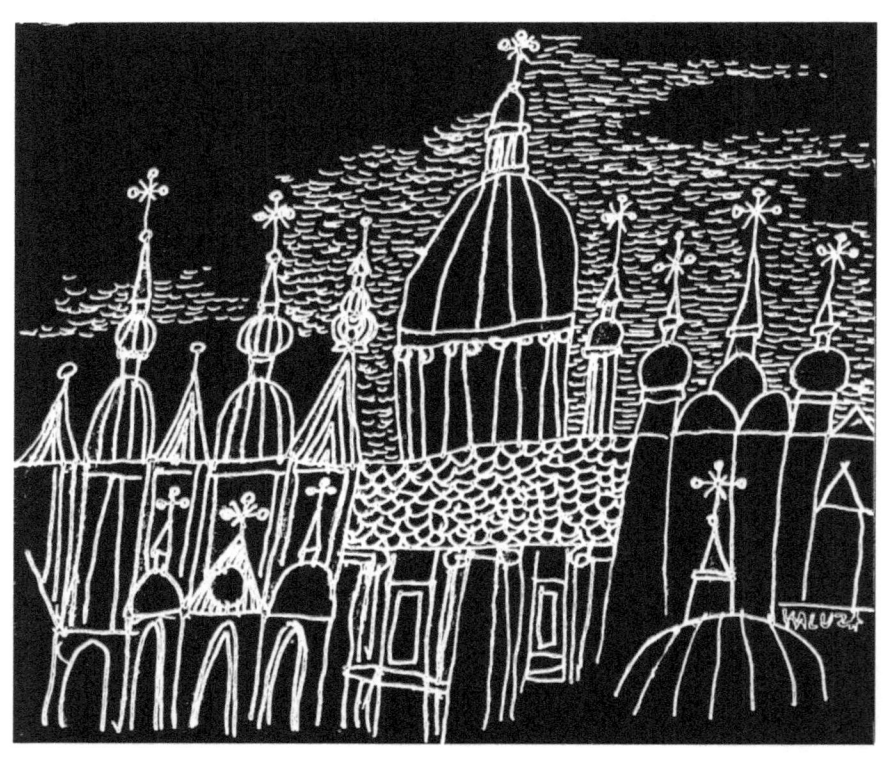

Churches

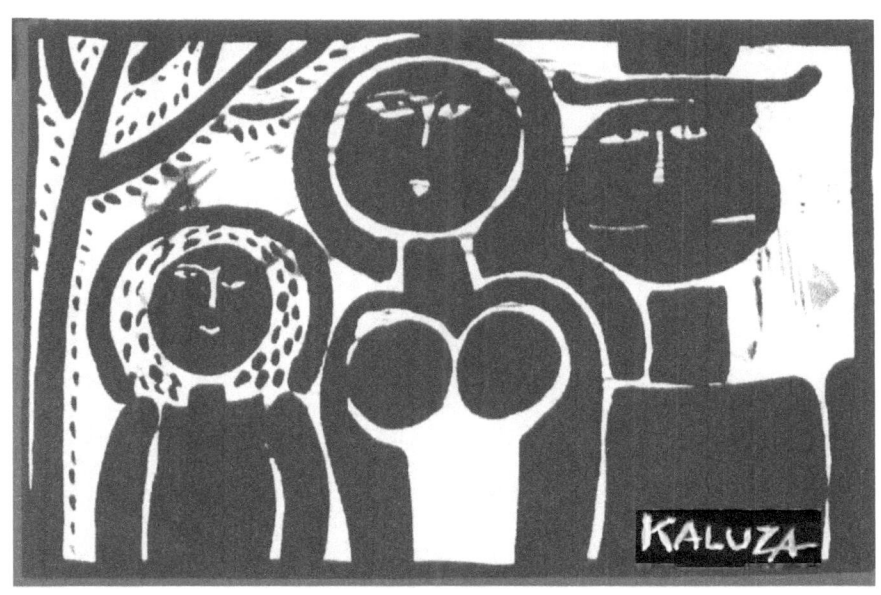

Family

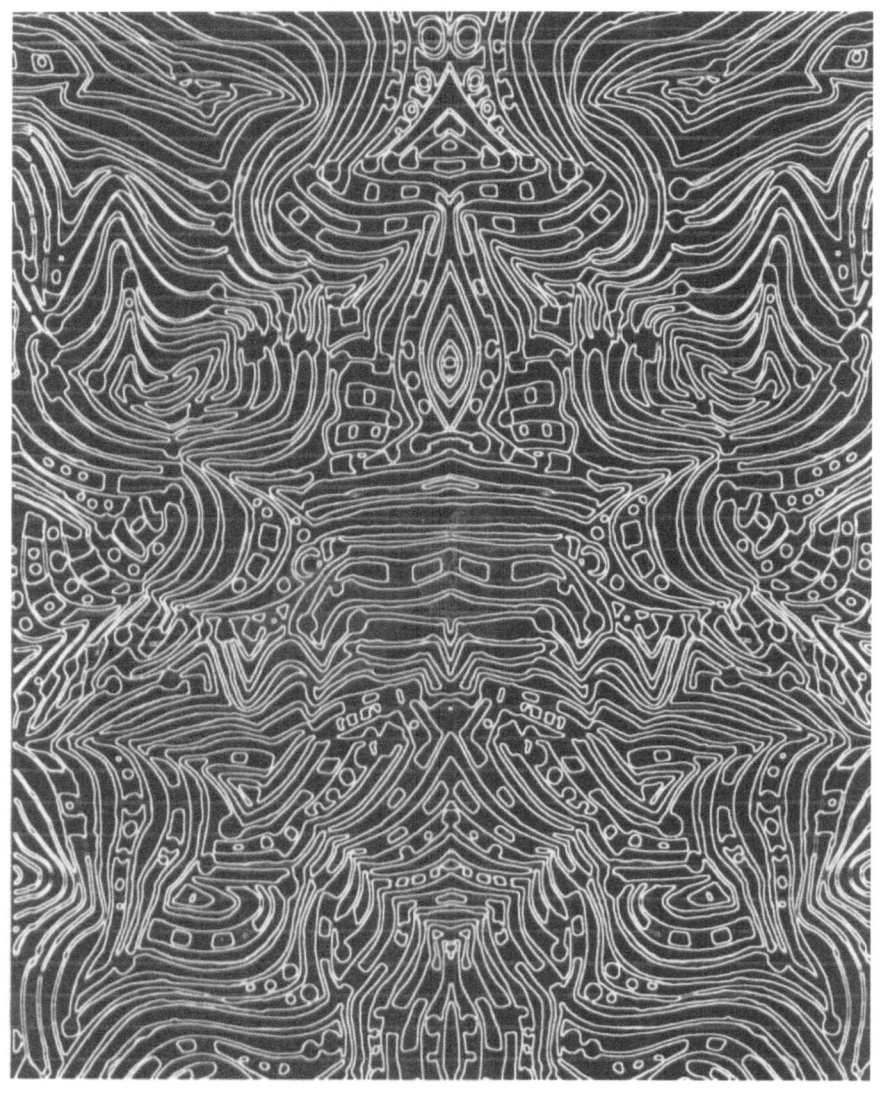

B&W Design

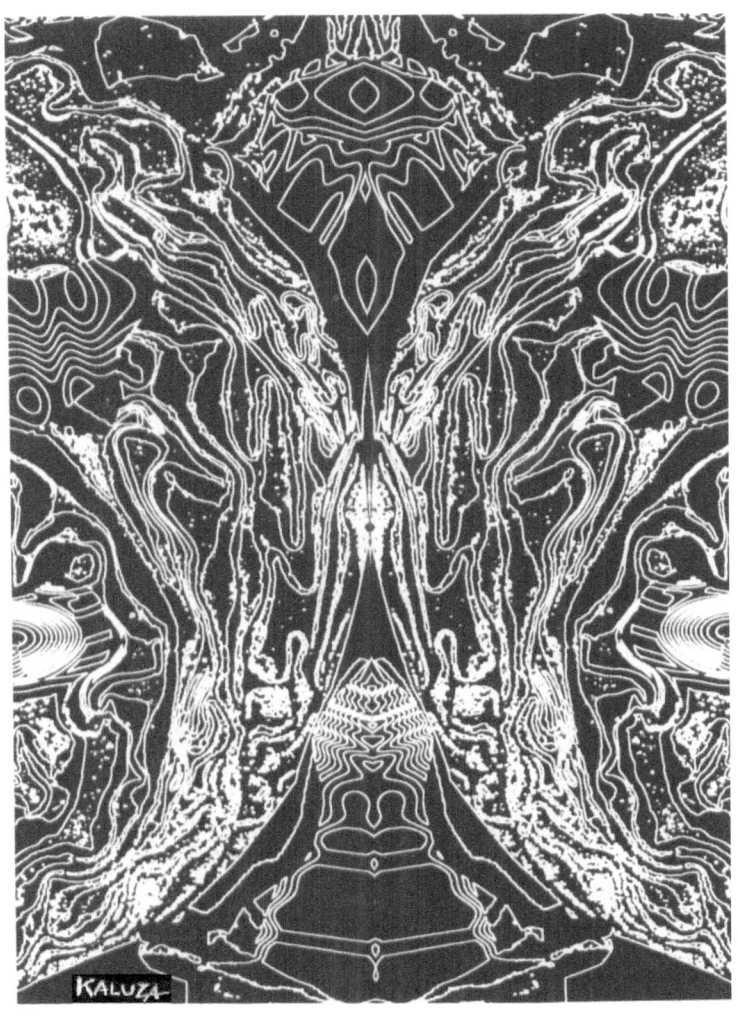

B&W Design 19

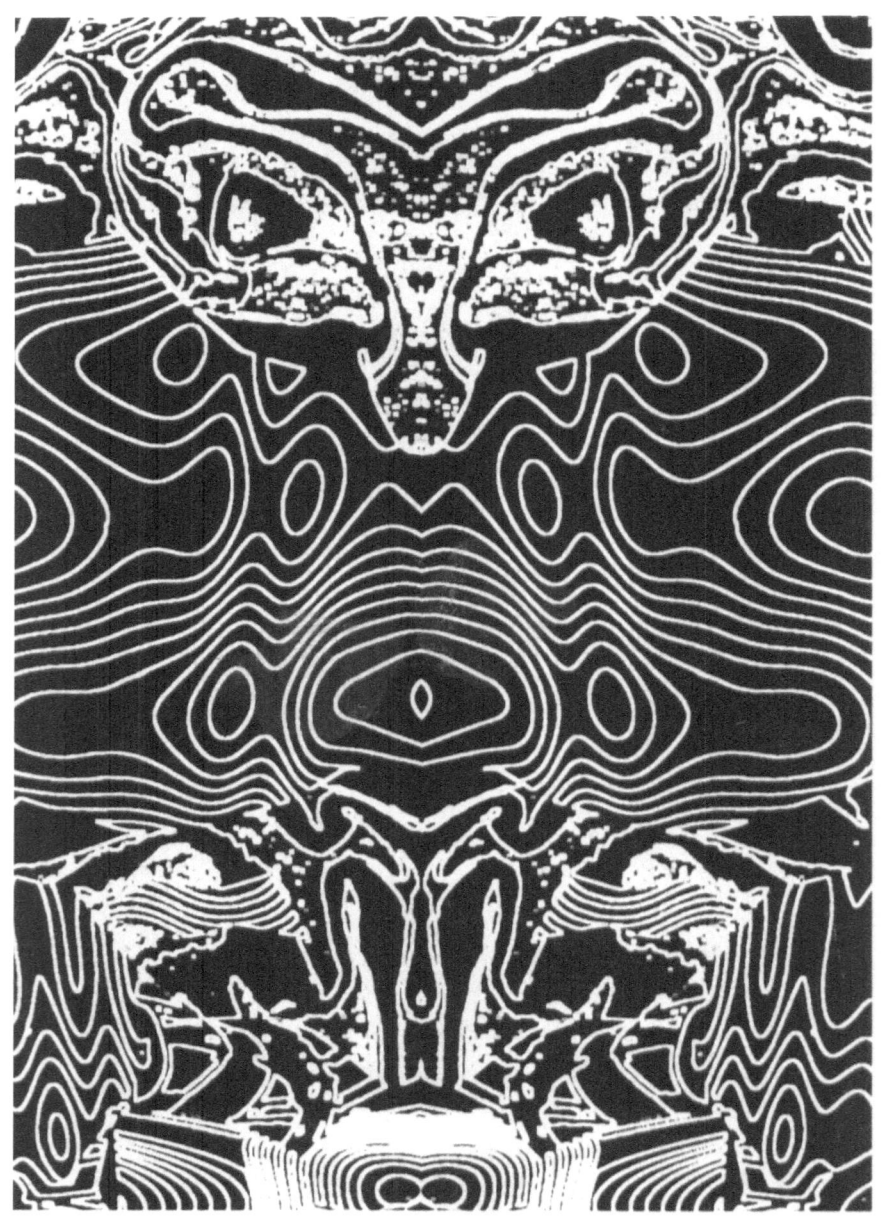

Creature Watching

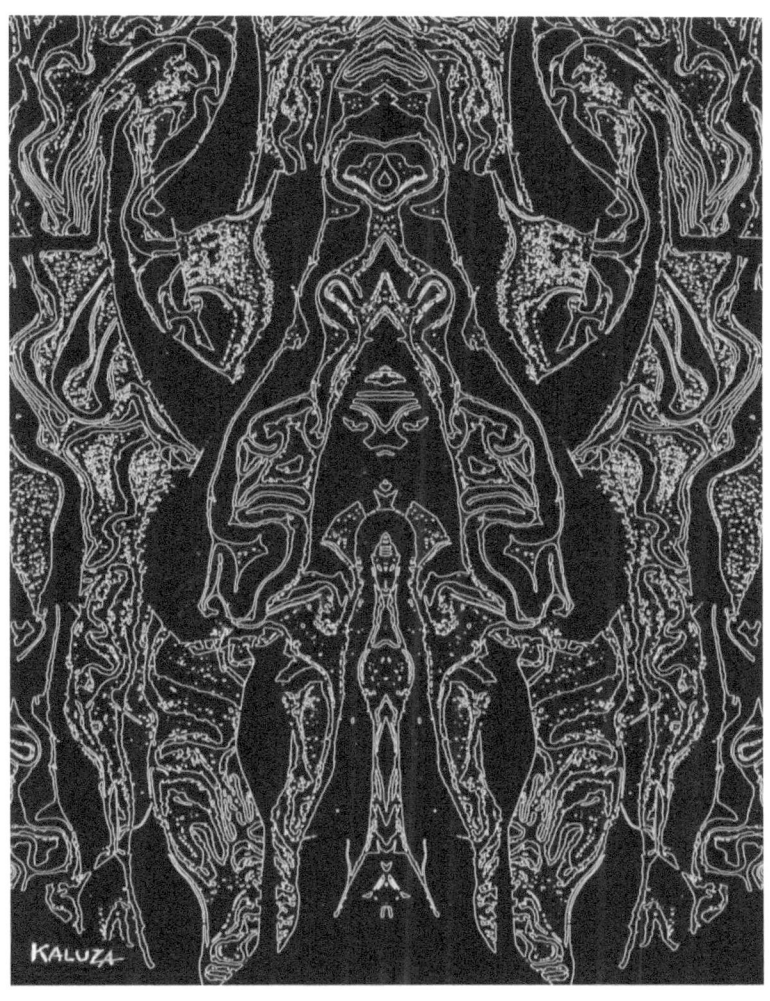

B&W Design 5

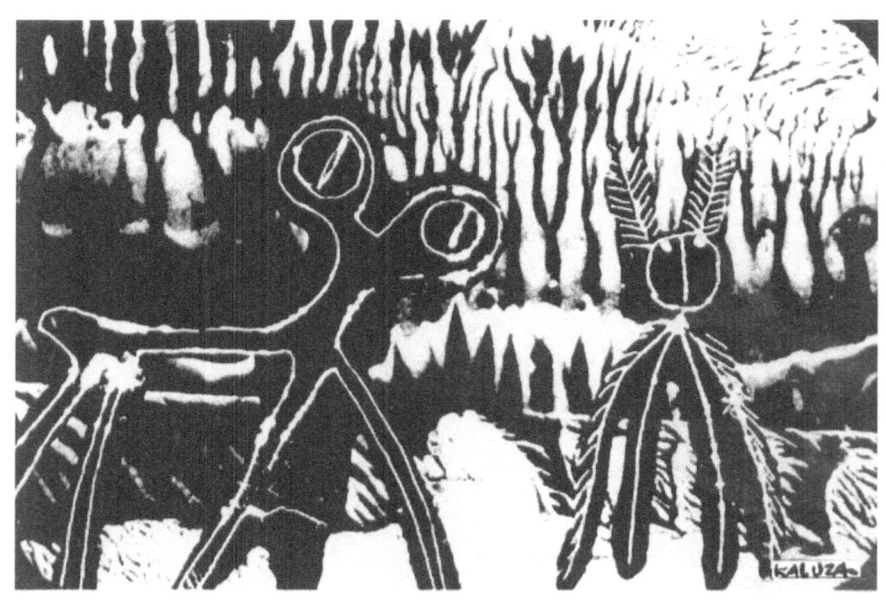

Strange Animals

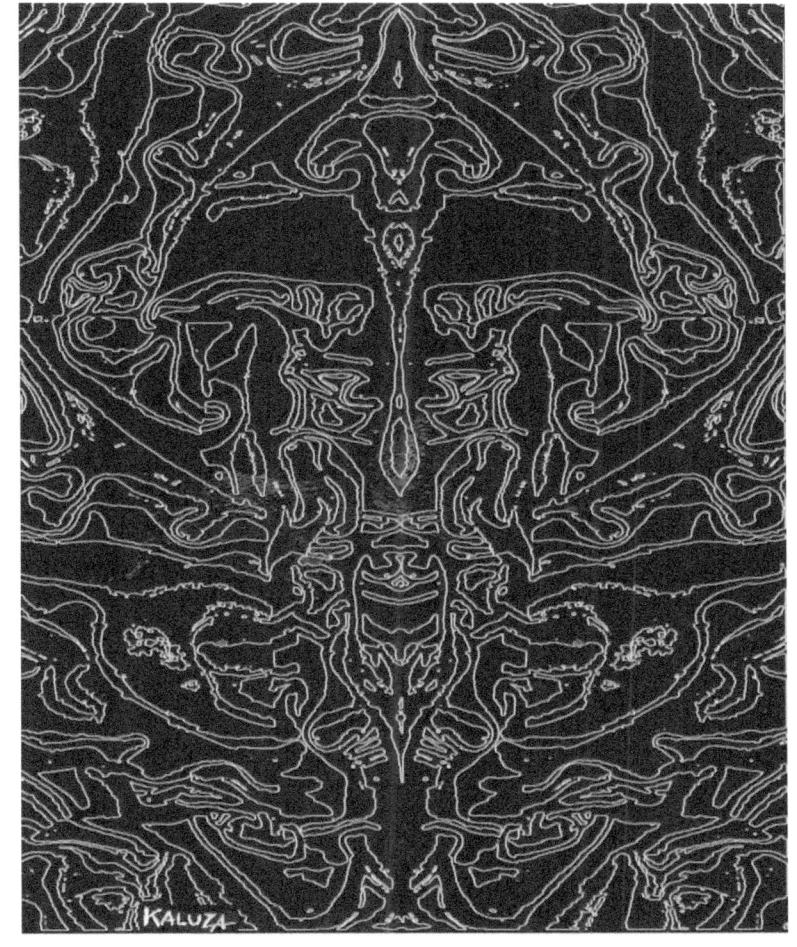

B&W Design 9

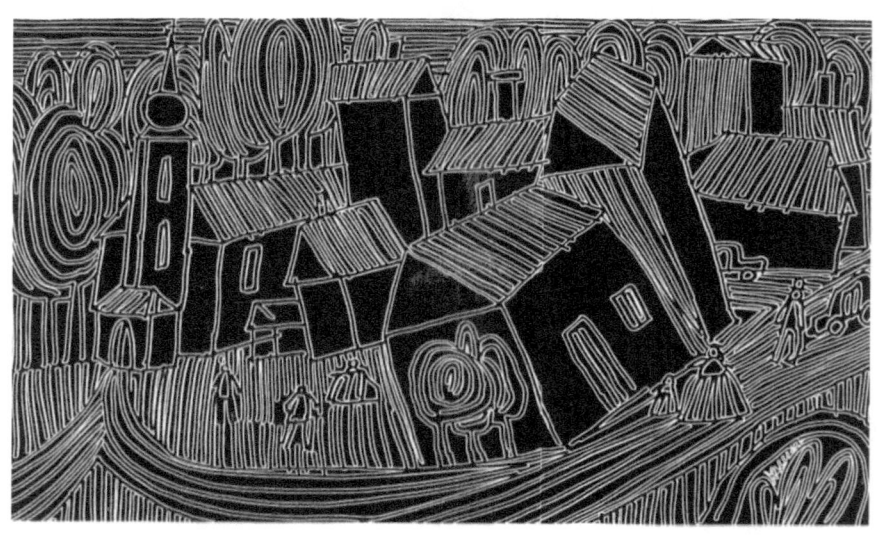

Village with Church

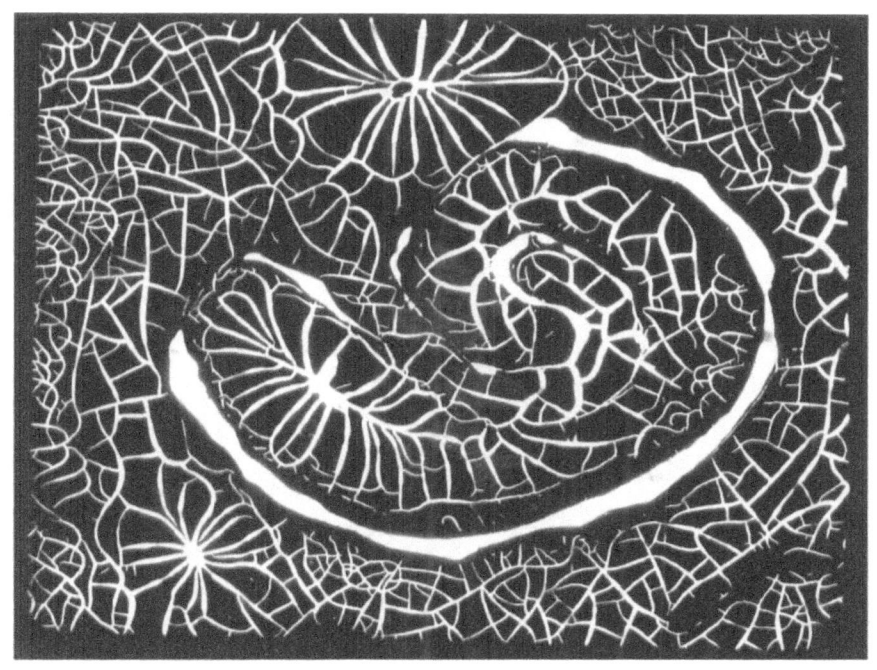

Microbes 3

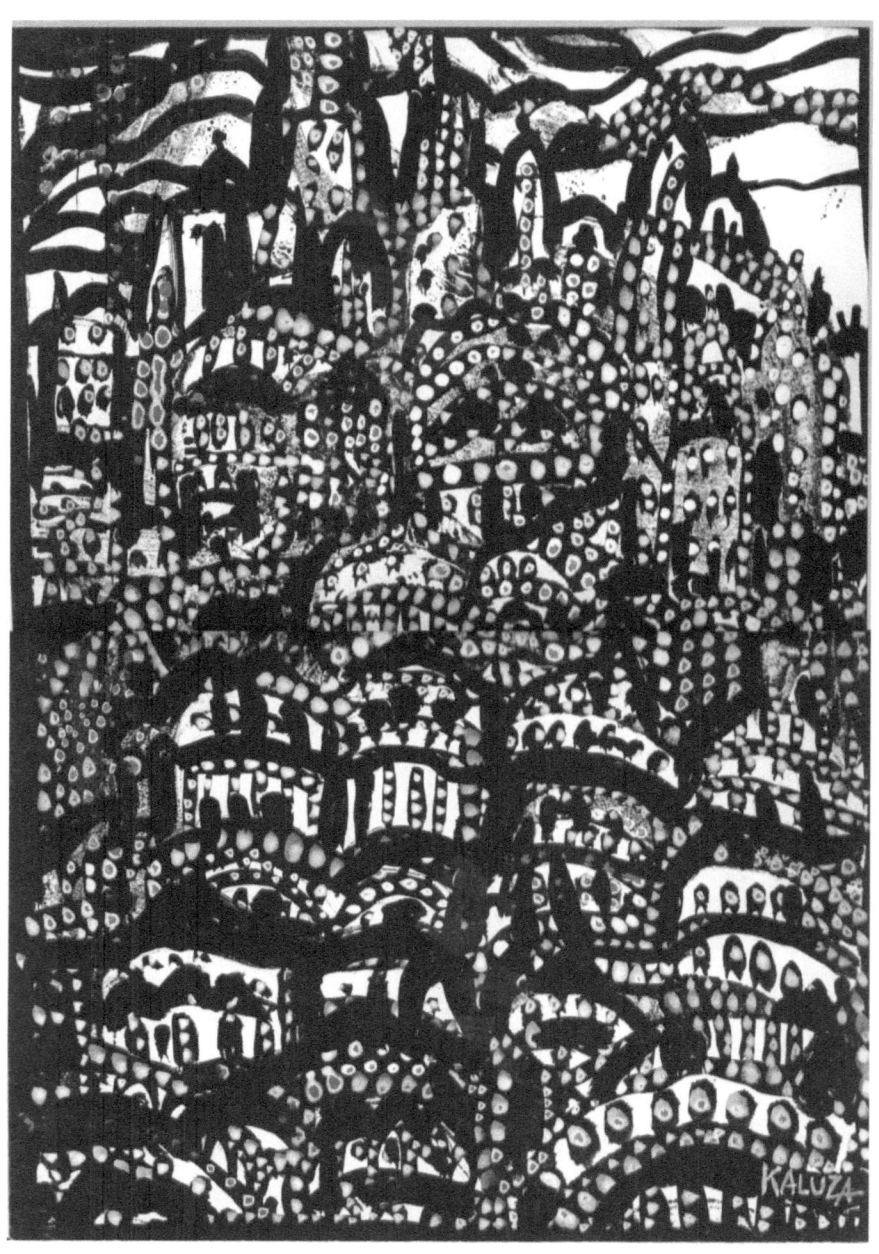

City

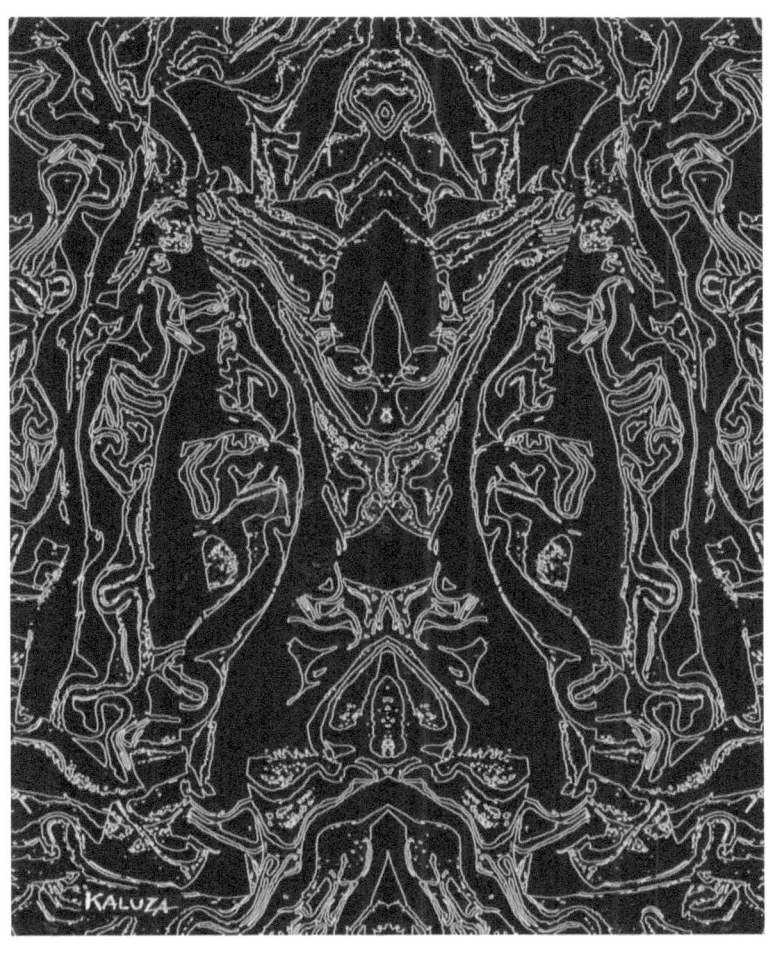

B&W Design 25

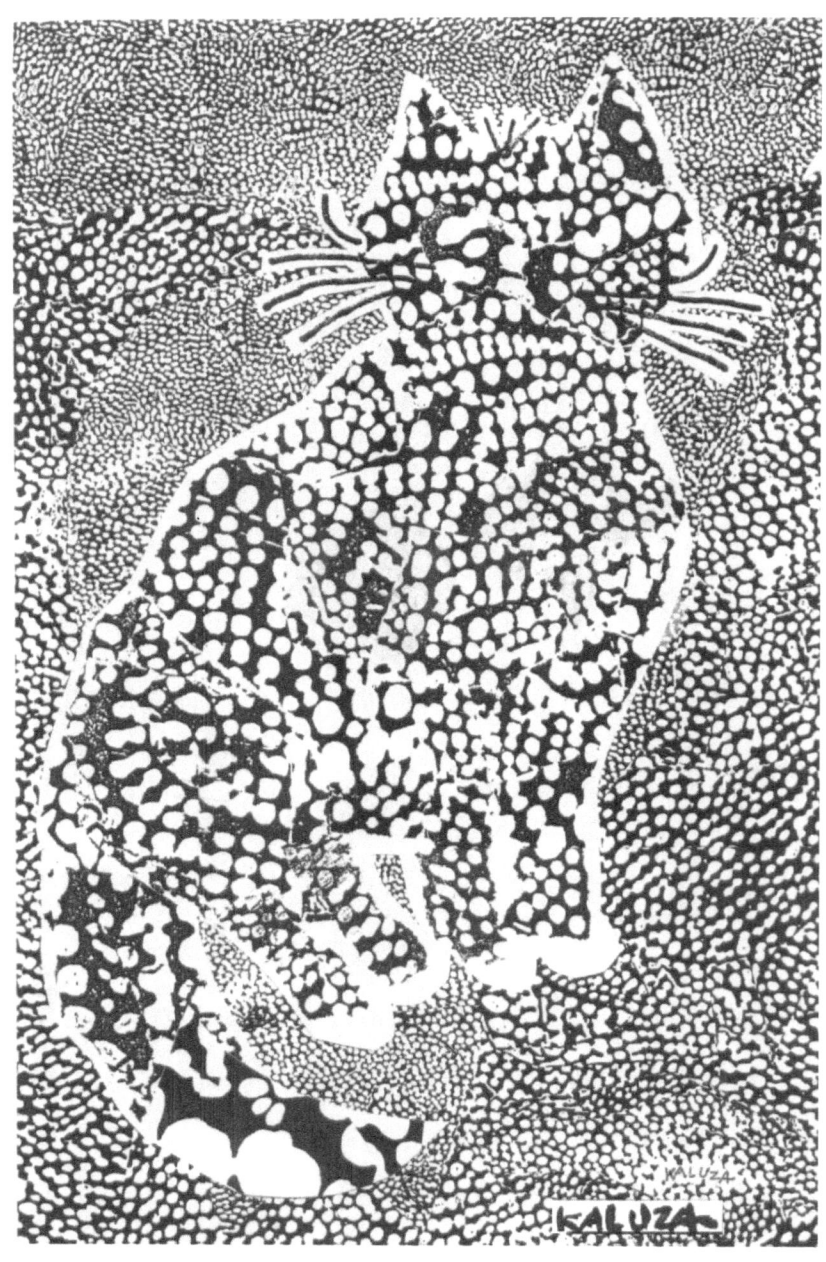

Cat in Dots

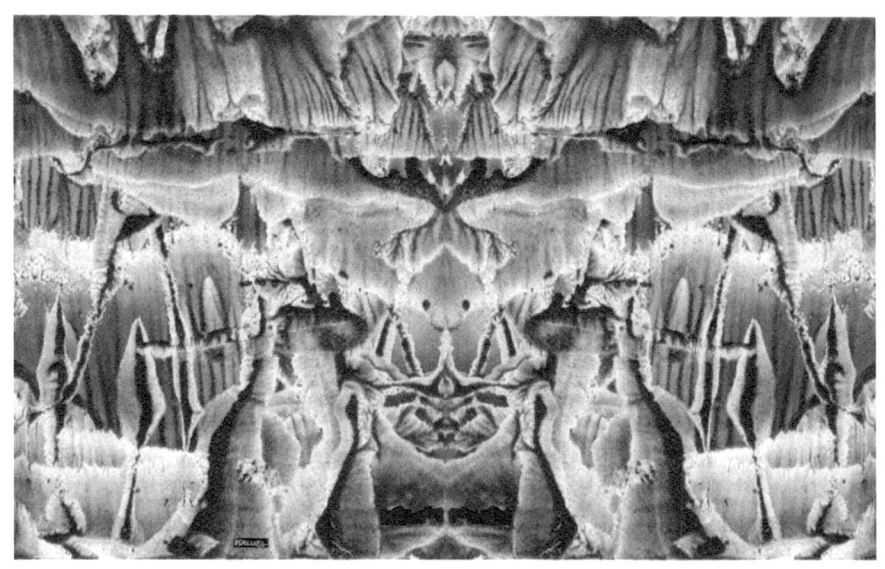

Mighty Thunderbird

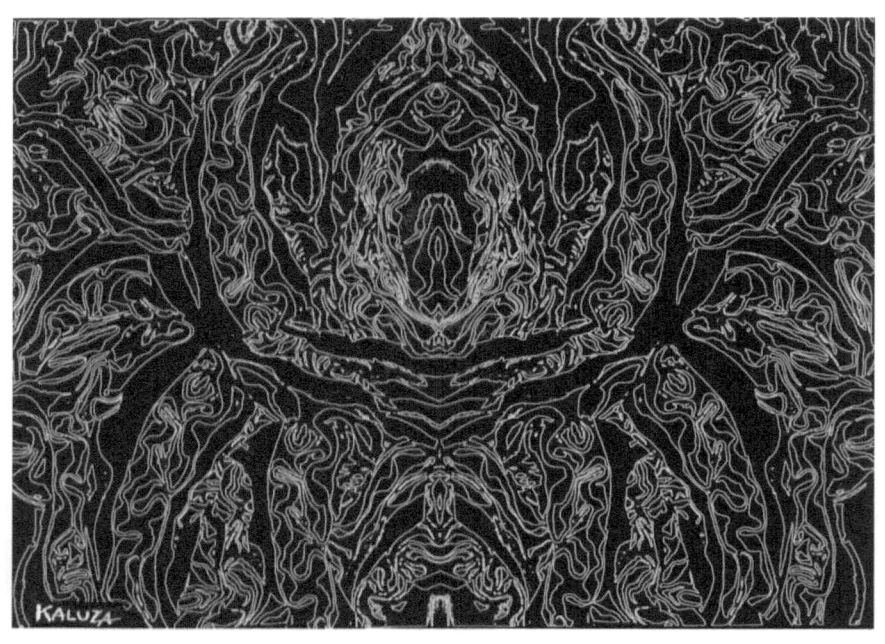

B&W Design 24

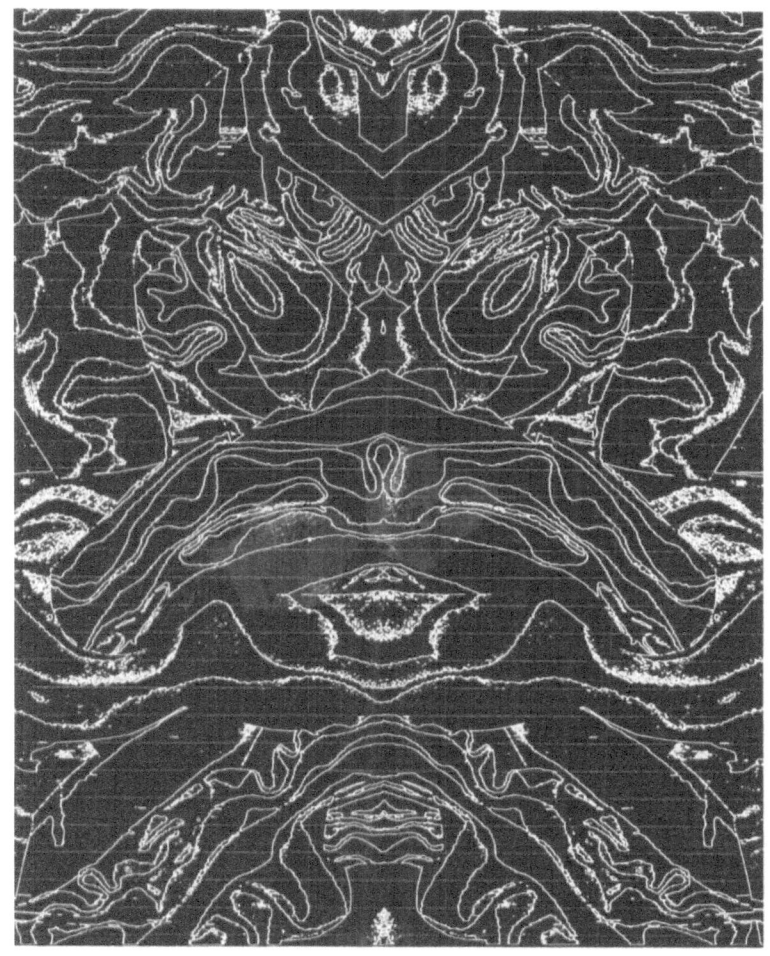

B&W Design 27

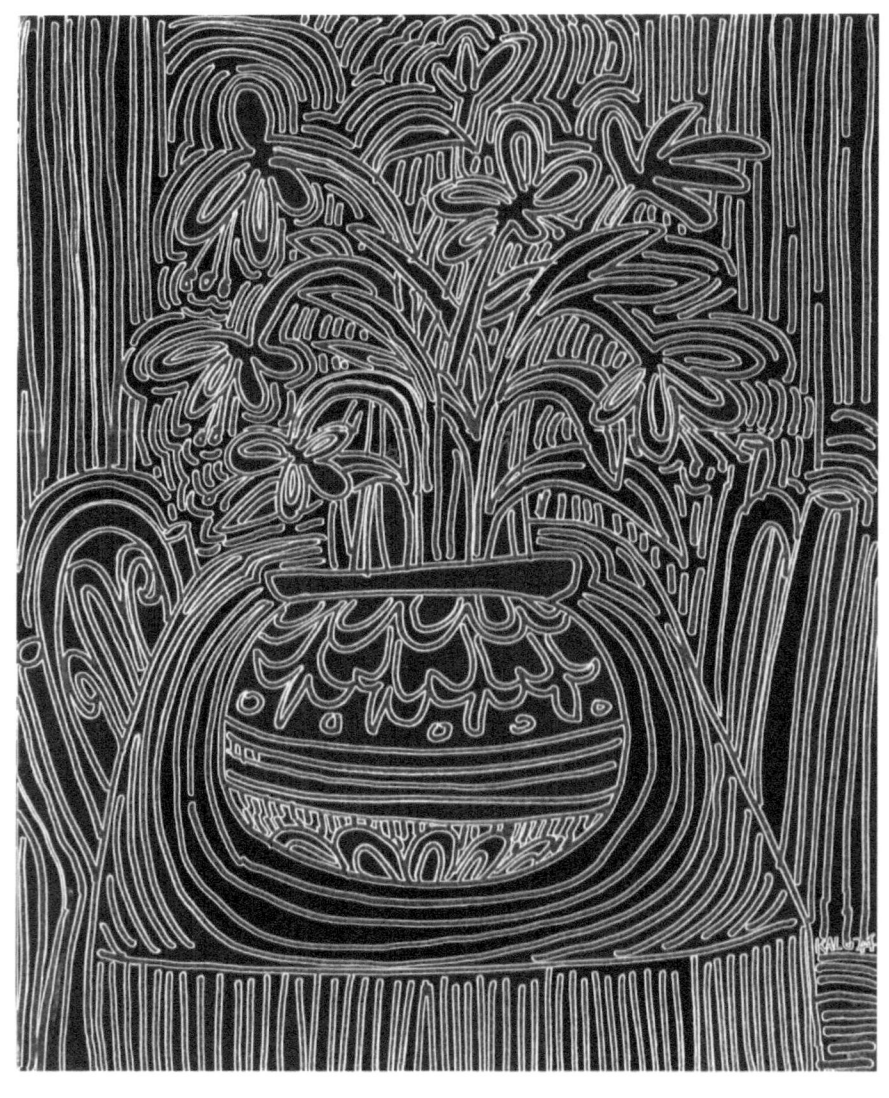

Flowers

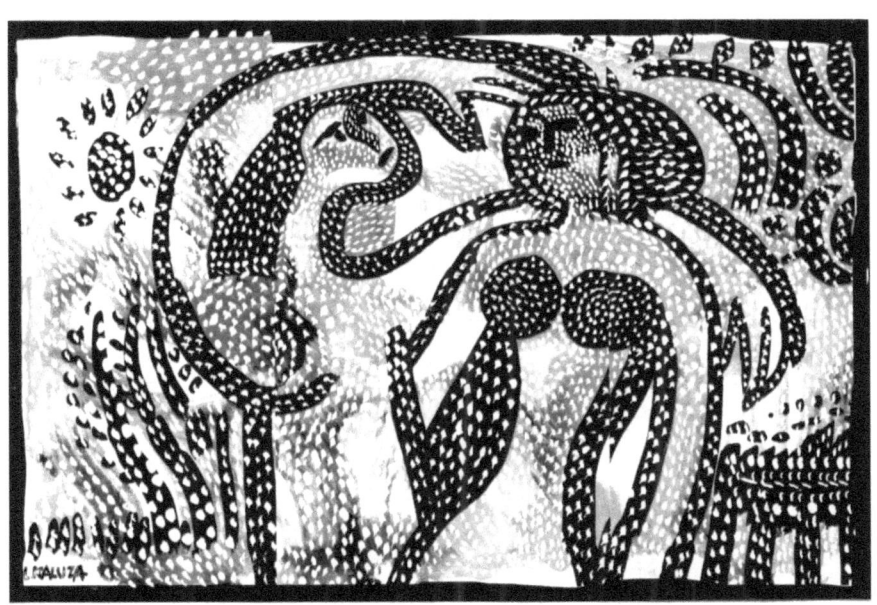

Two Women

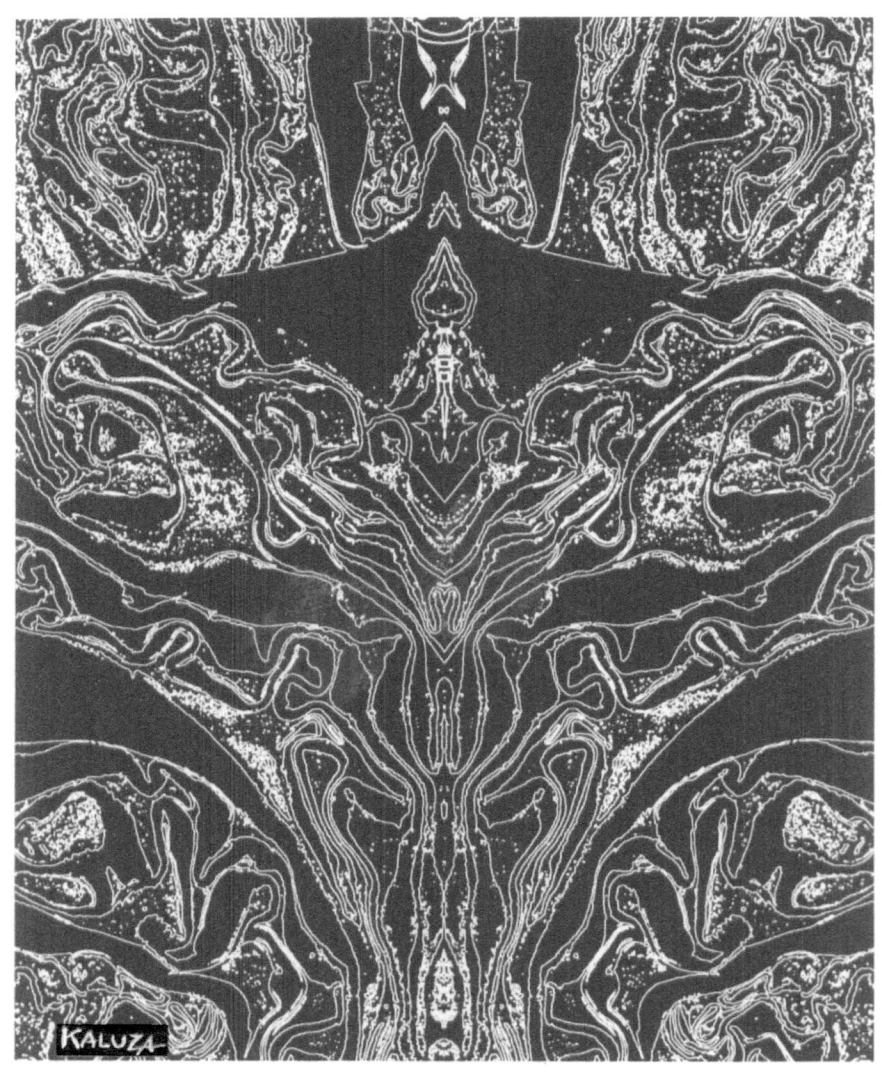

B&W Design 39

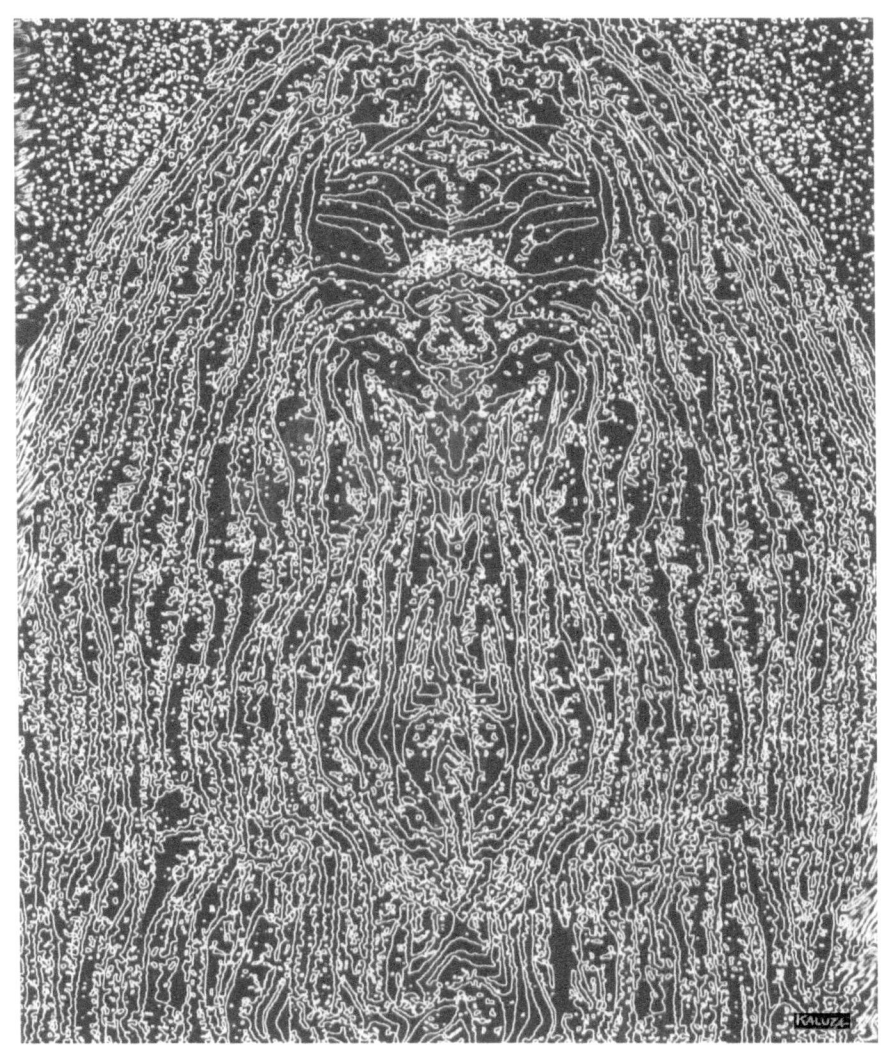

Yeti

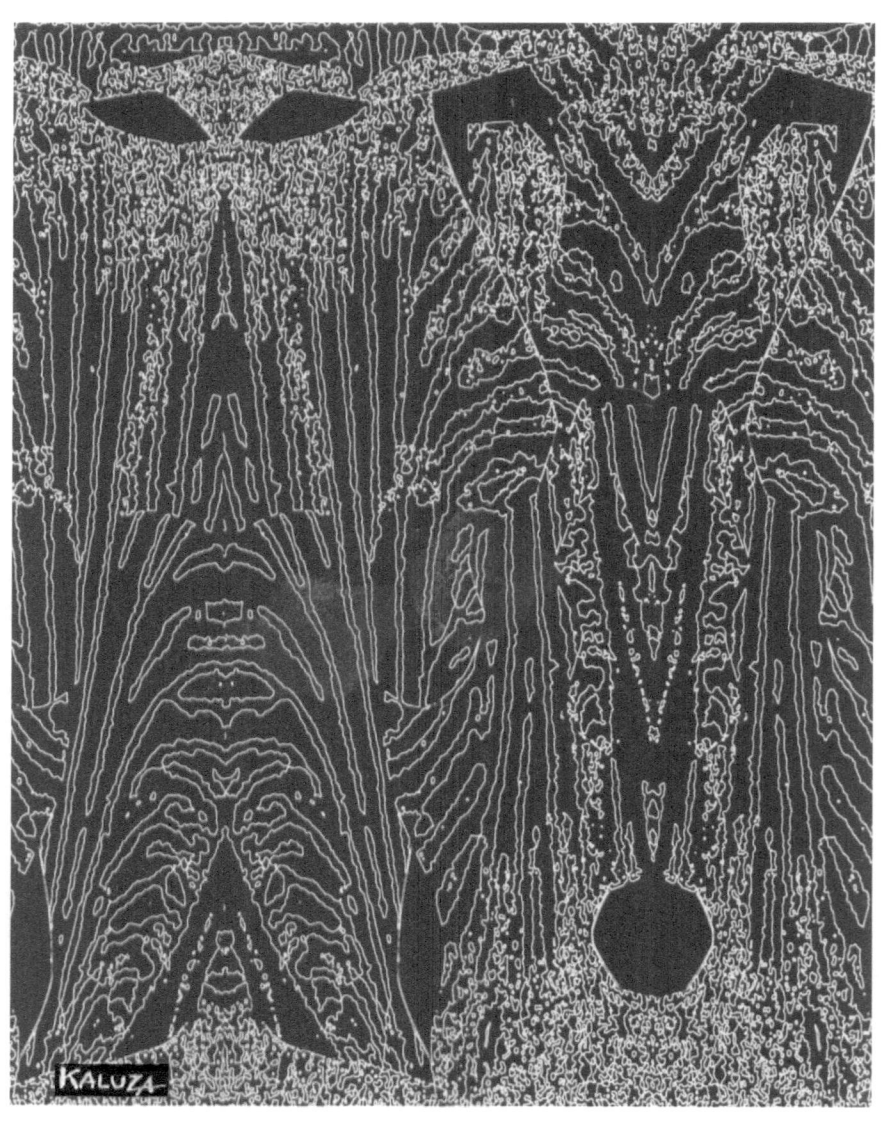

B&W Design 38

ART IN BLACK & WHITE

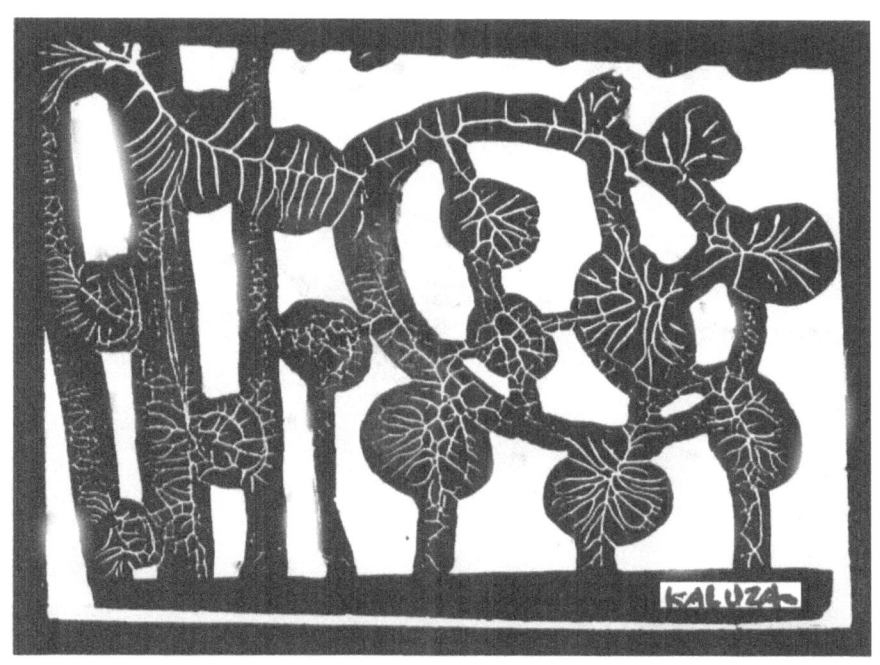

Microbes 2

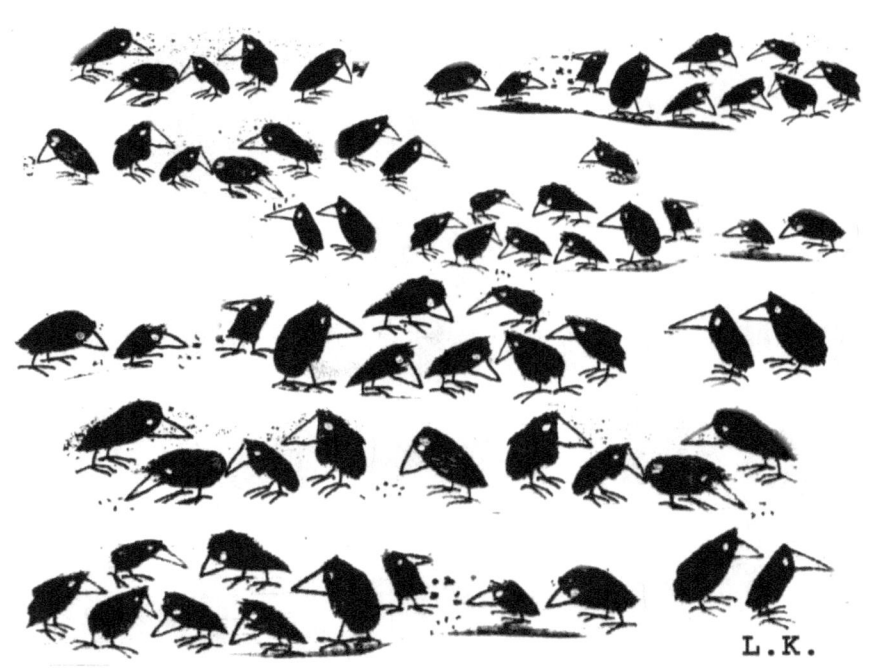

Crows

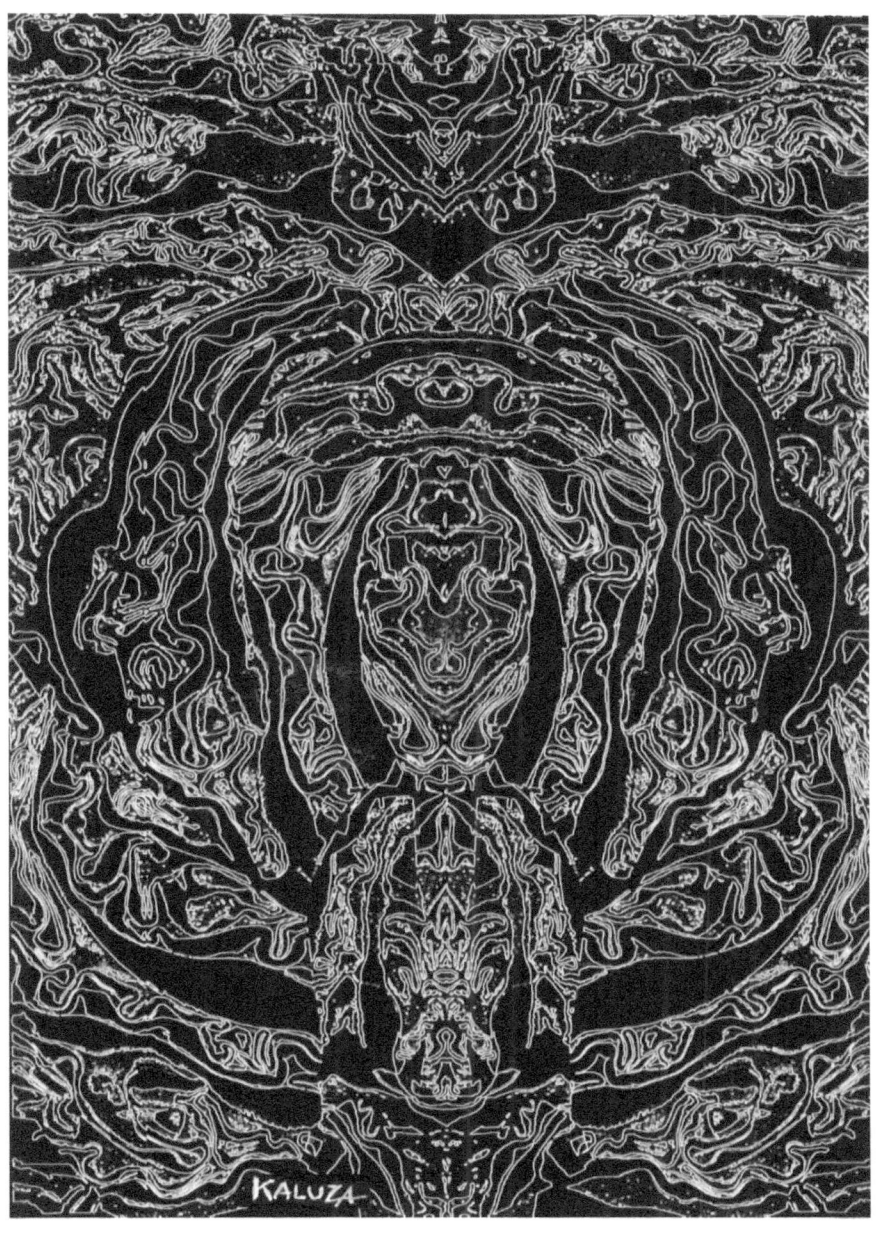

B&W Design 35

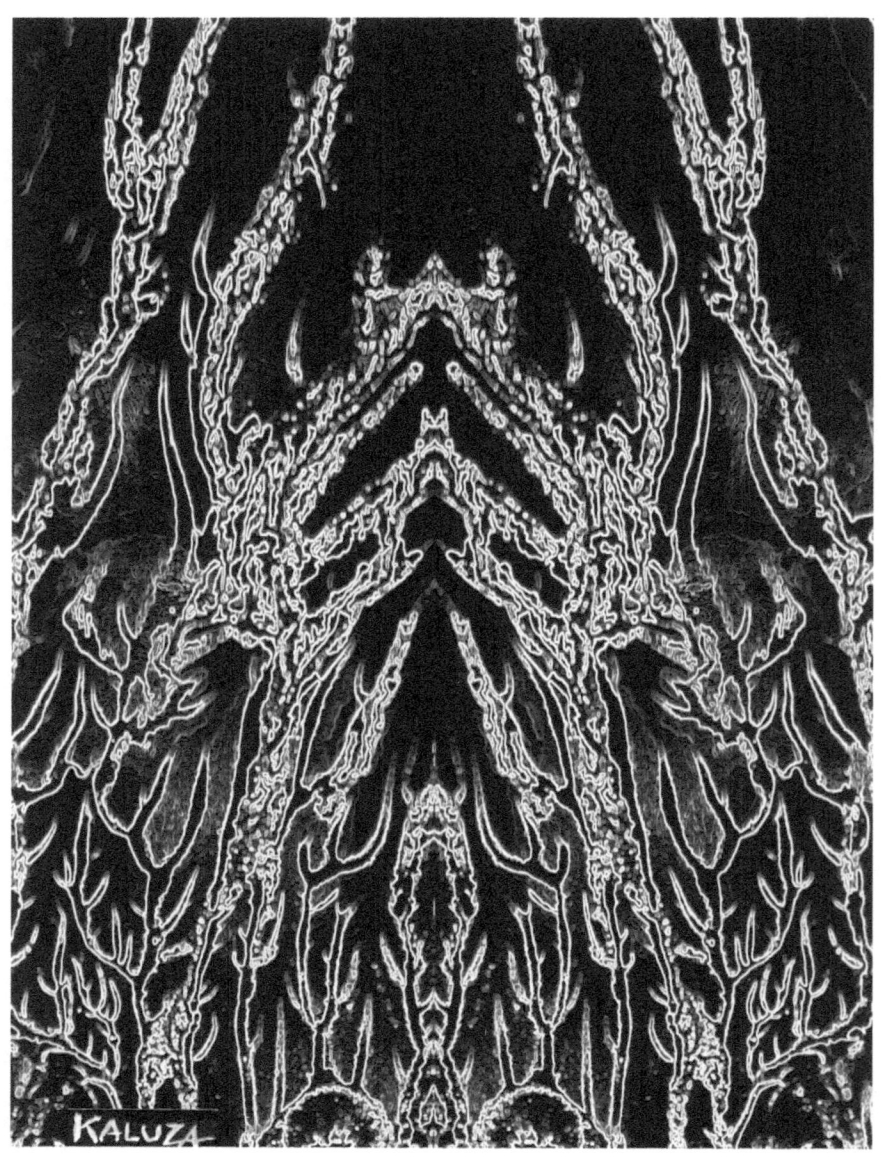

Bug in B&W

ART IN BLACK & WHITE

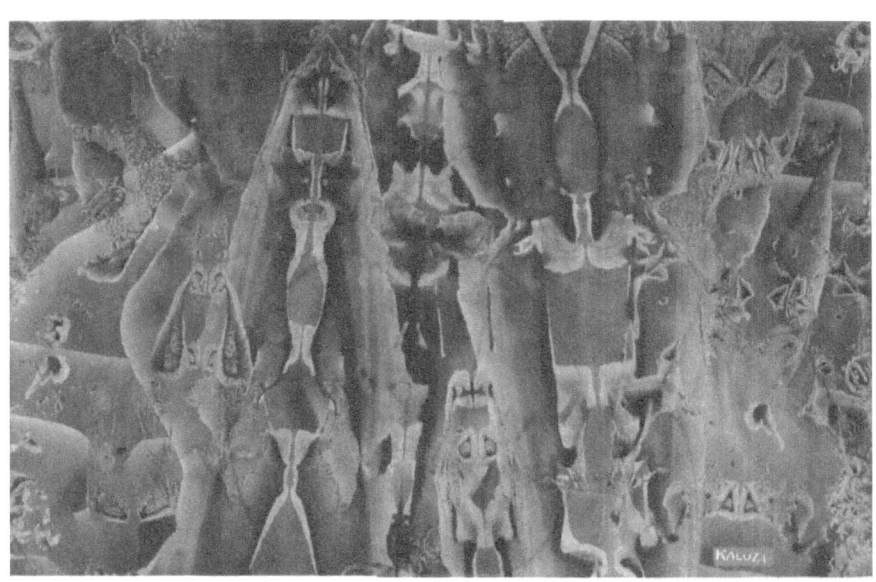

Phantasma

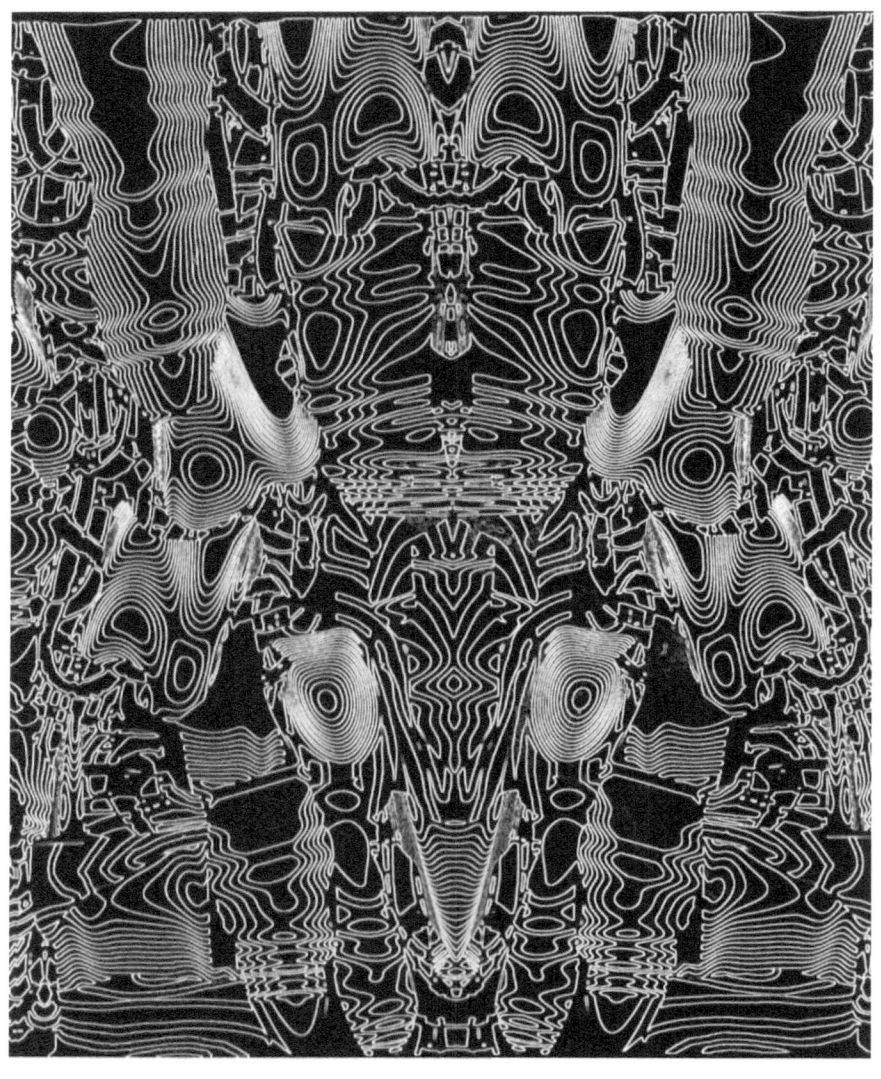

B&W Design 45

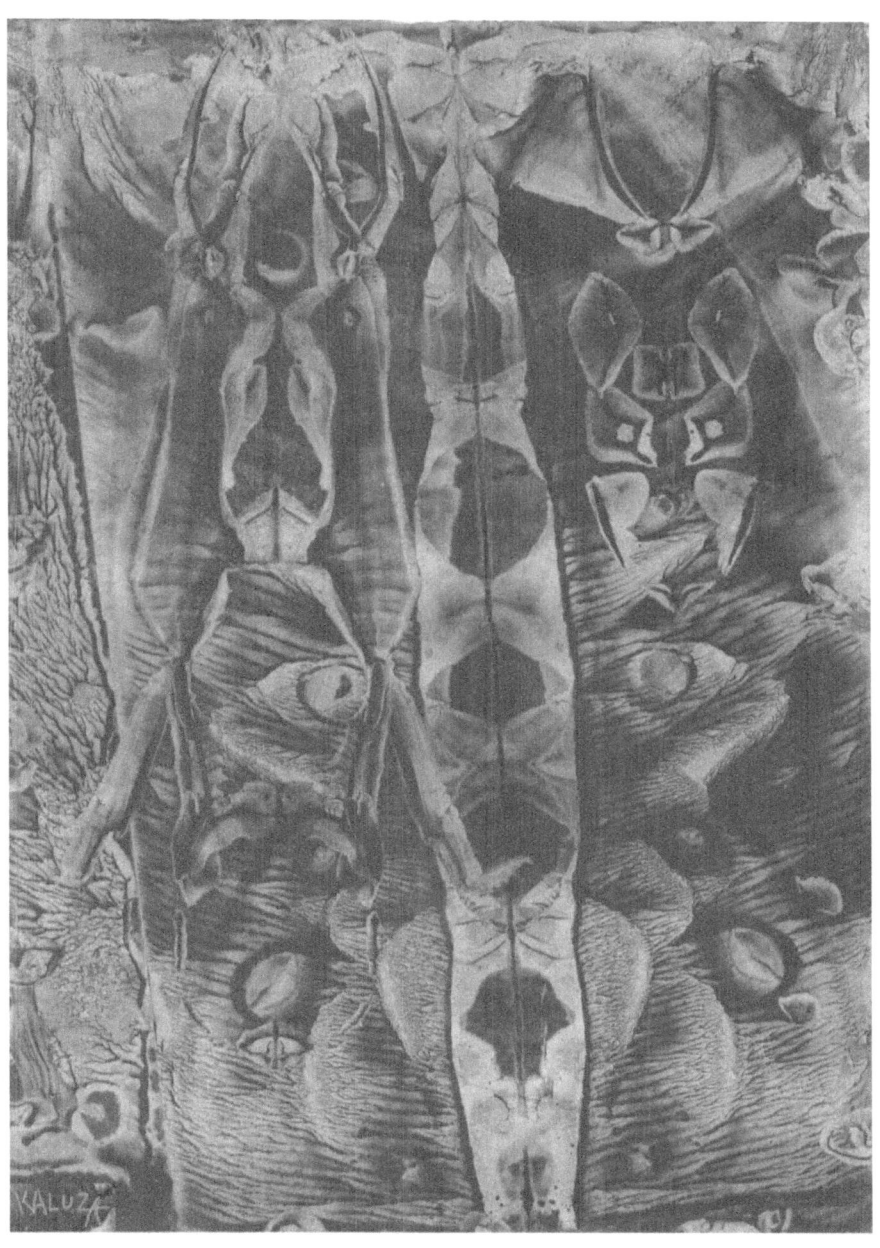

Creatures of the Night

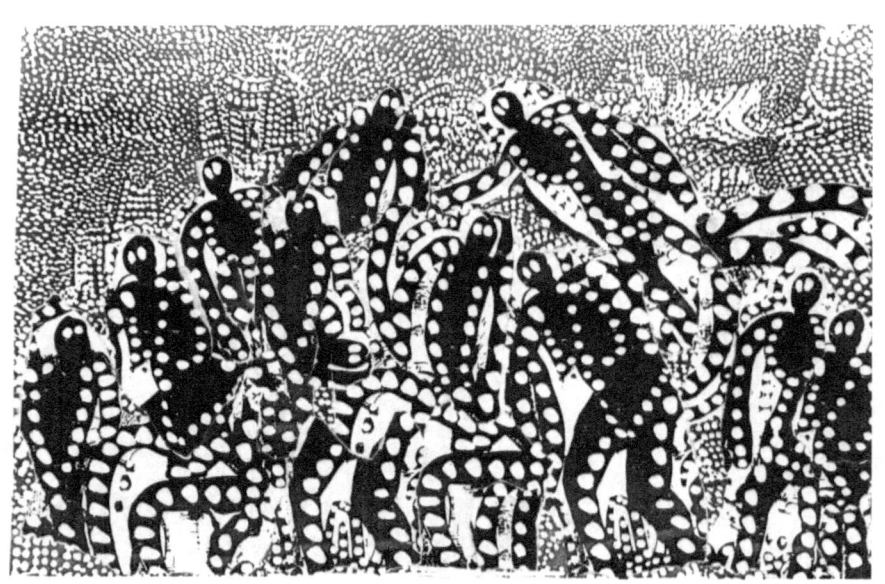

Figures

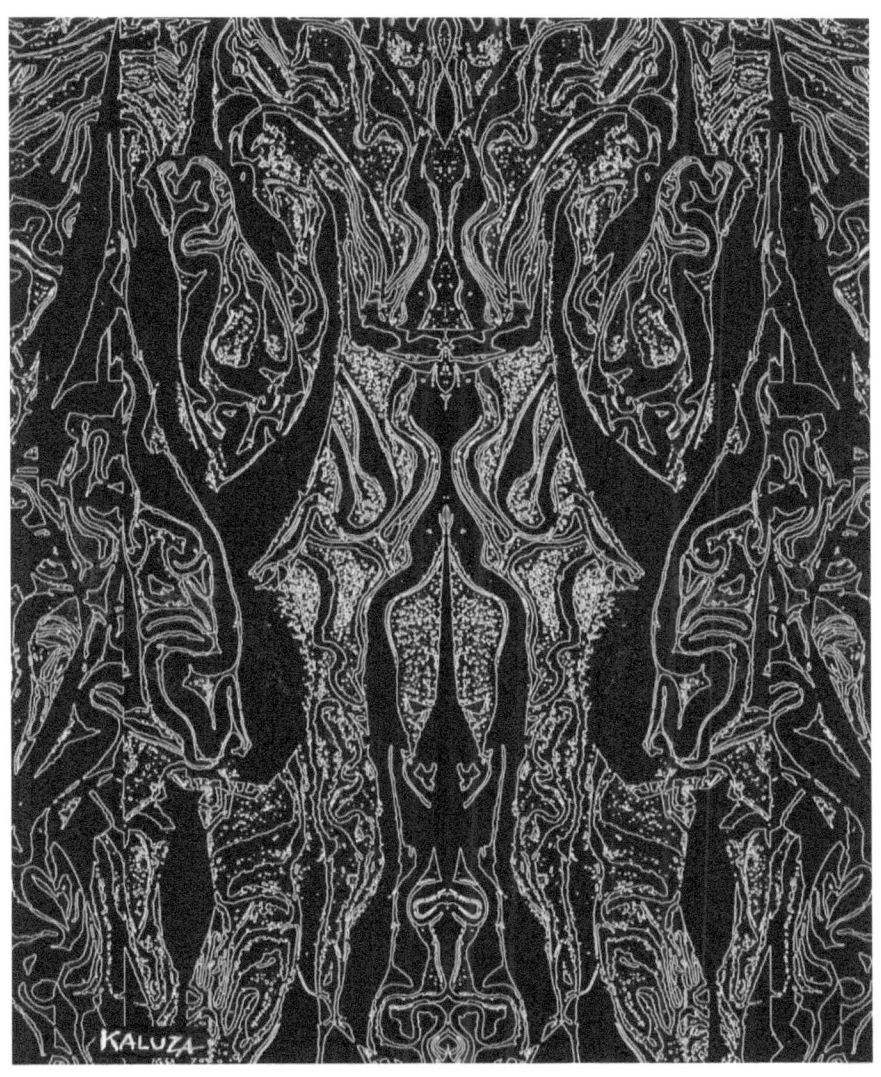

Design 31

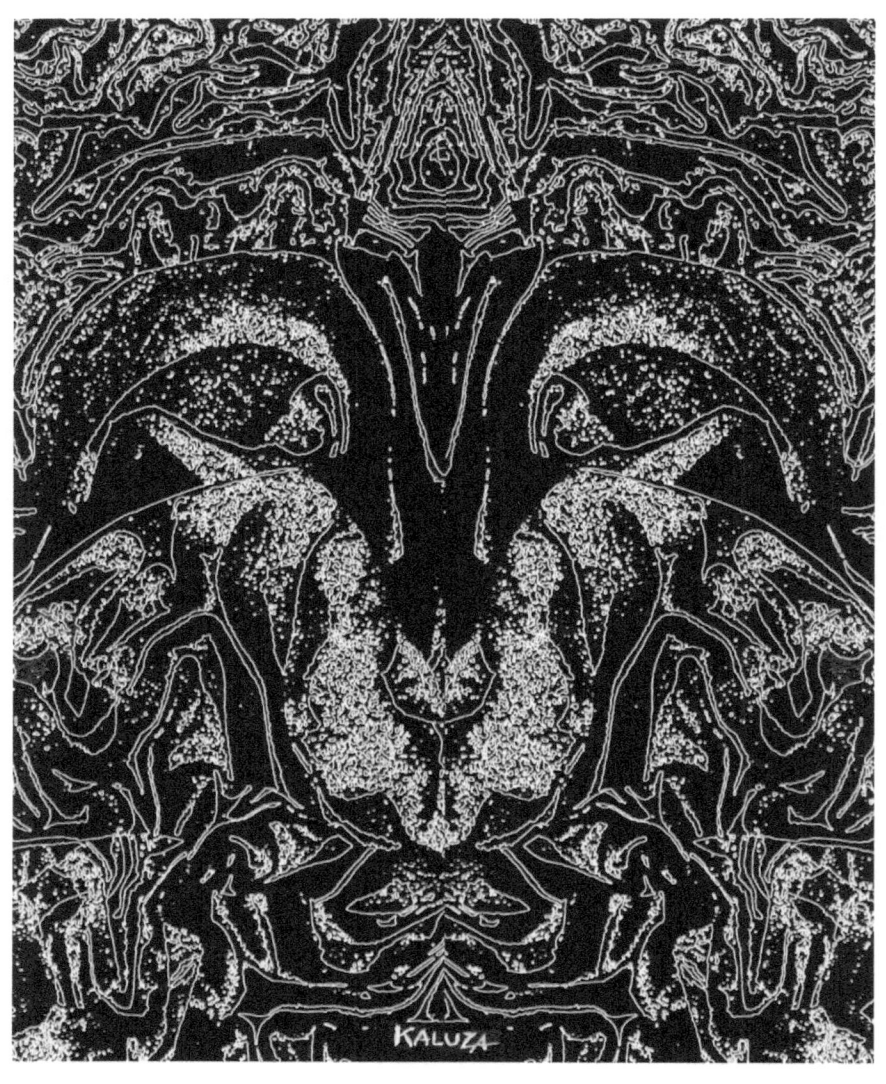

Puppy

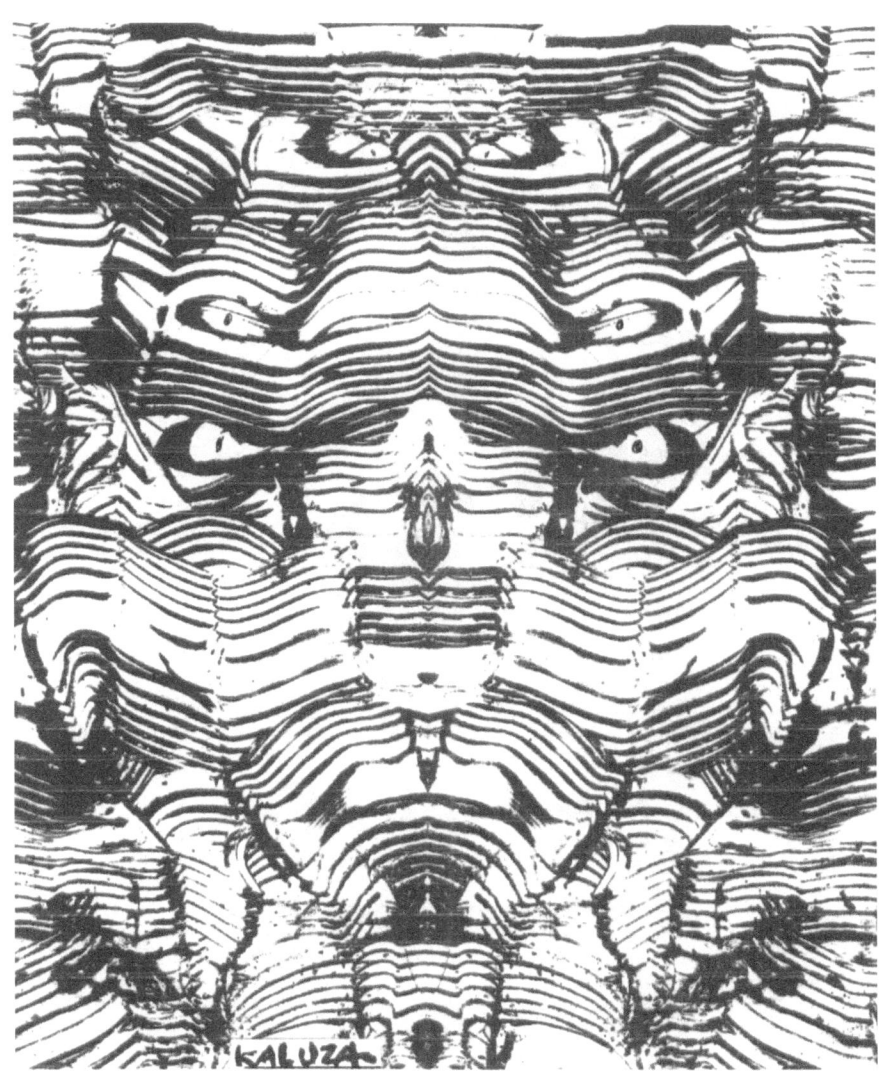

Sinister Being

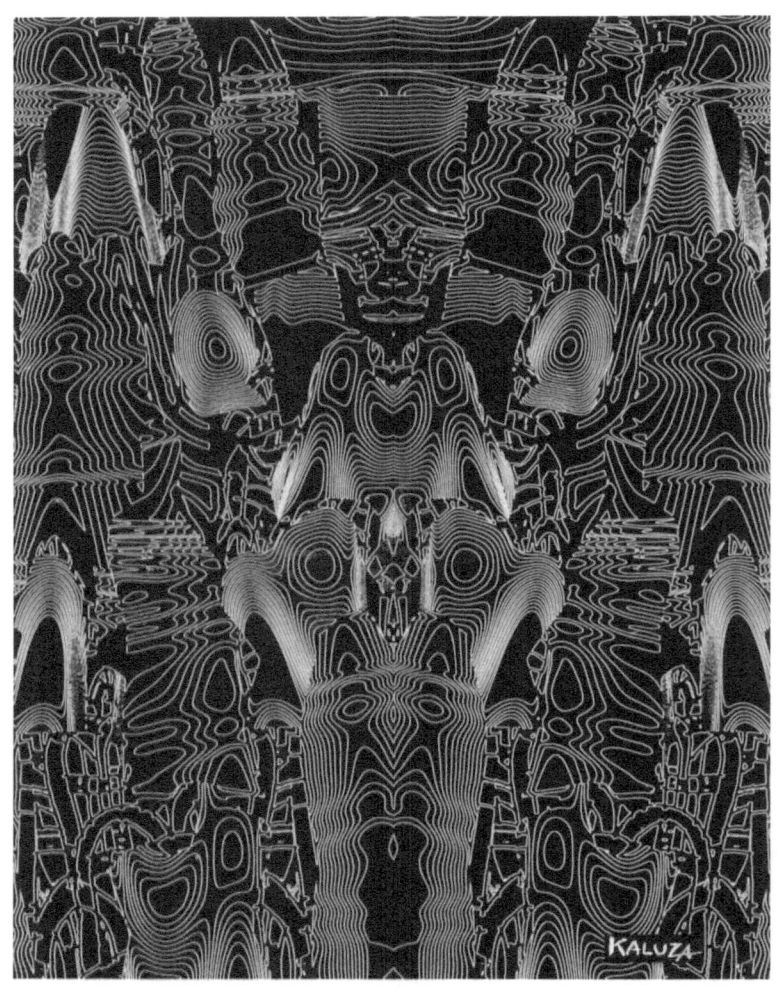

Alien

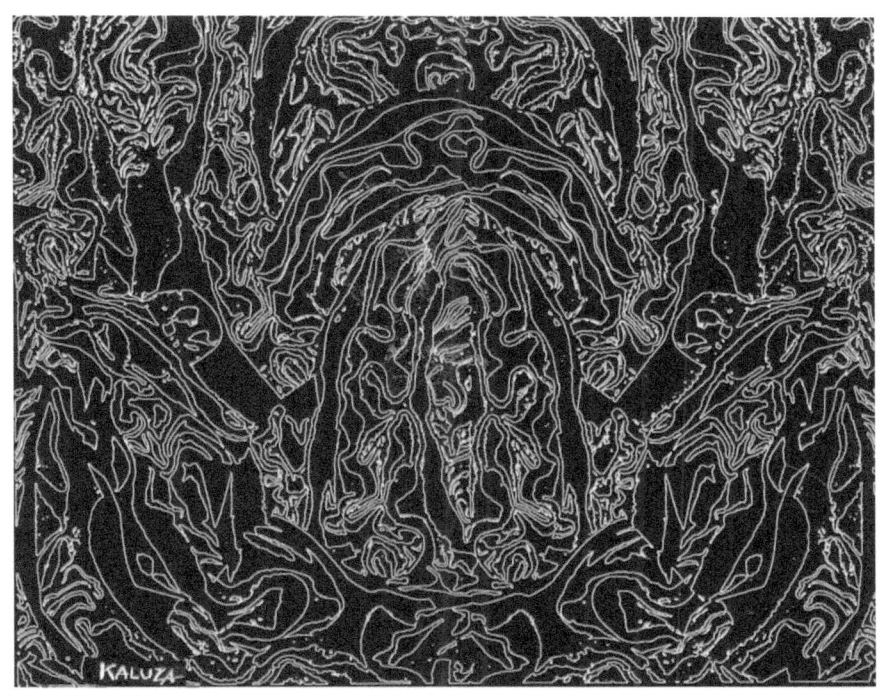

Design 18

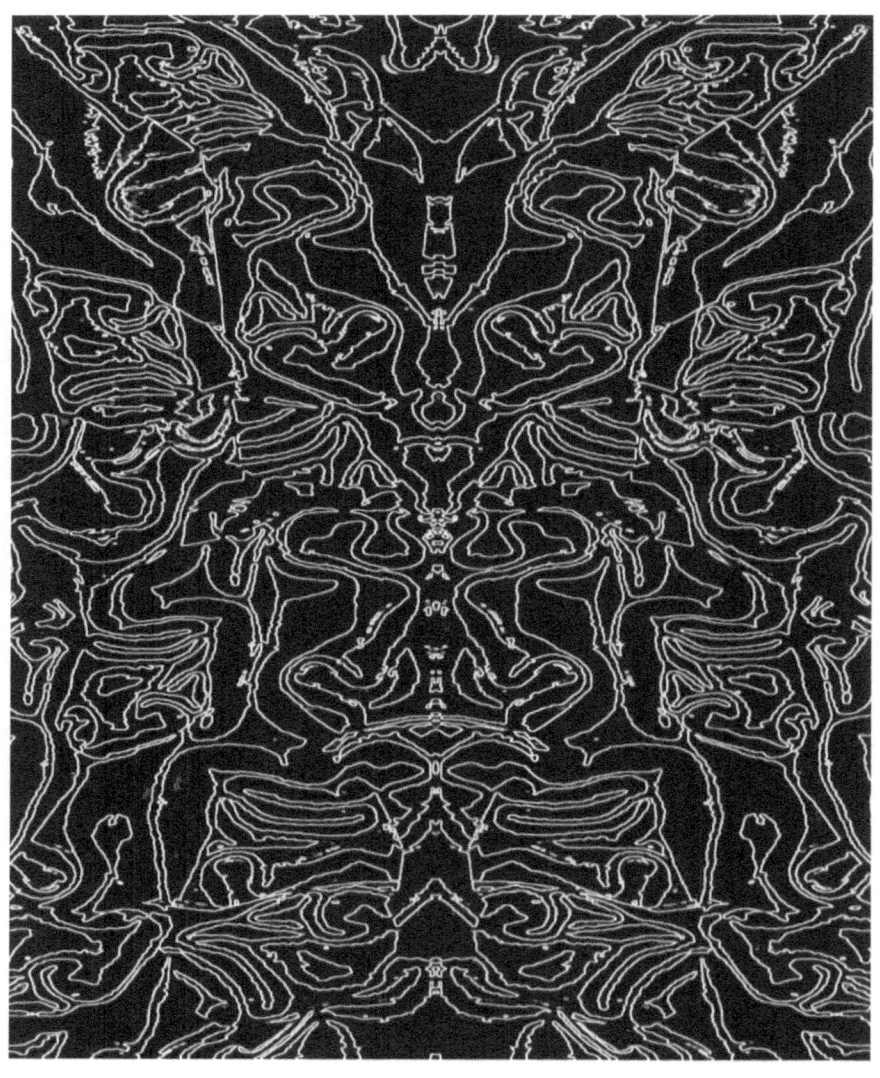

Dark Vision

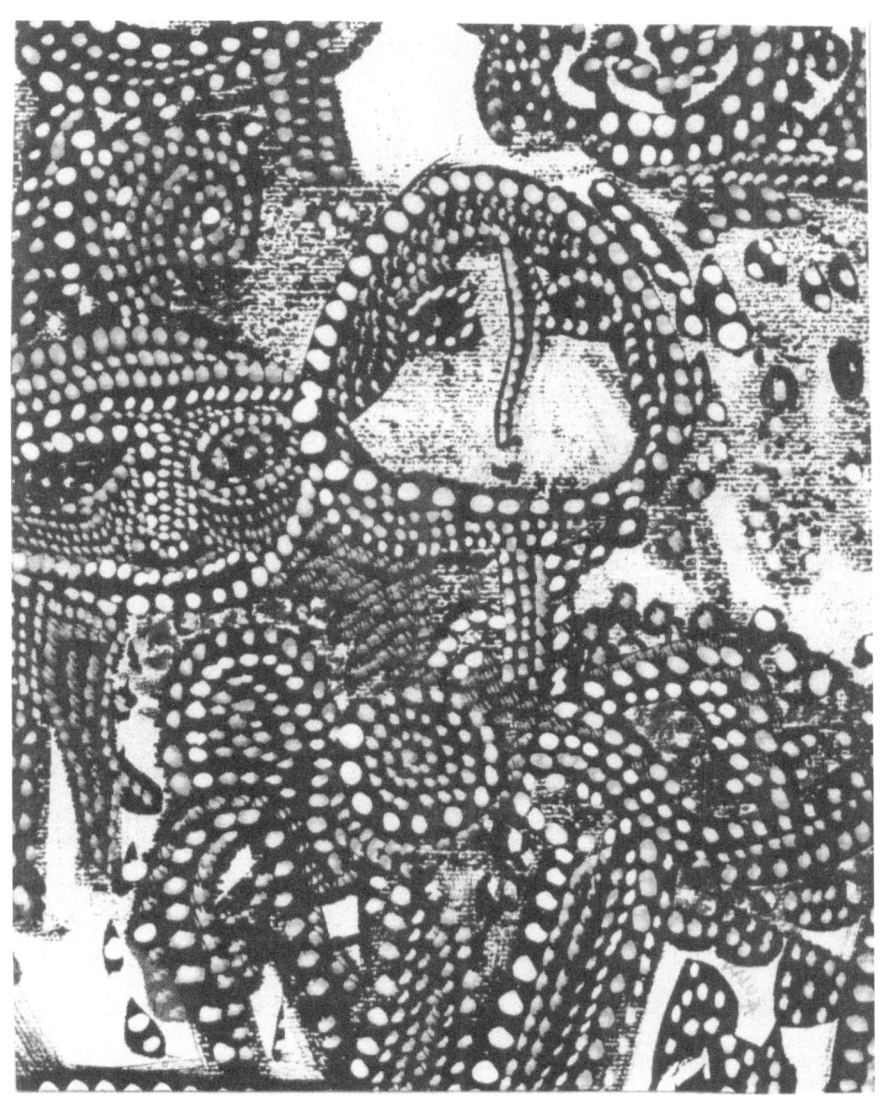

Two Aliens

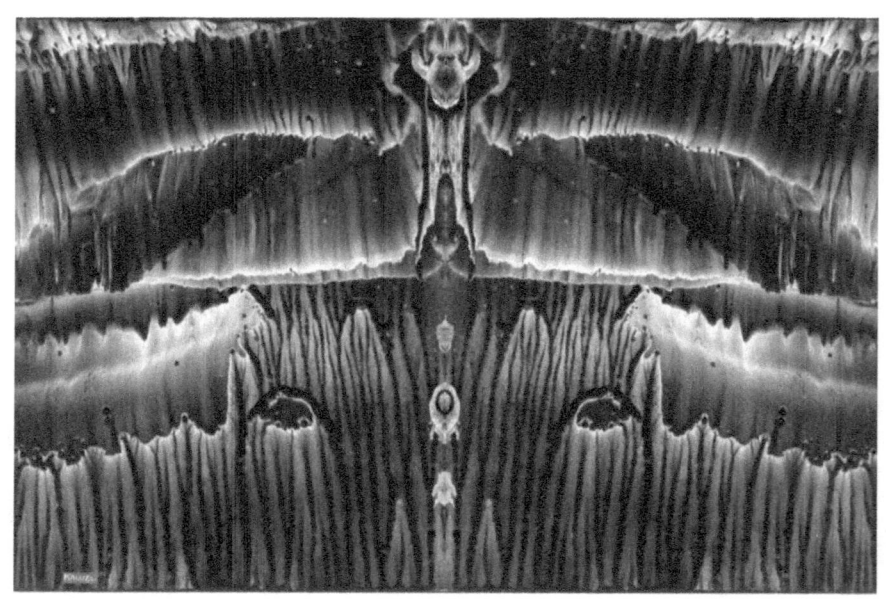

Winged Apparition

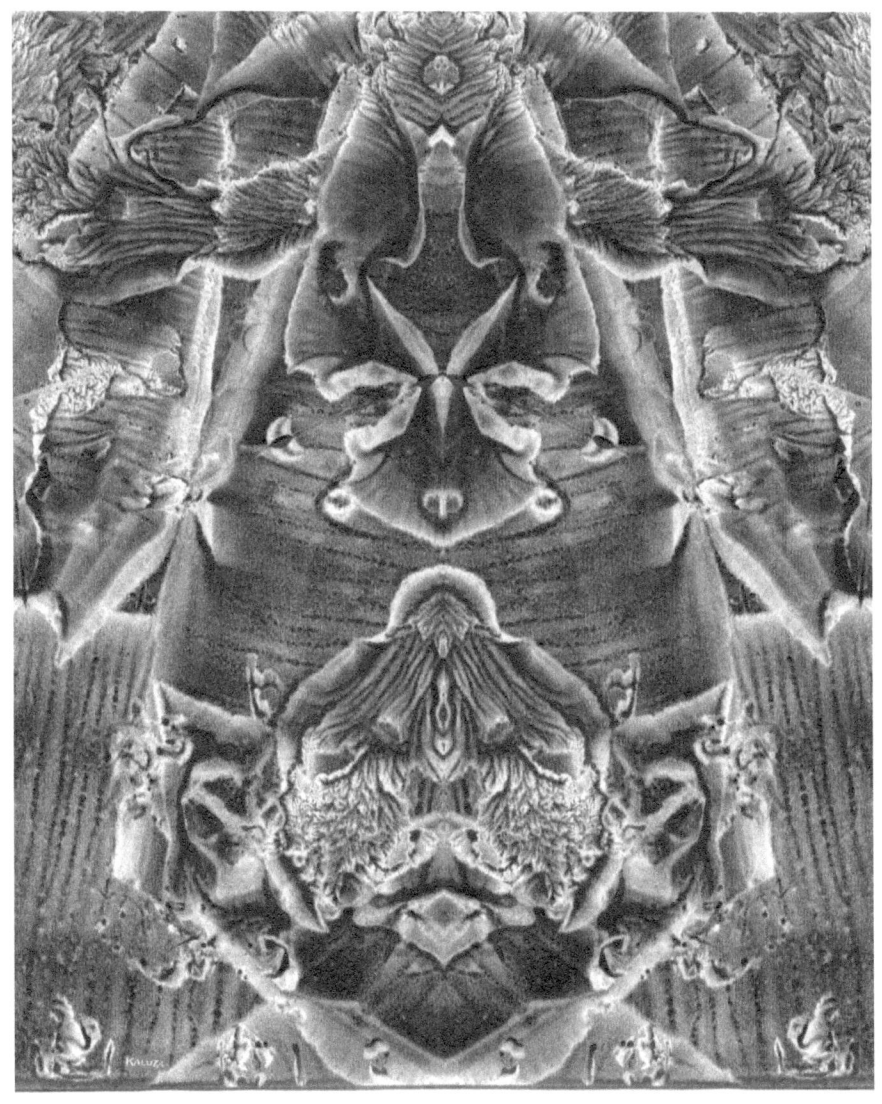

Trolls

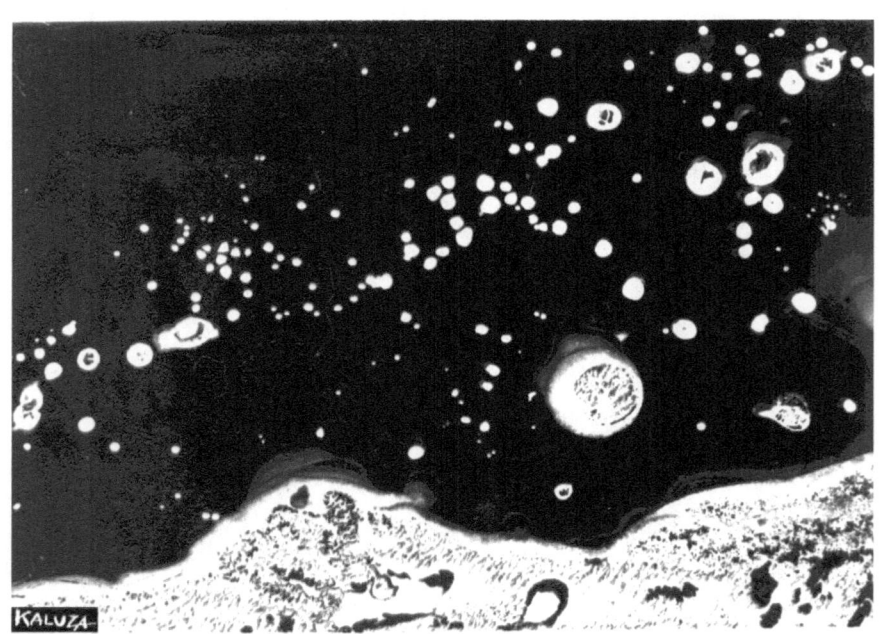

Outer Space

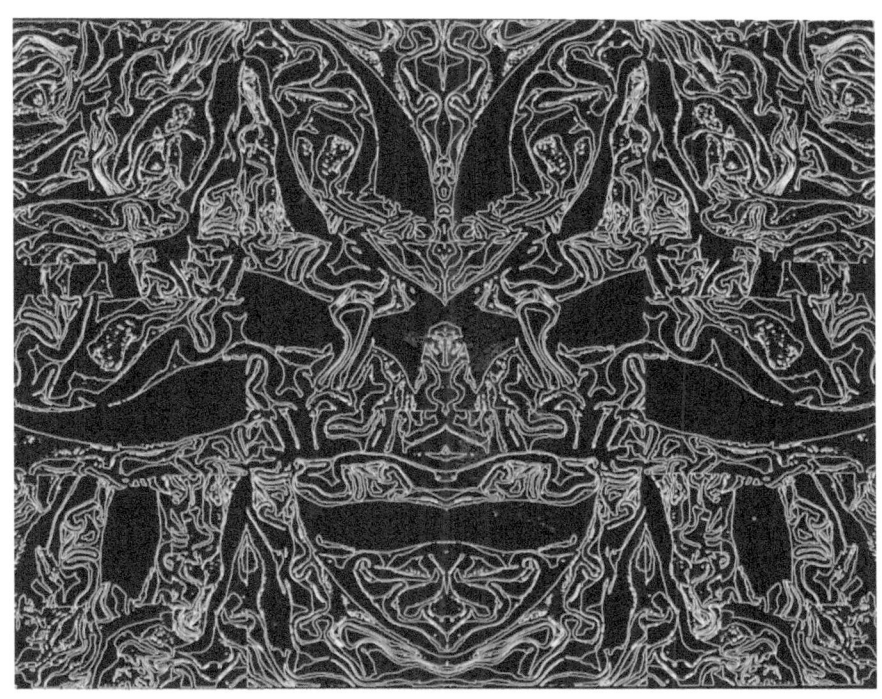

Design 46

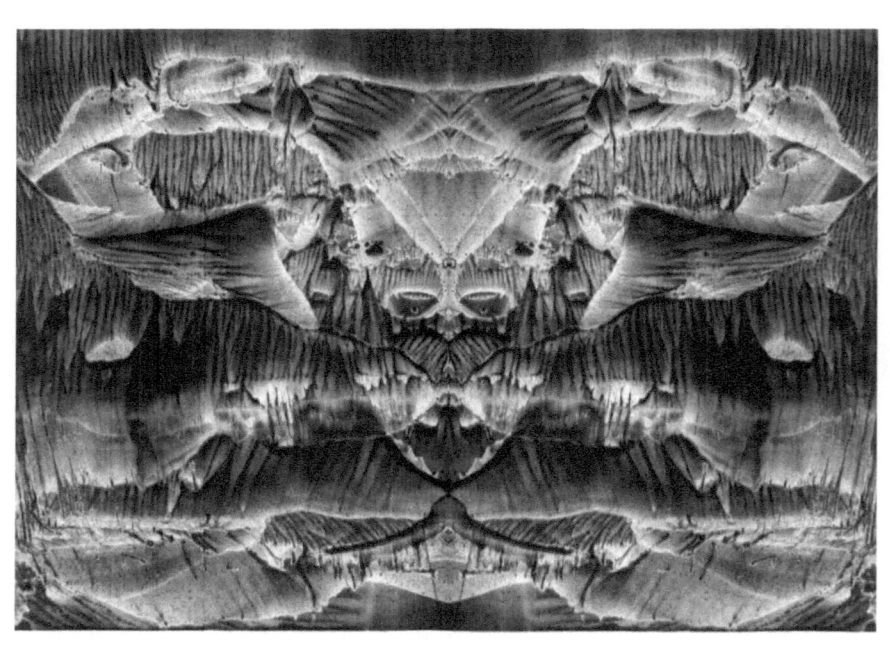

Mighty Wizard

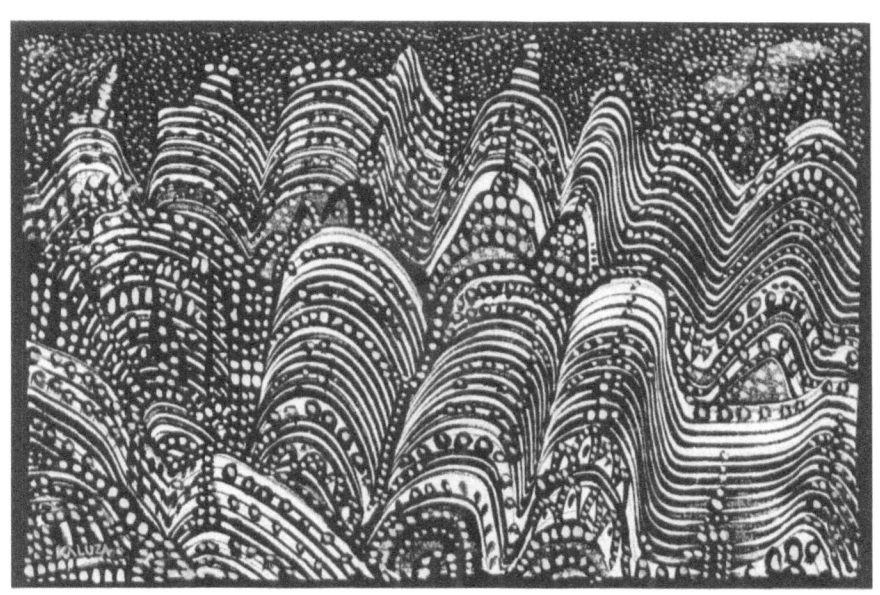

City at Night

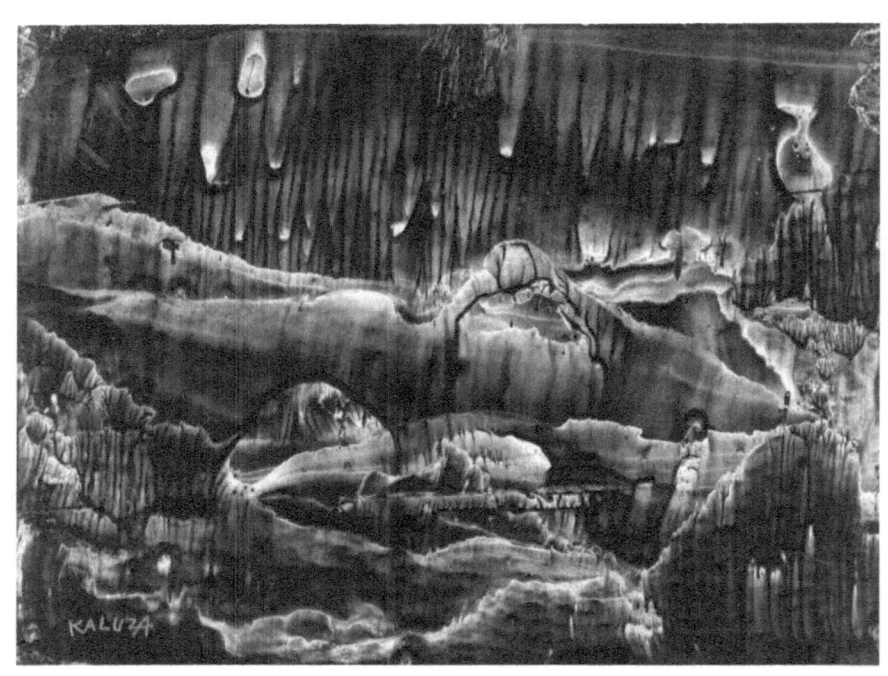

Meteor Shower

Village 2

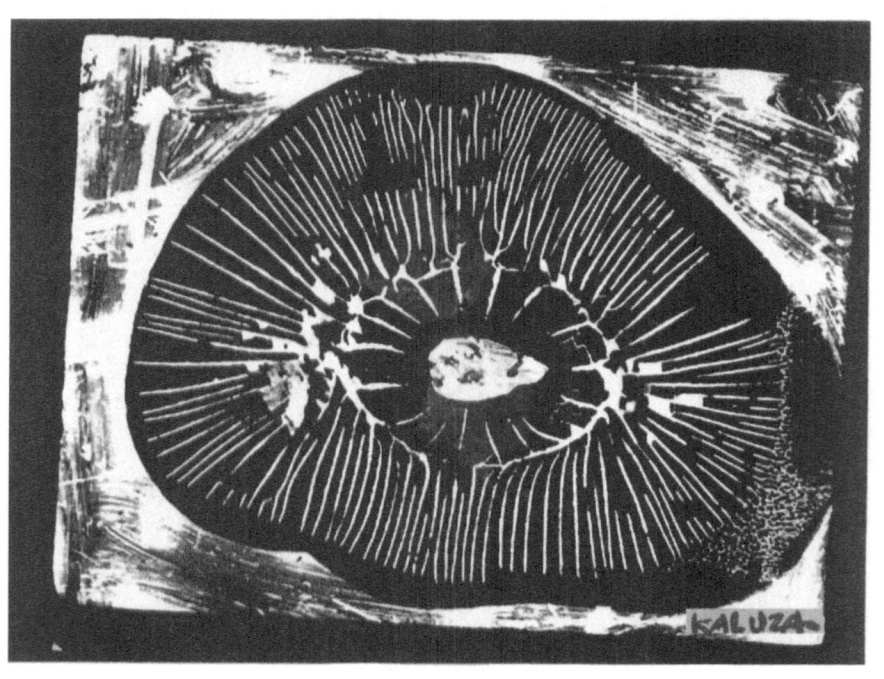

Microbe

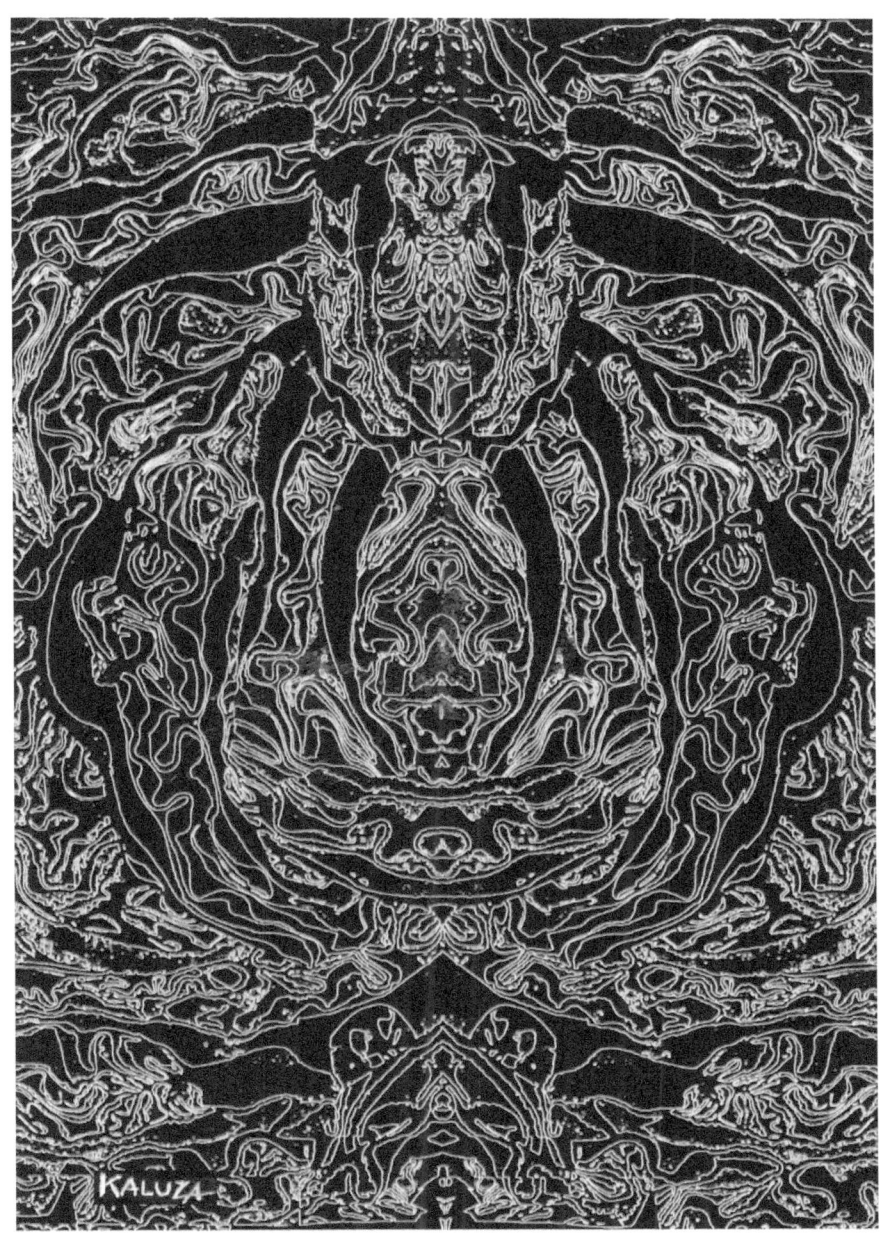

Design 32

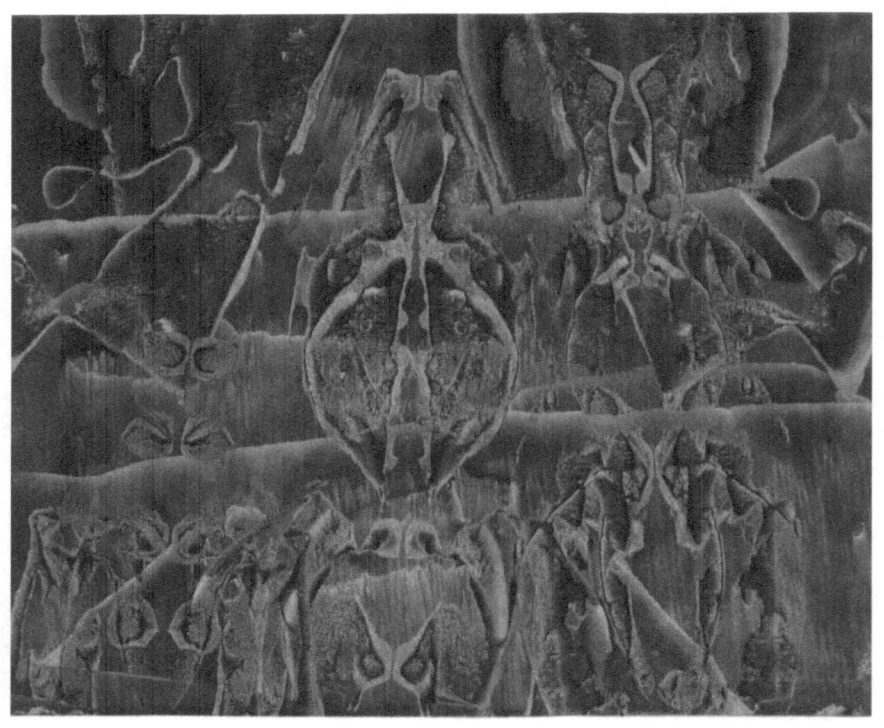

Clowns

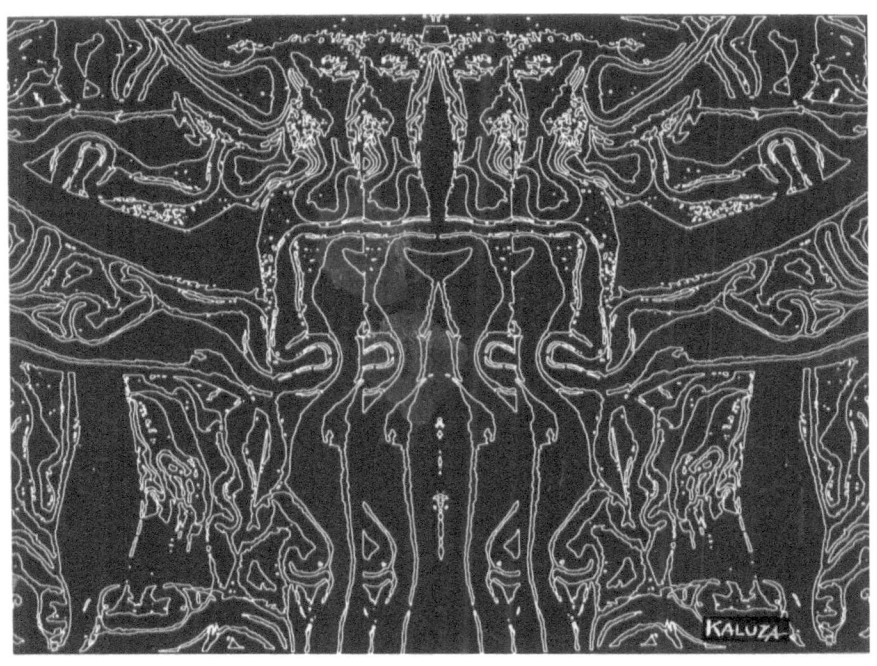

Design 7

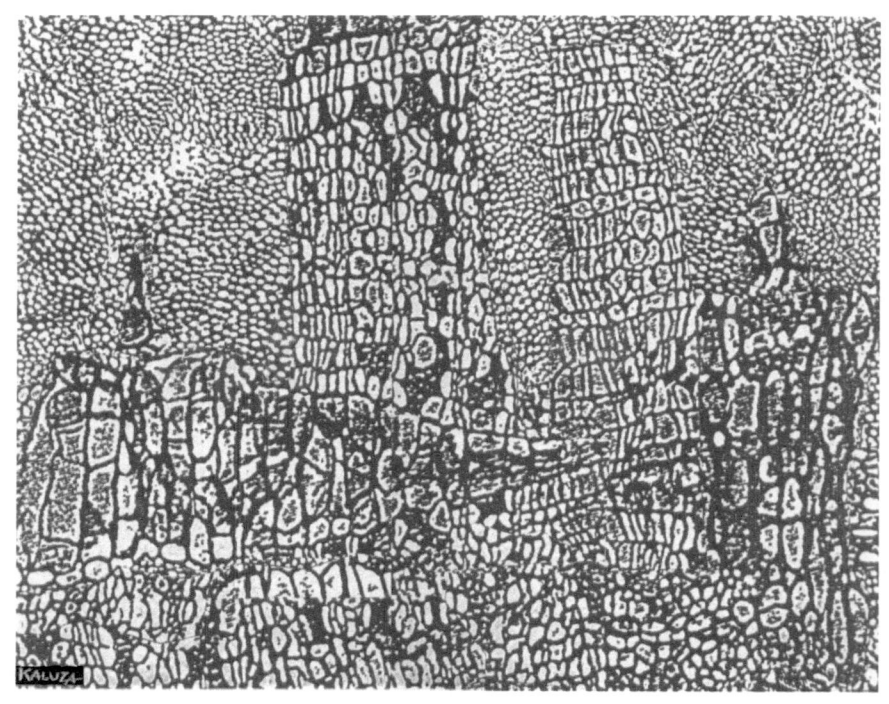

Churches and Skyscrapers

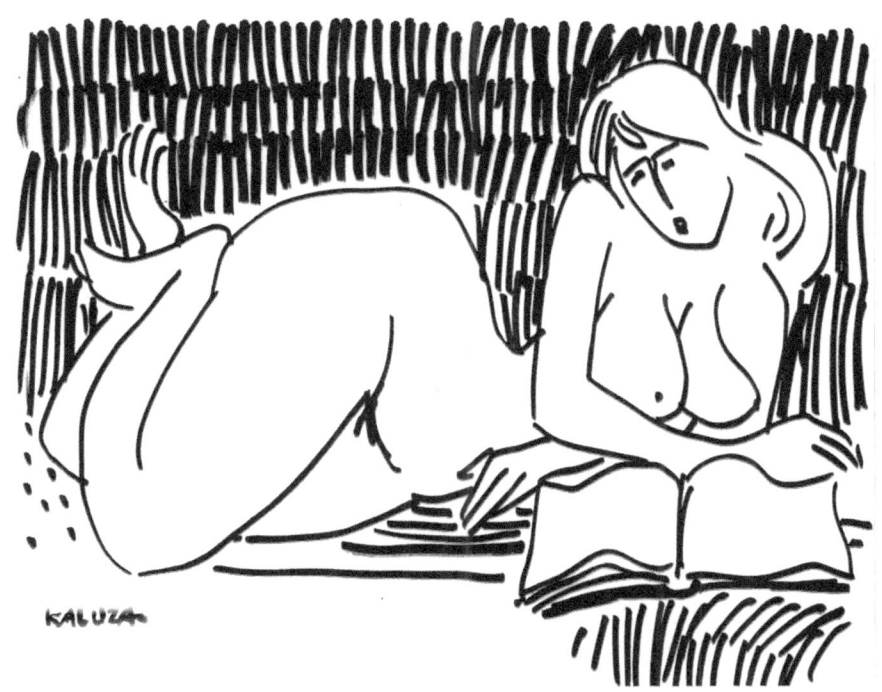

Woman with Book

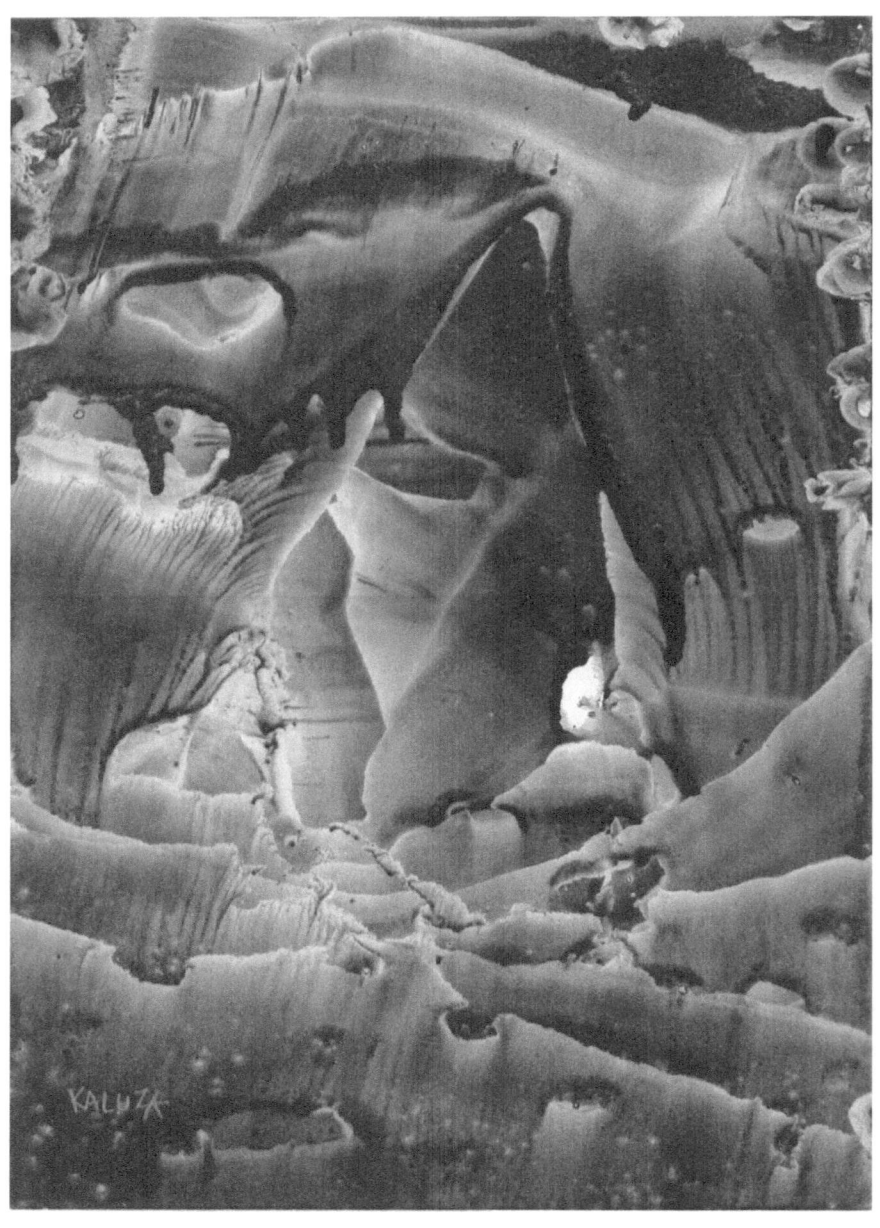

Strange Landscape

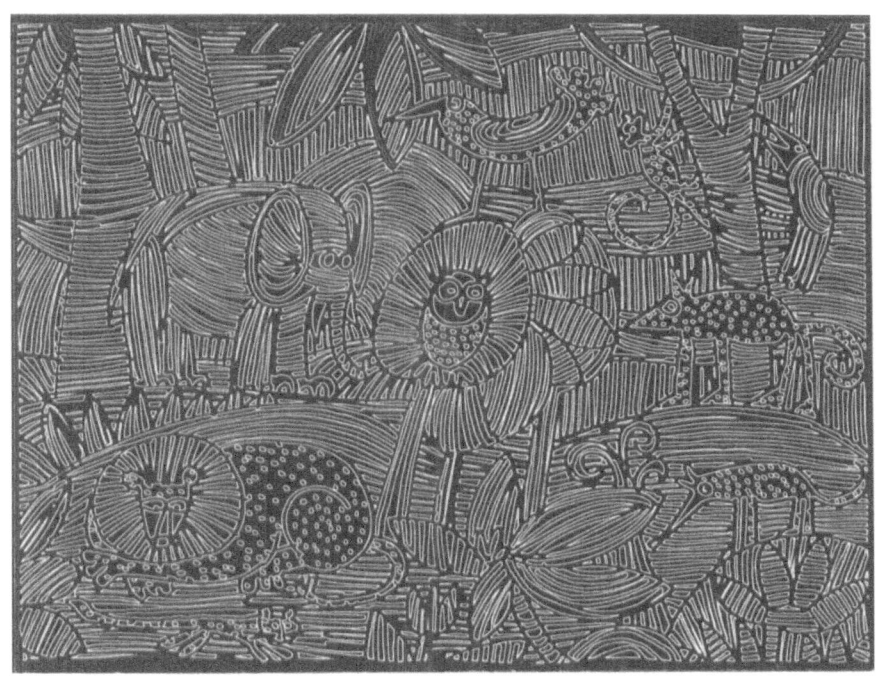

Jungle

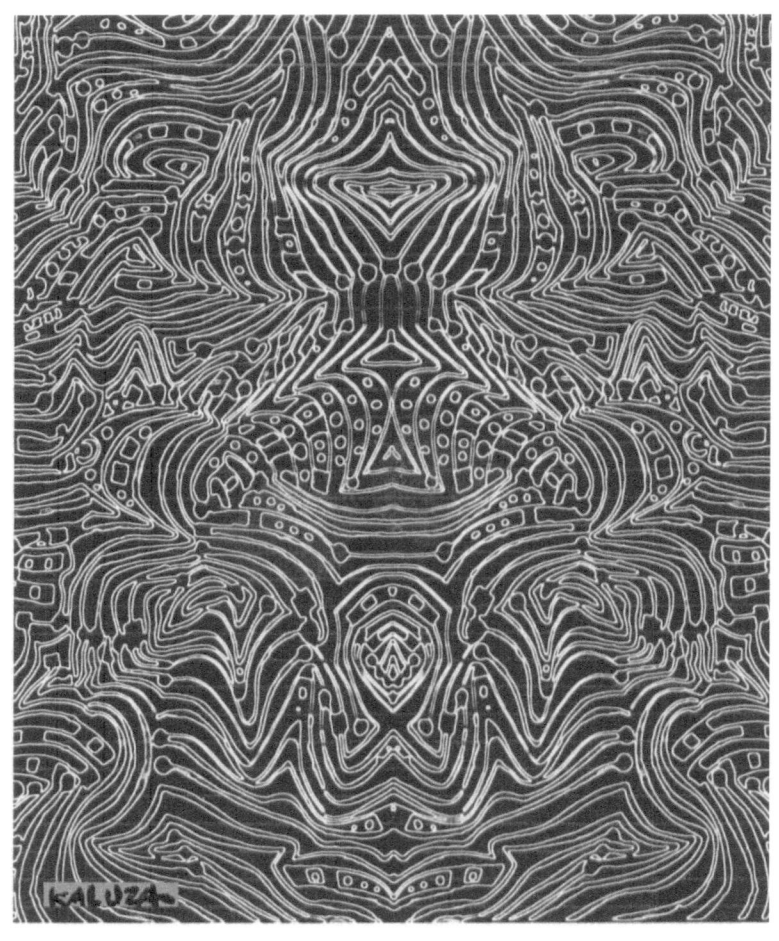

Design 2

ART IN BLACK & WHITE

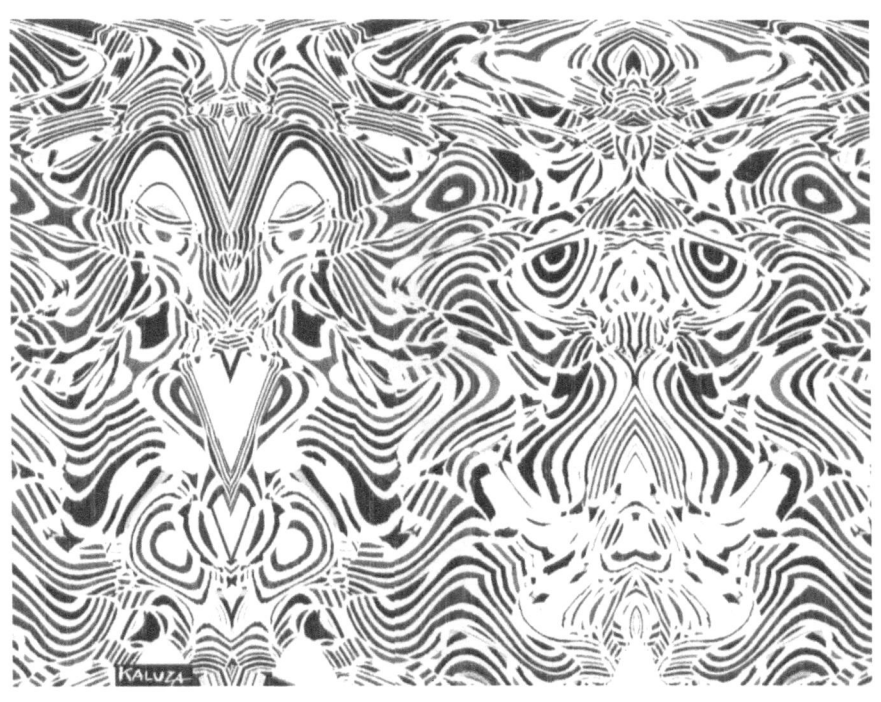

Two Cuties

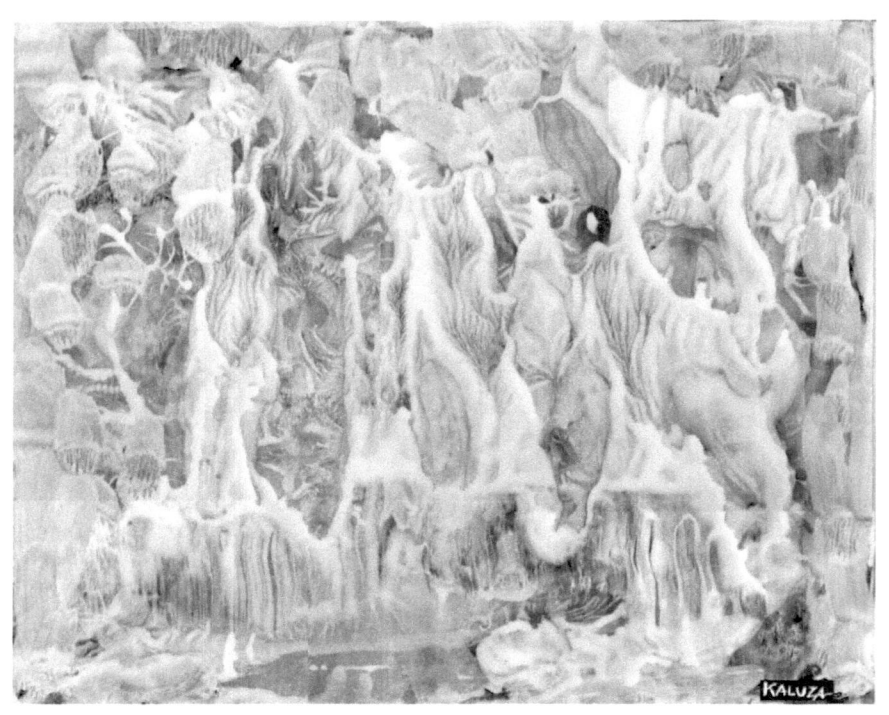

Frosty Landscape 3

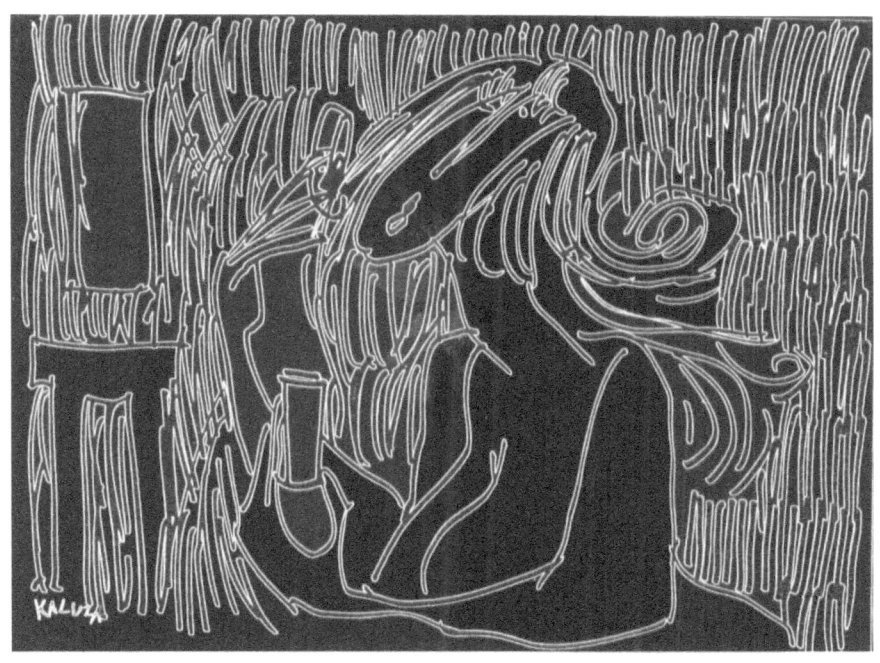

Woman

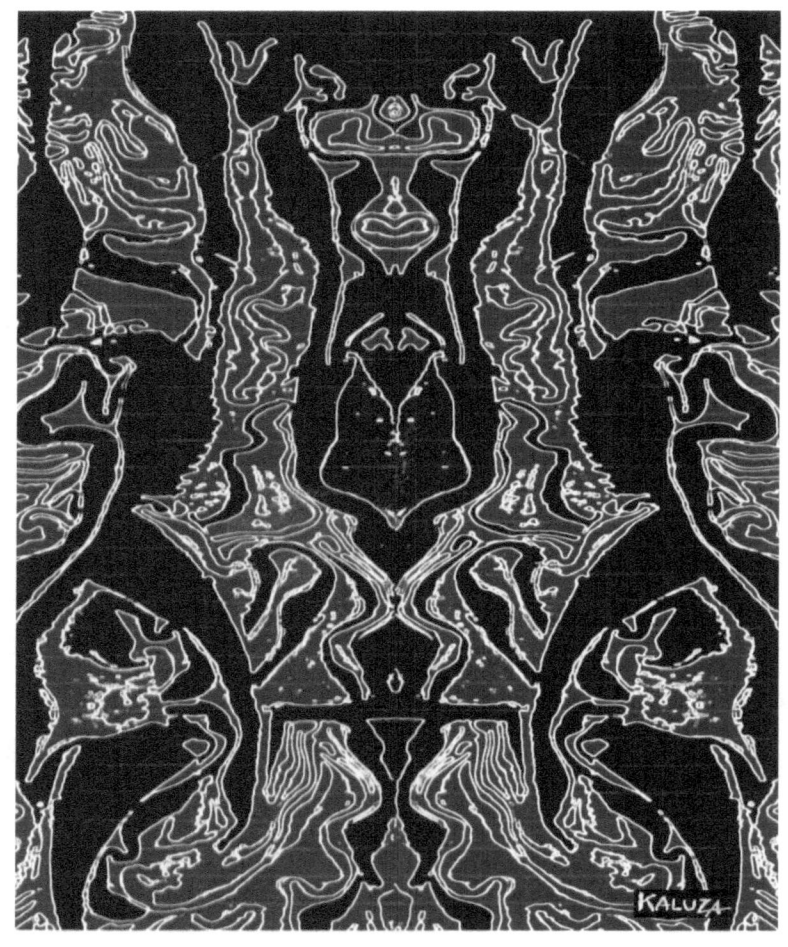

Design 4

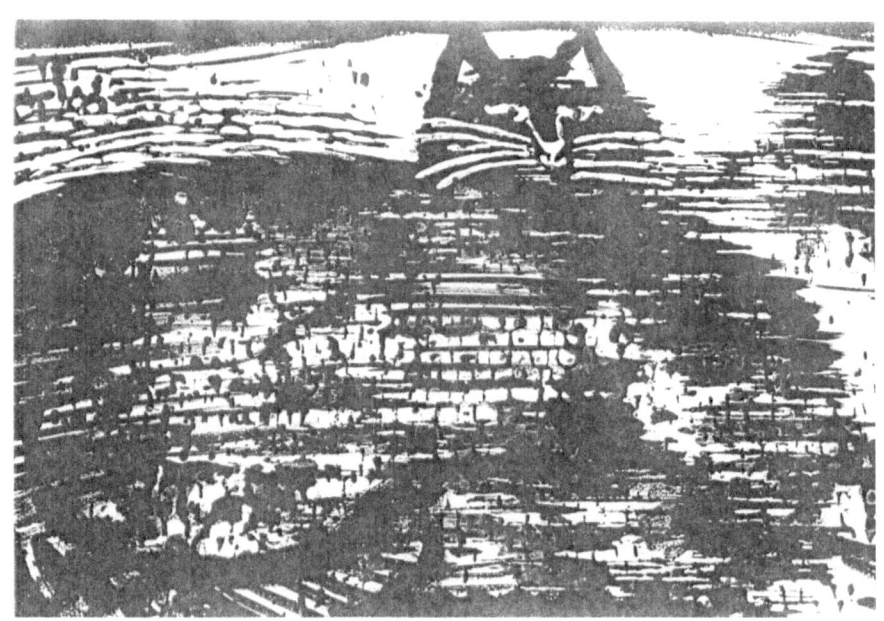

Fat Cat

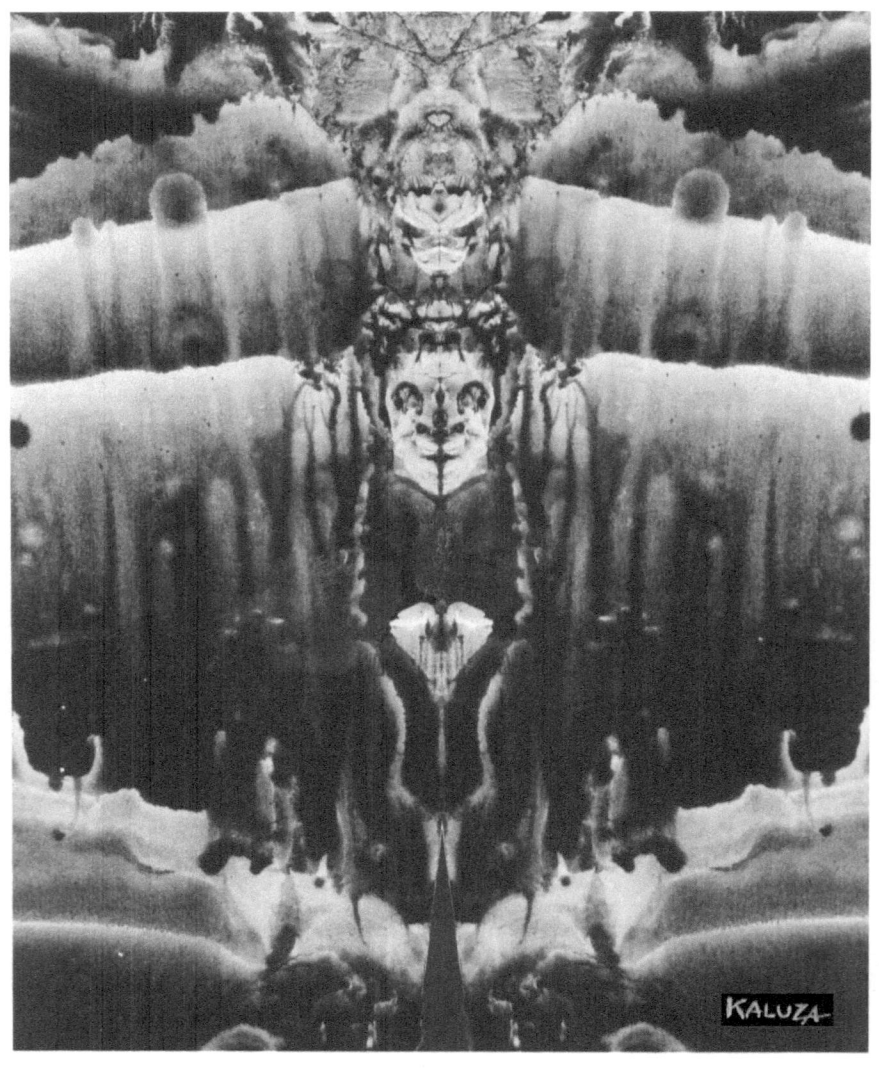

Strange Being

ART IN BLACK & WHITE

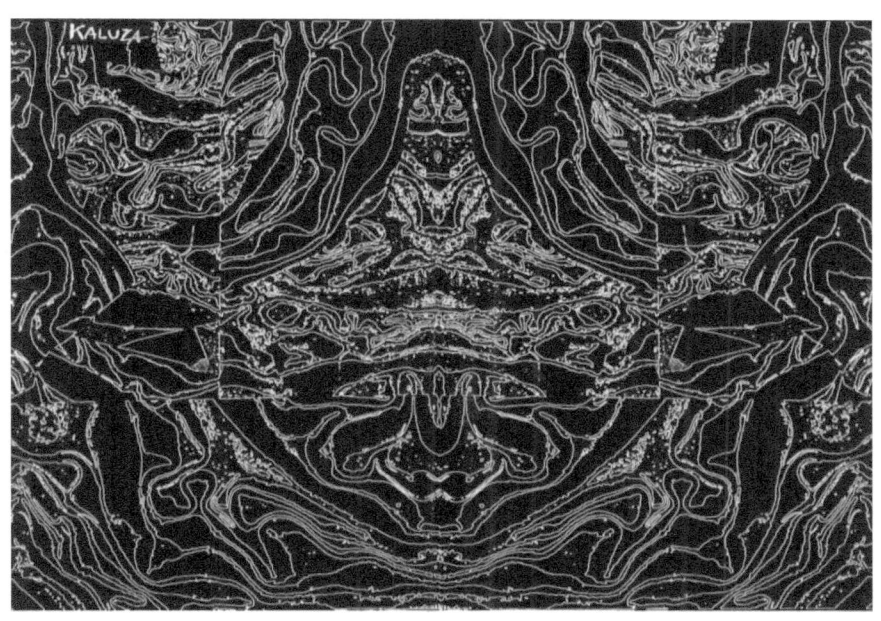

Design 10

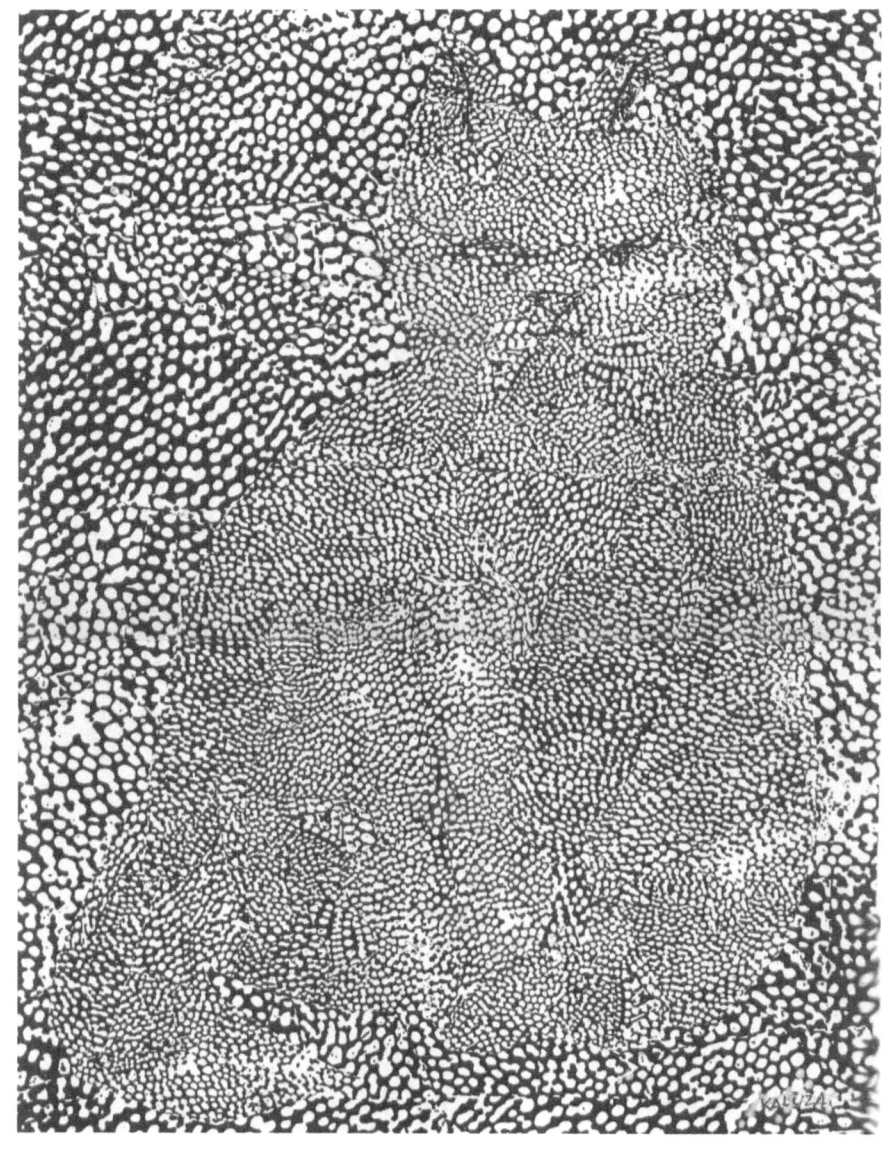

Camouflage Cat 3

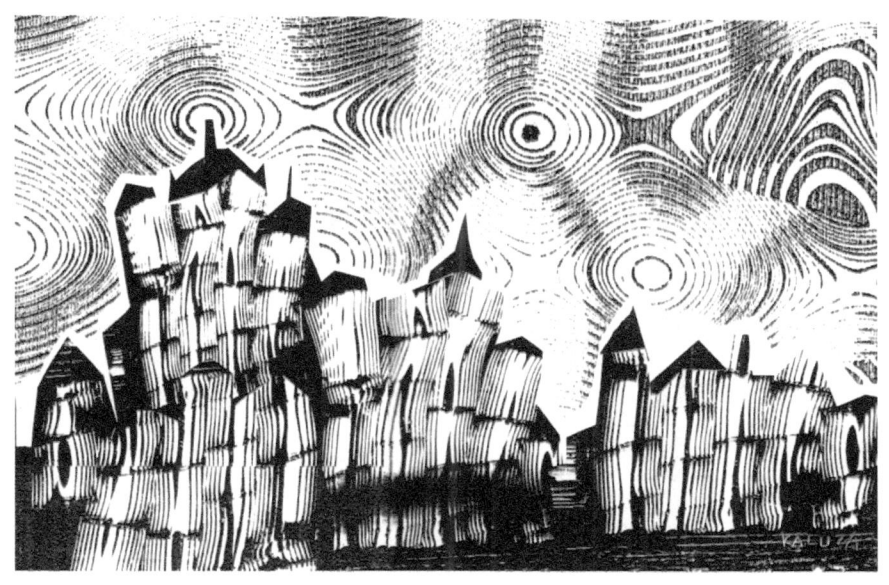

City 2

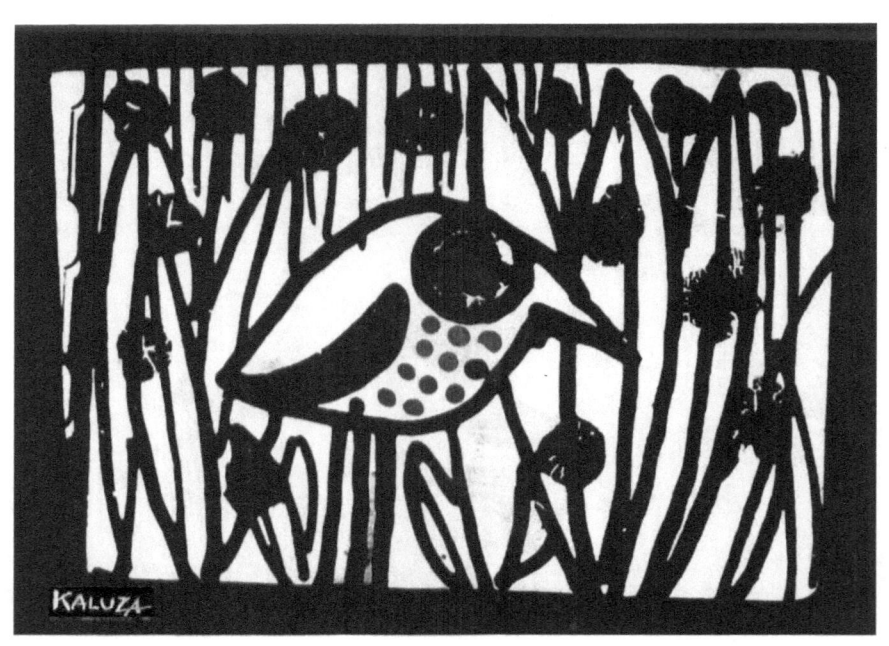

Bird

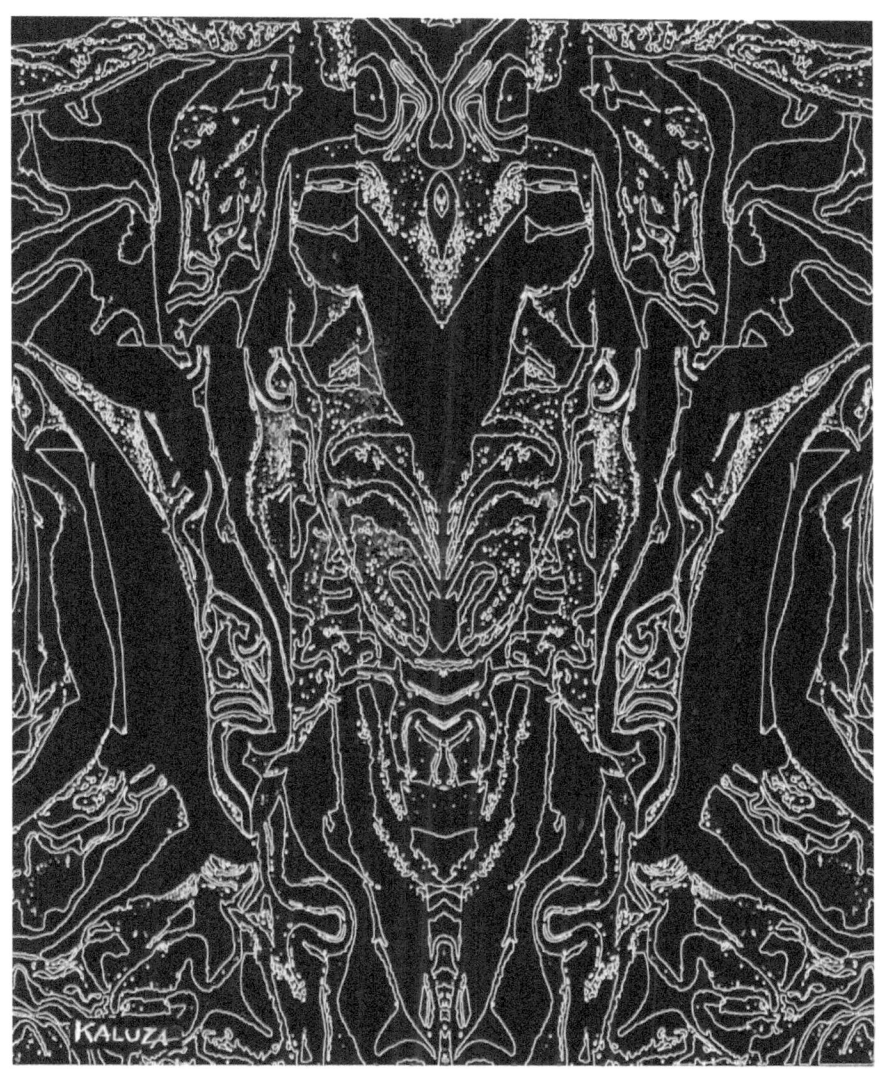

Design 37

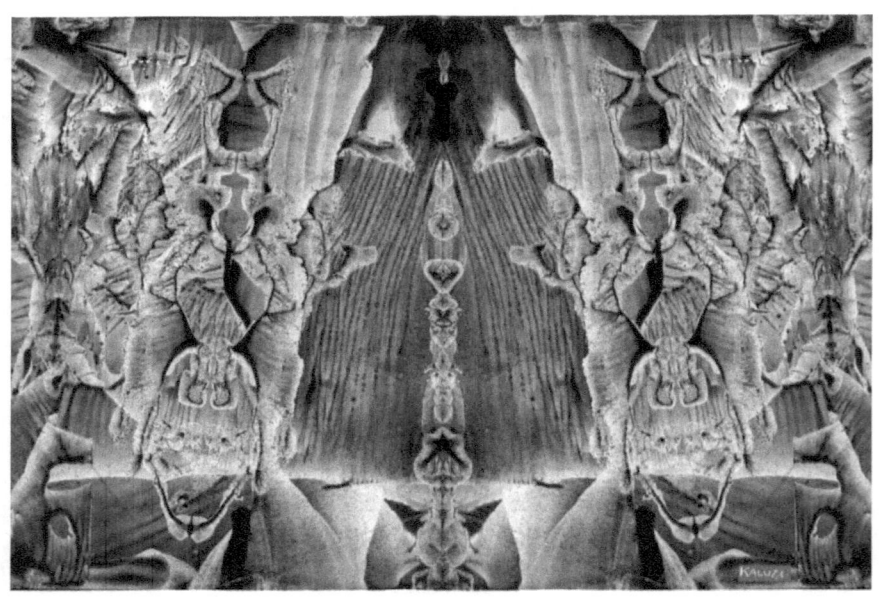

The Oracle

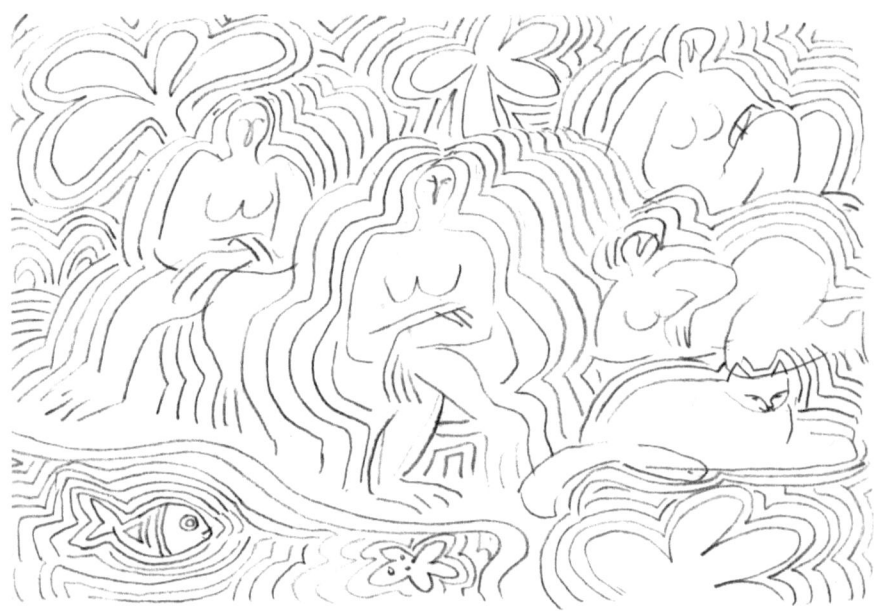

At the Beach

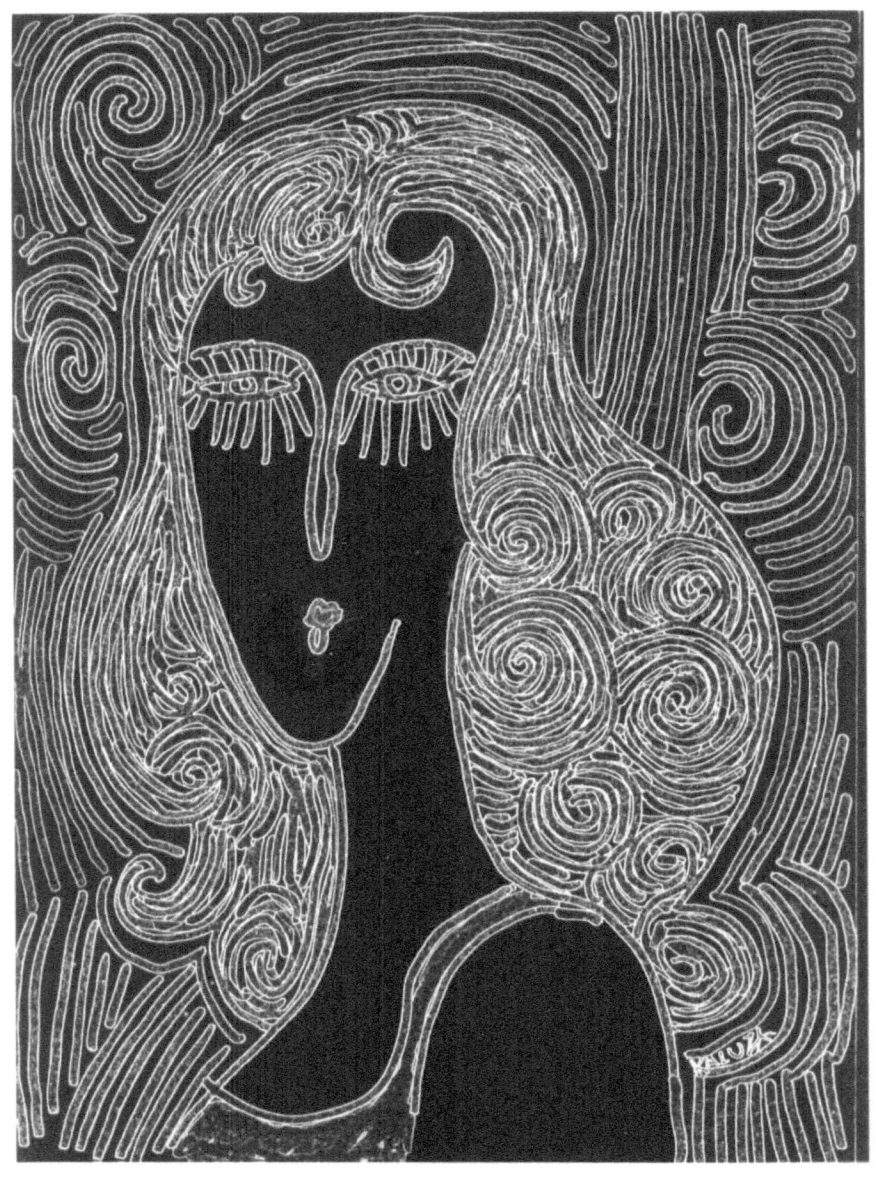

Face 3

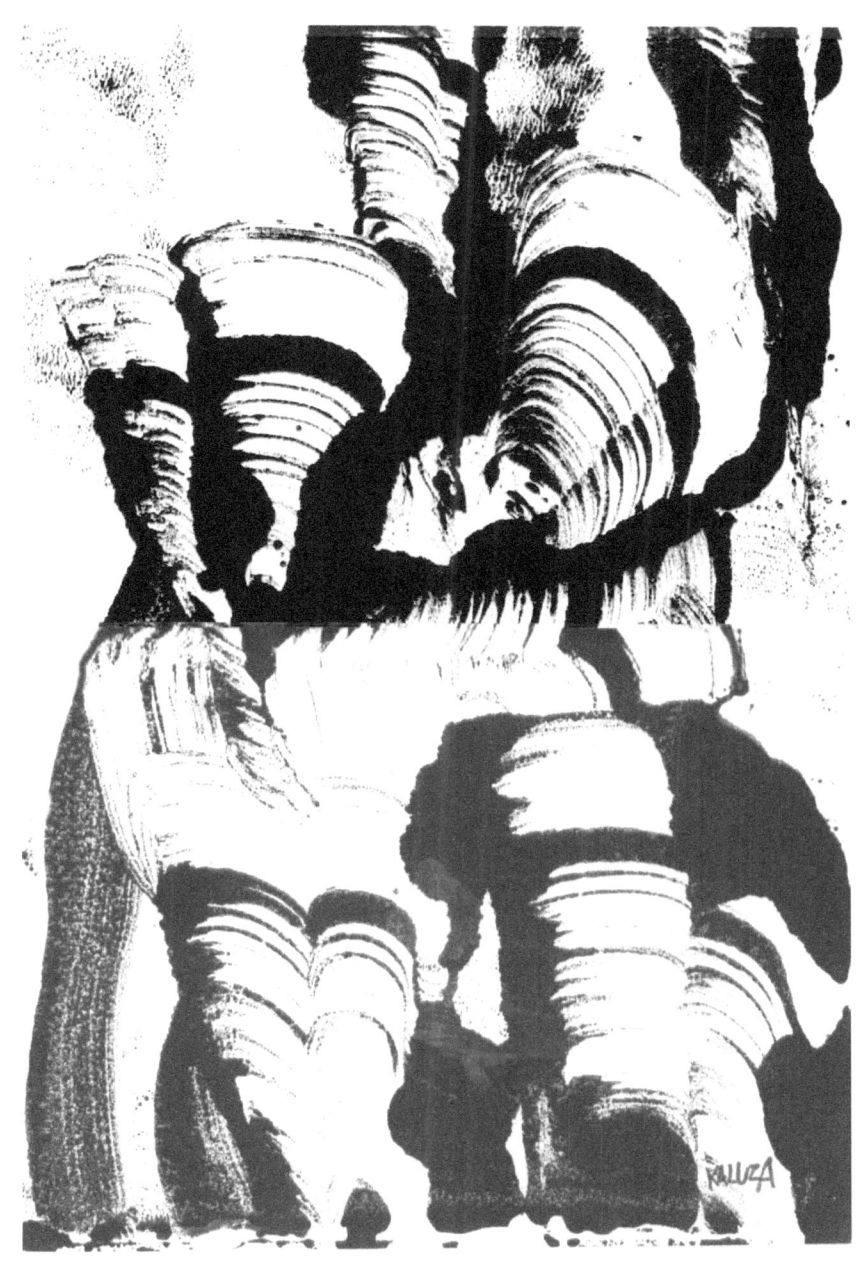

Twisters

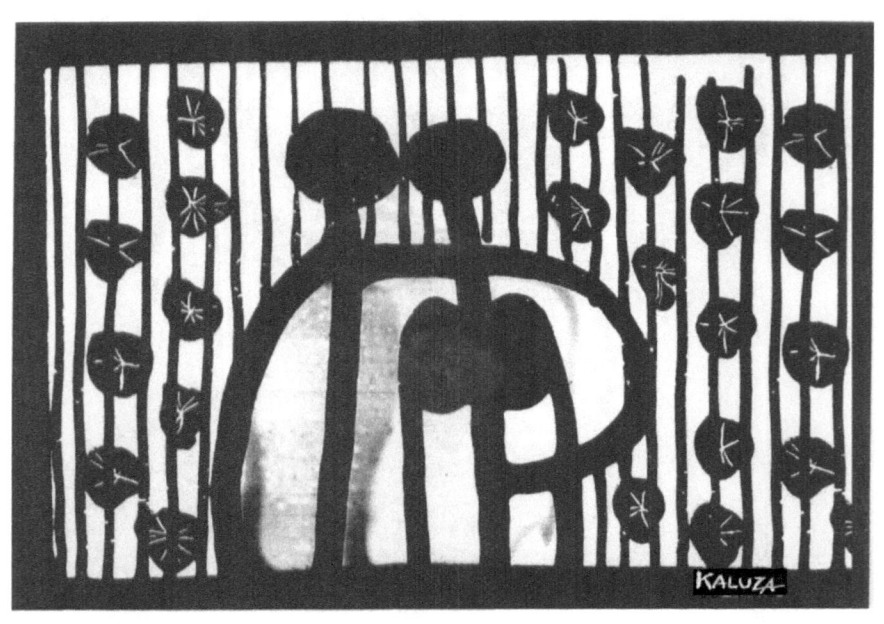

Couple

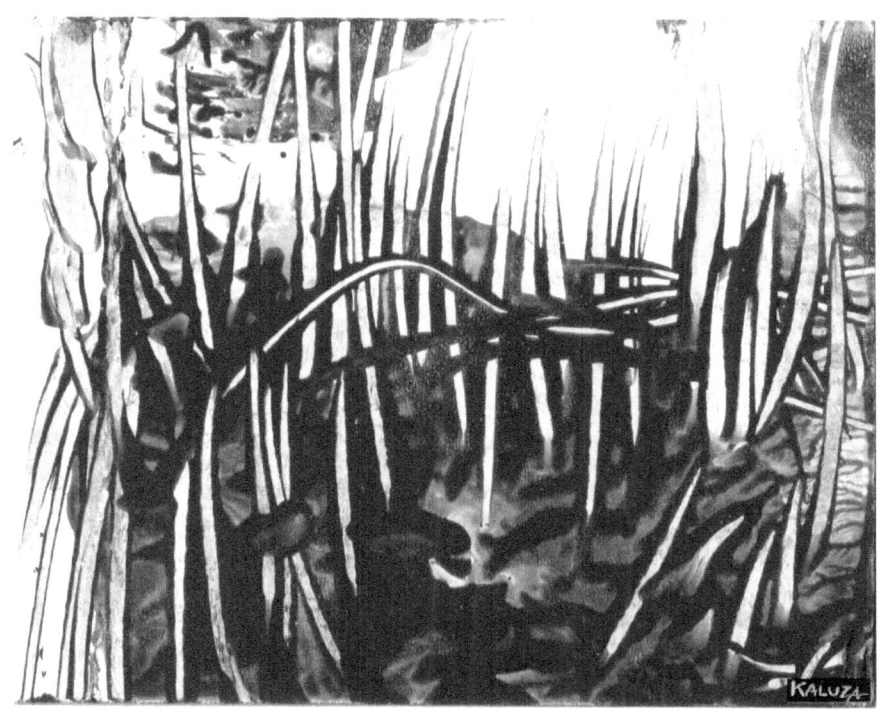

Spires

Cat

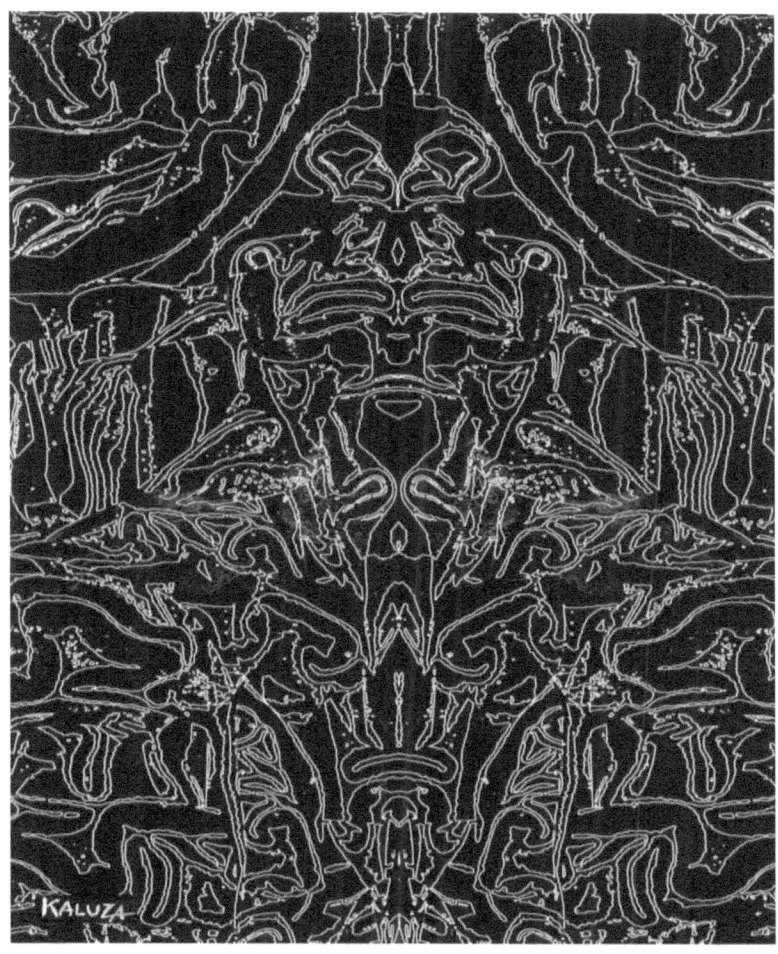

Design 21

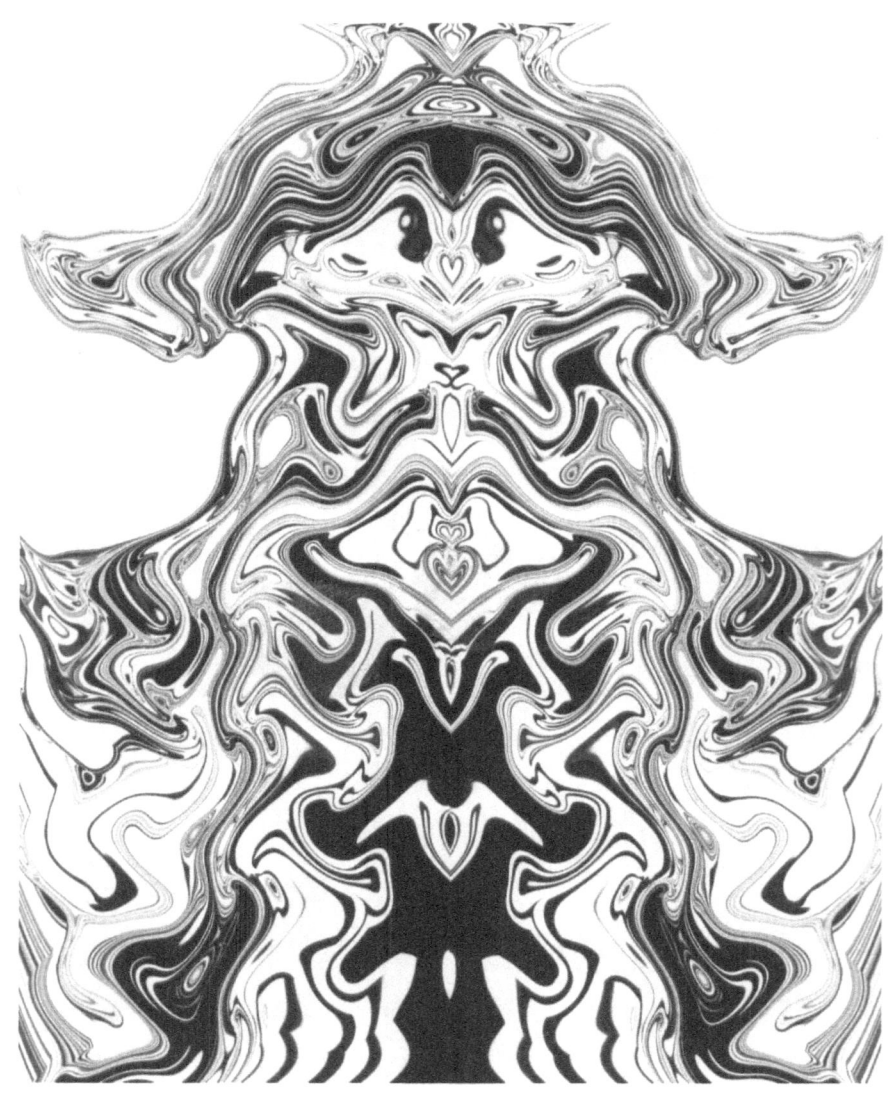

Little Girl

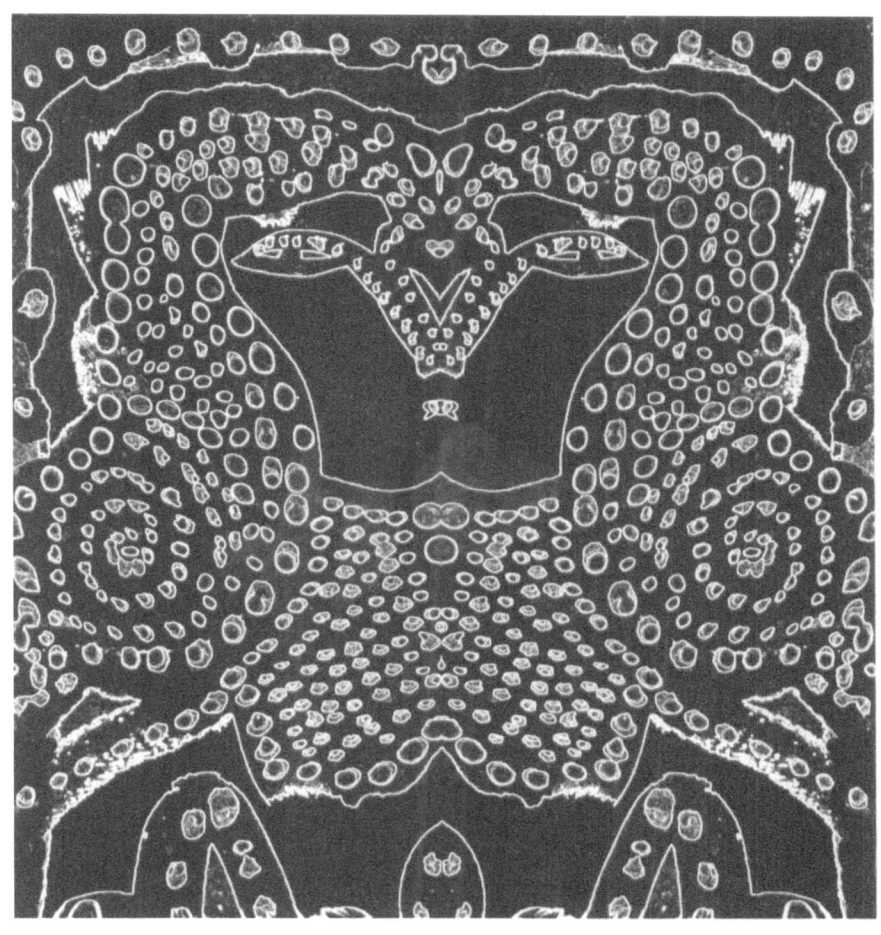

Dowager

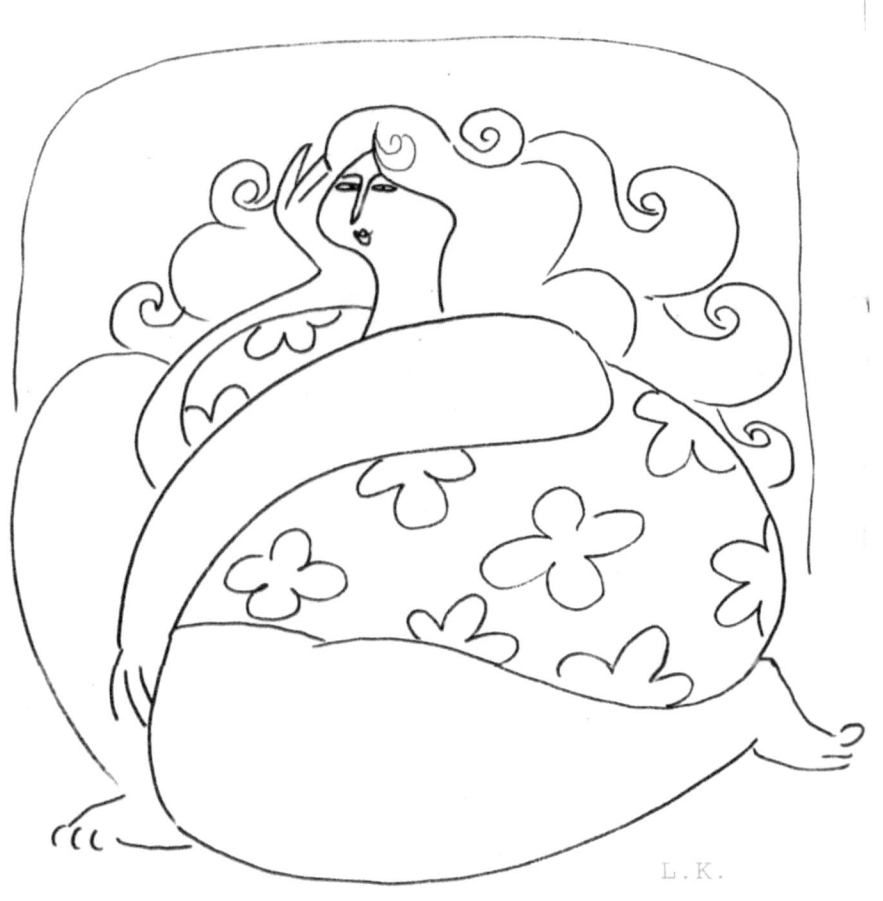

Woman Resting

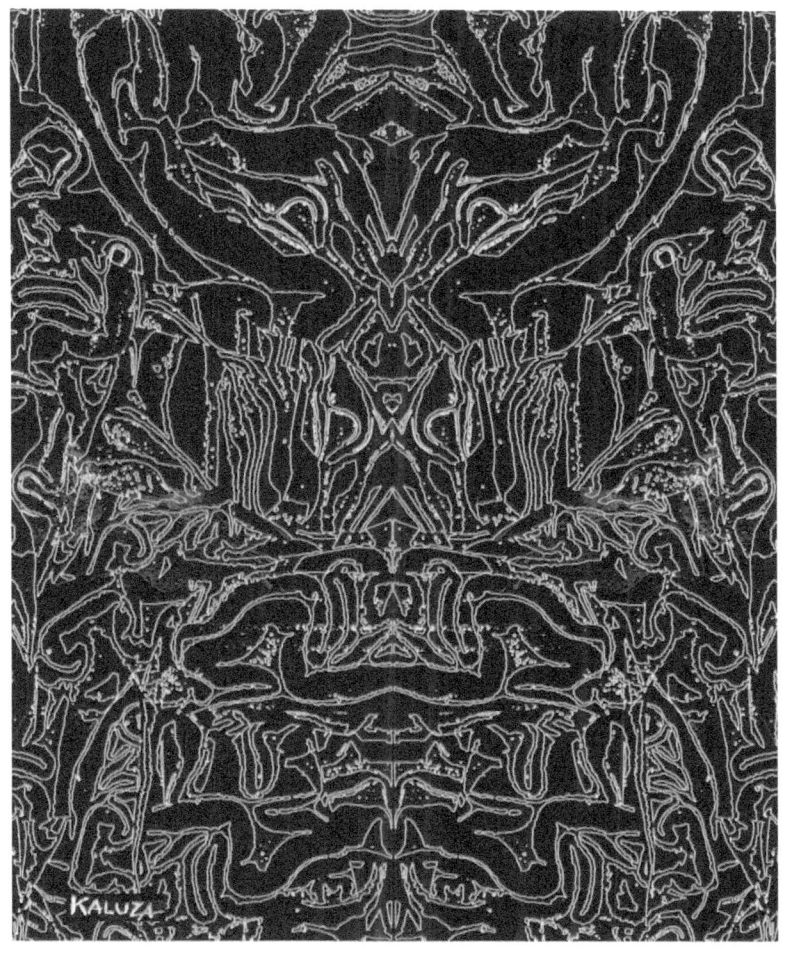

Design 20

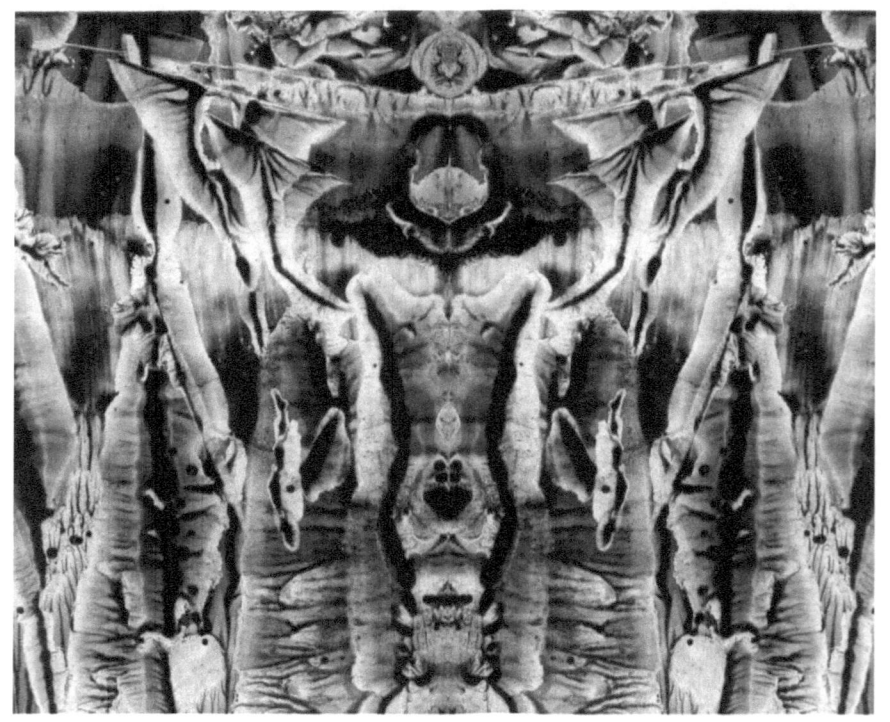

Divine Being

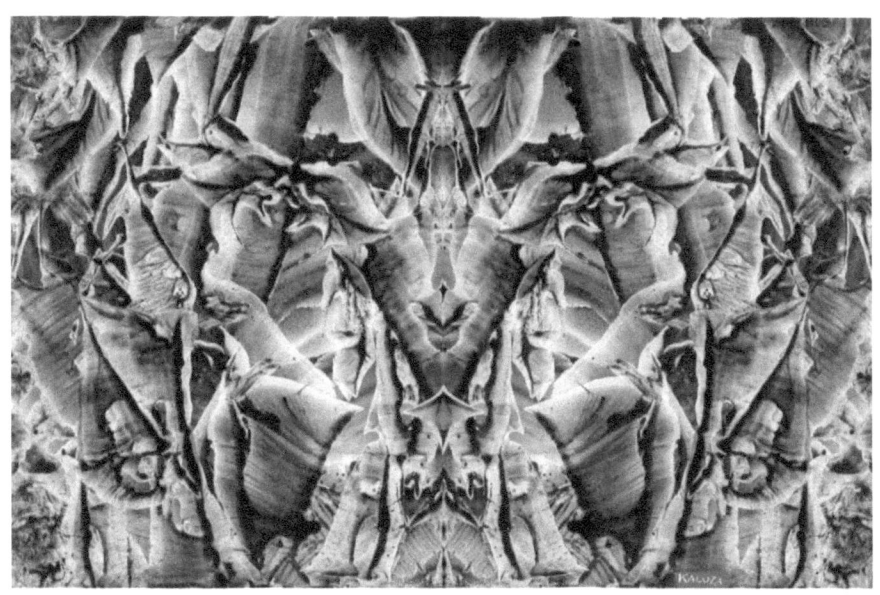

The Priestess

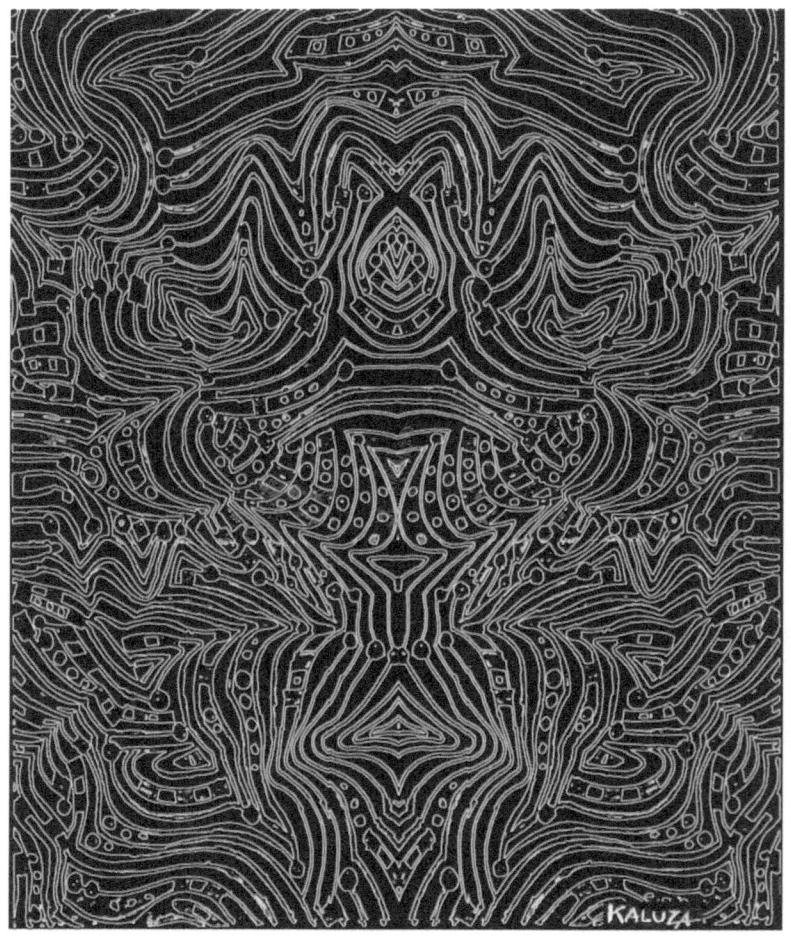

Design 16

ART IN BLACK & WHITE

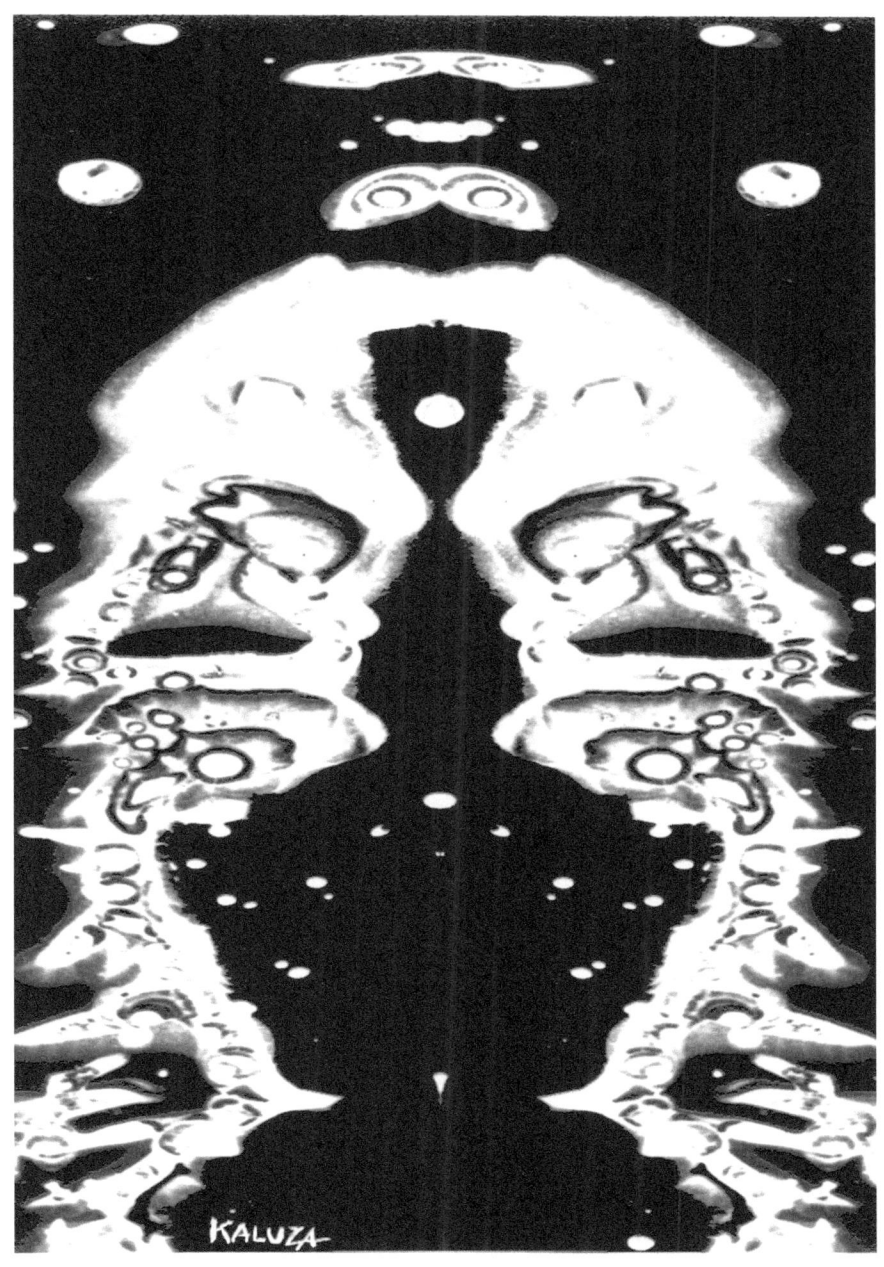

Clown 2

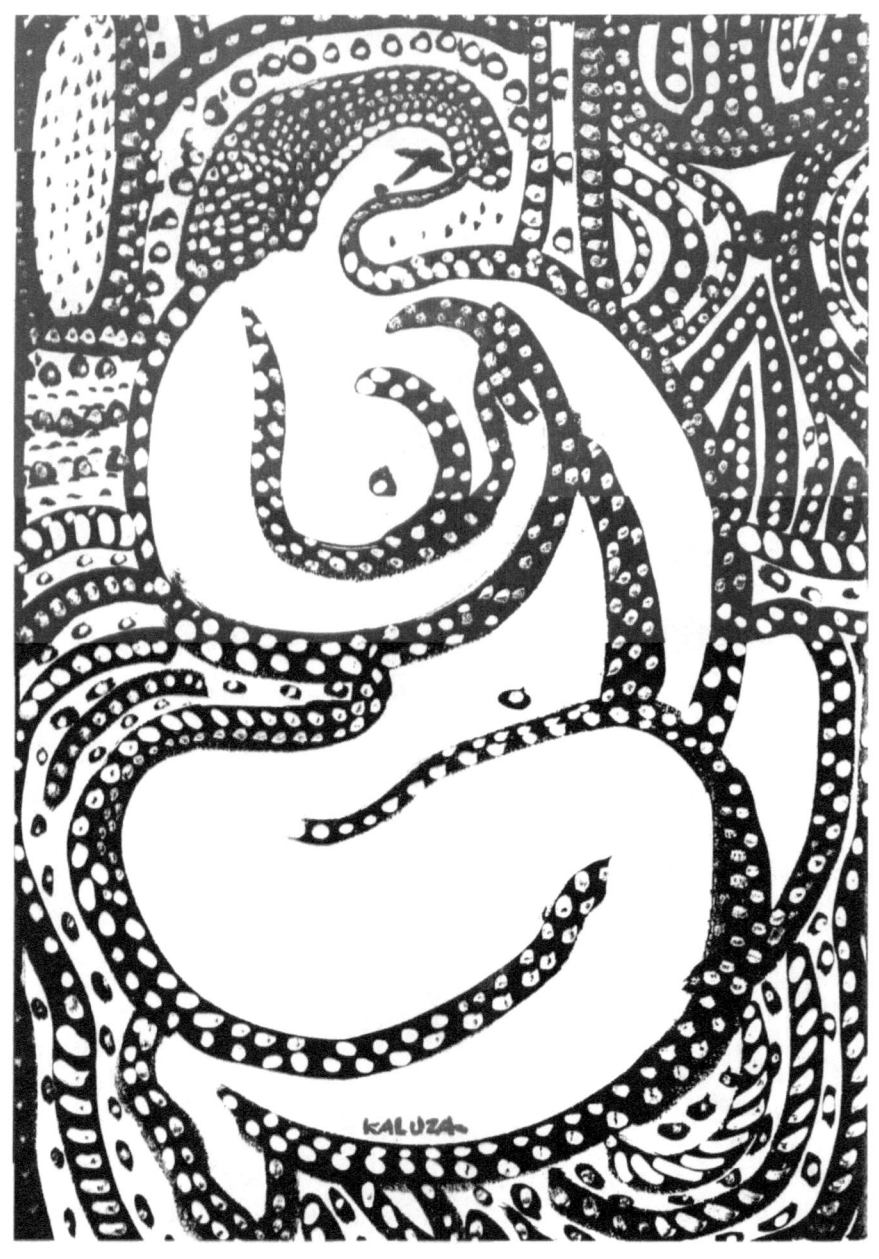

Woman Relaxing

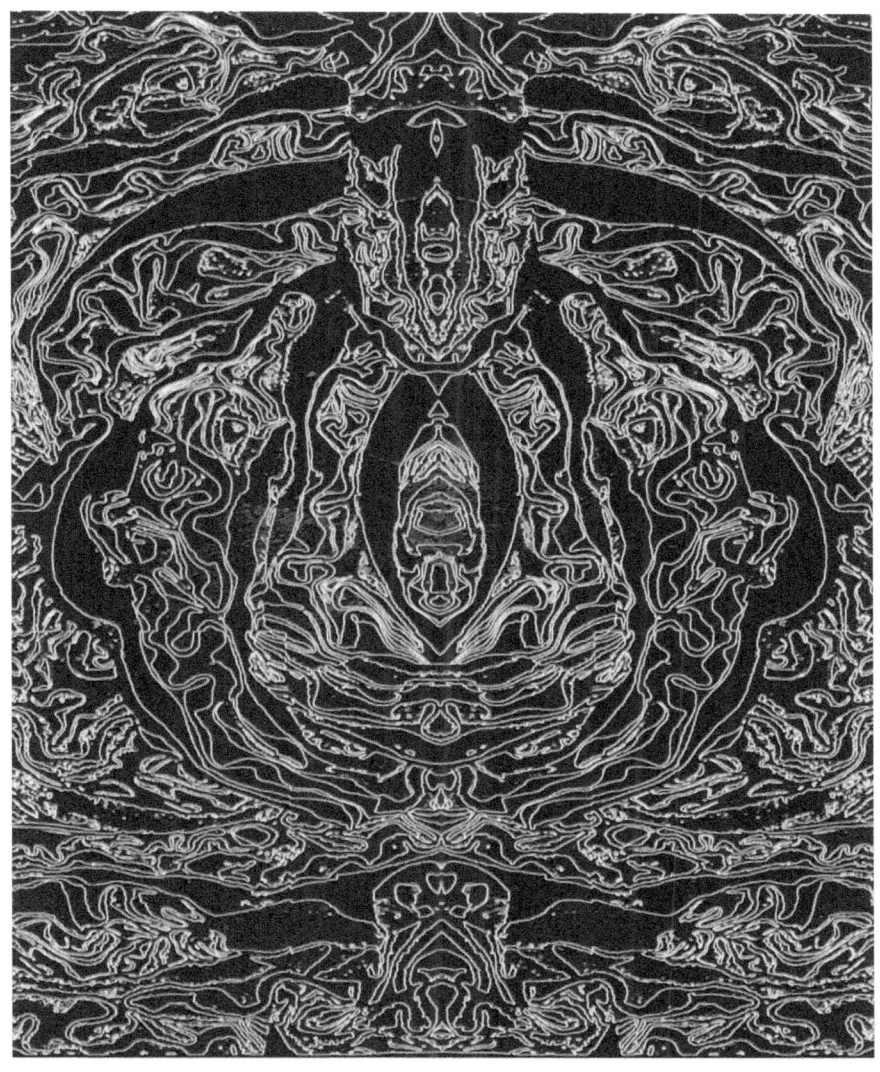

Design 36

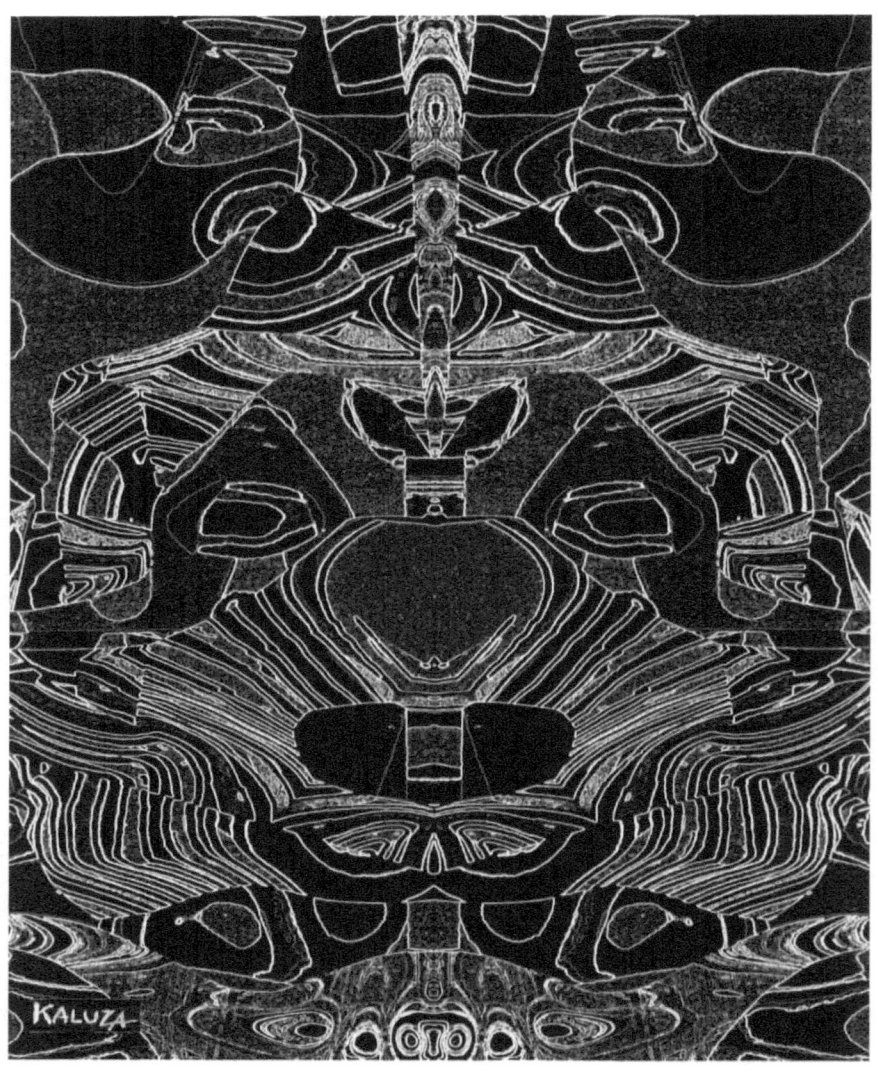

Face

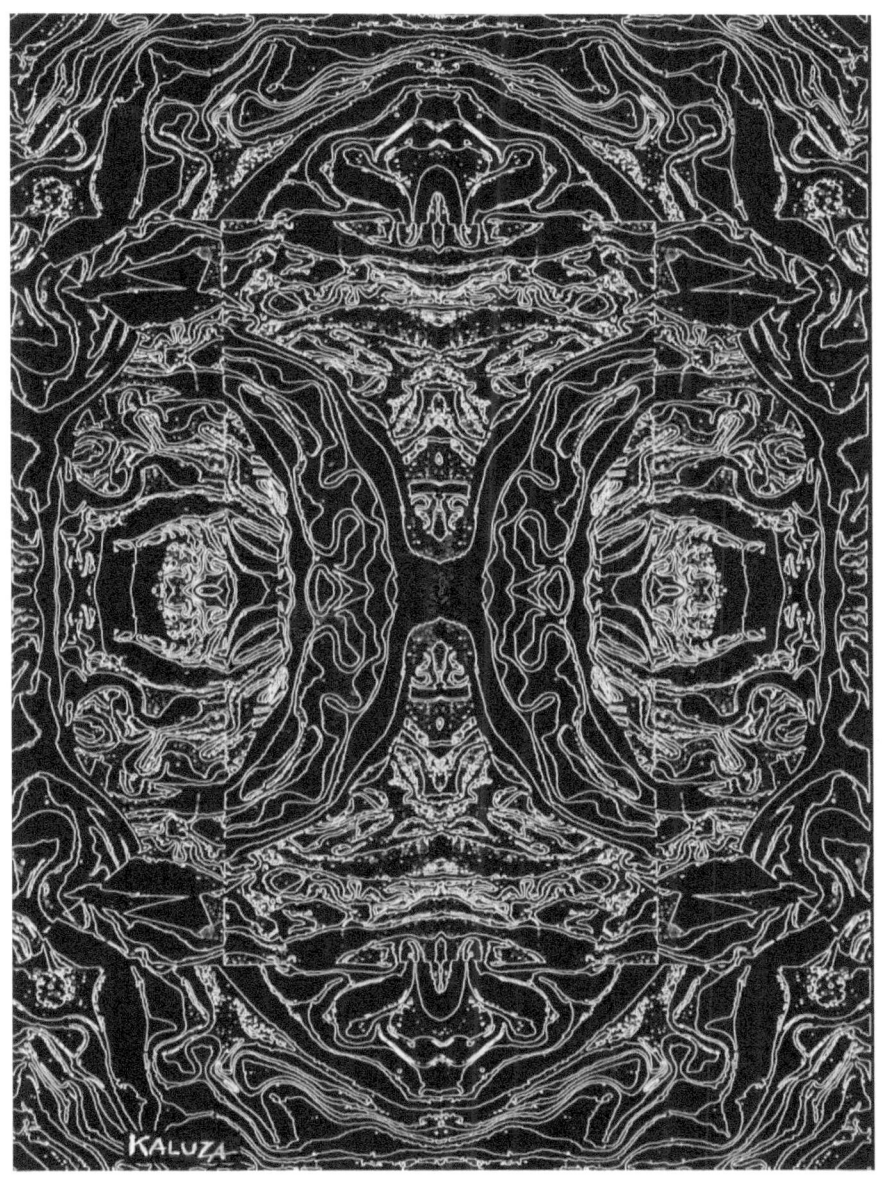

Design 17

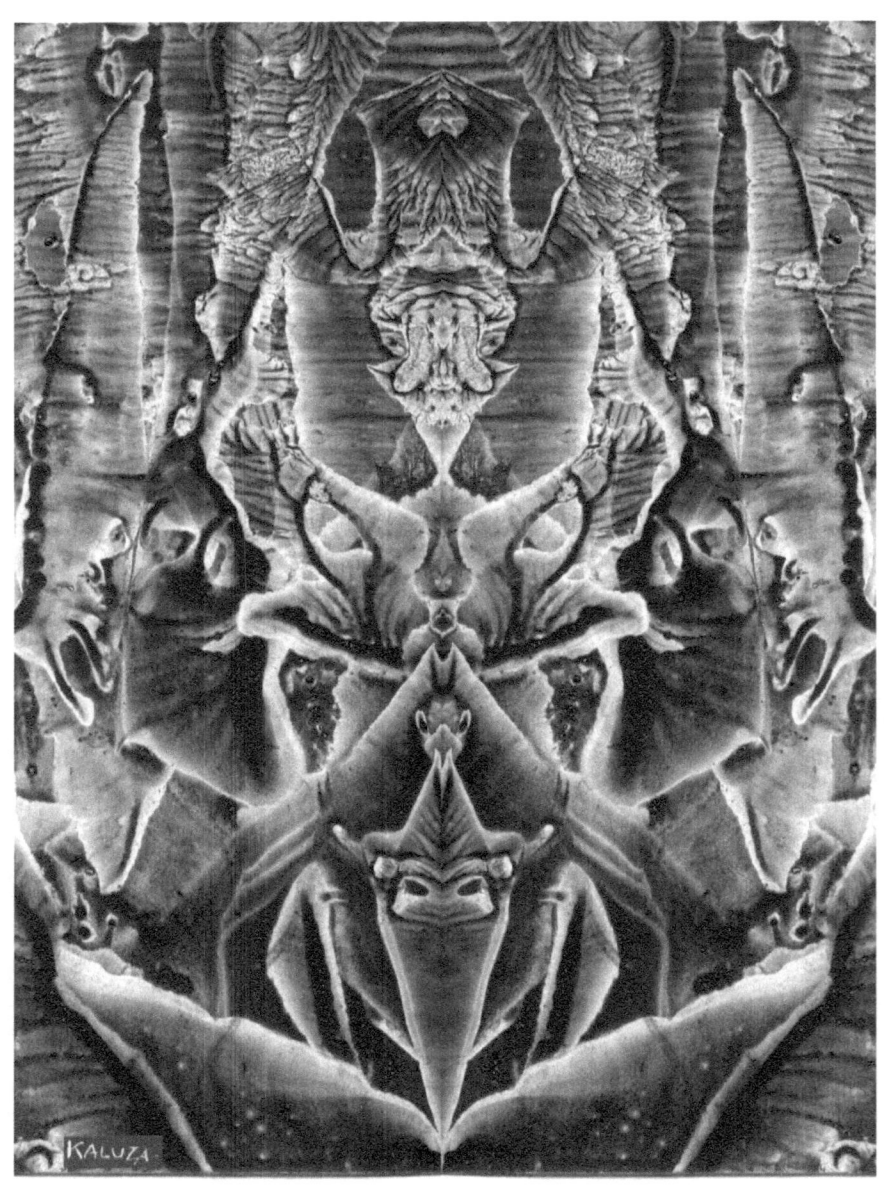

The Sorceress

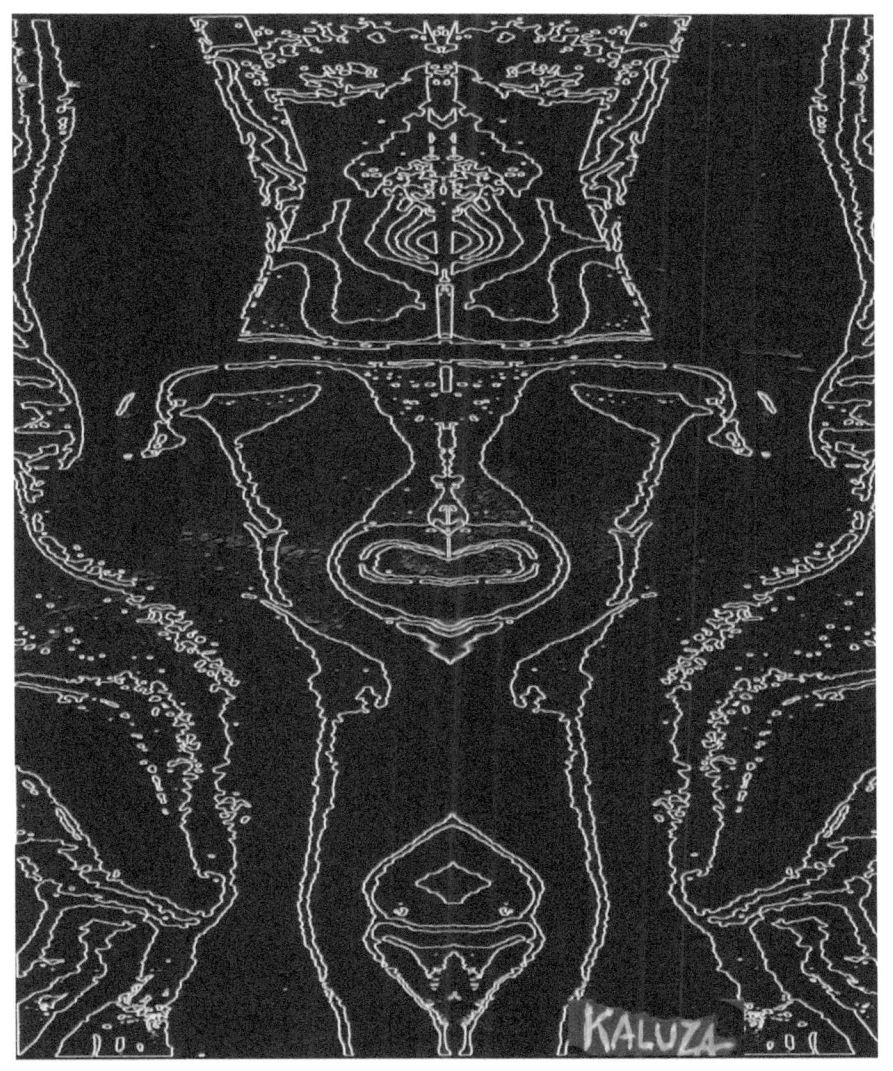

Face 2

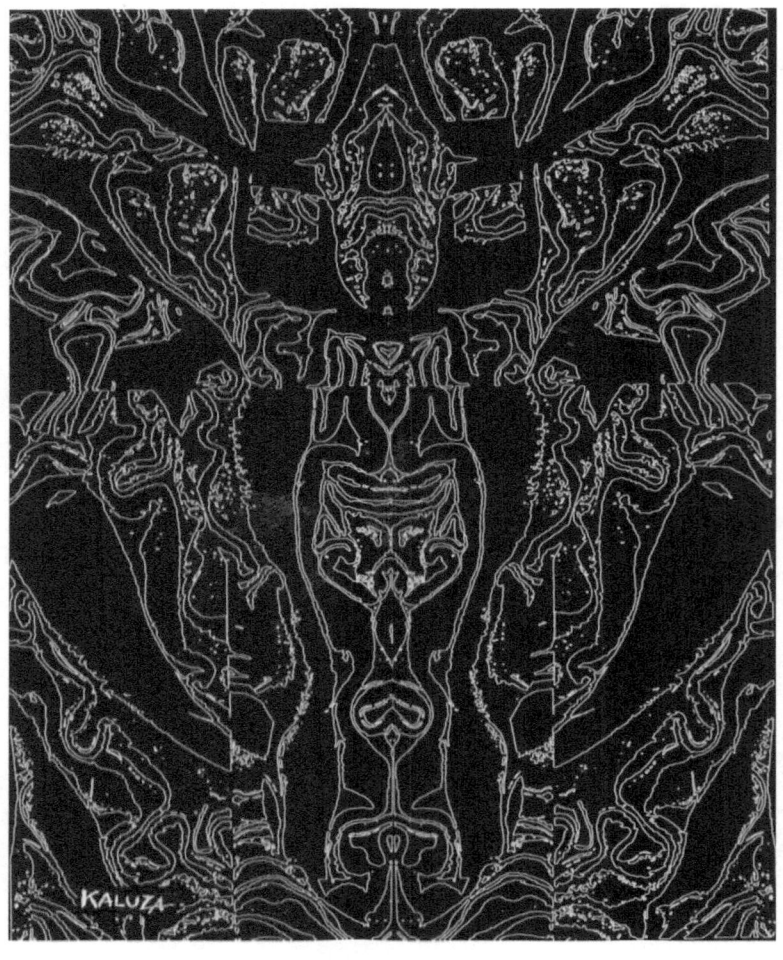

Design 11

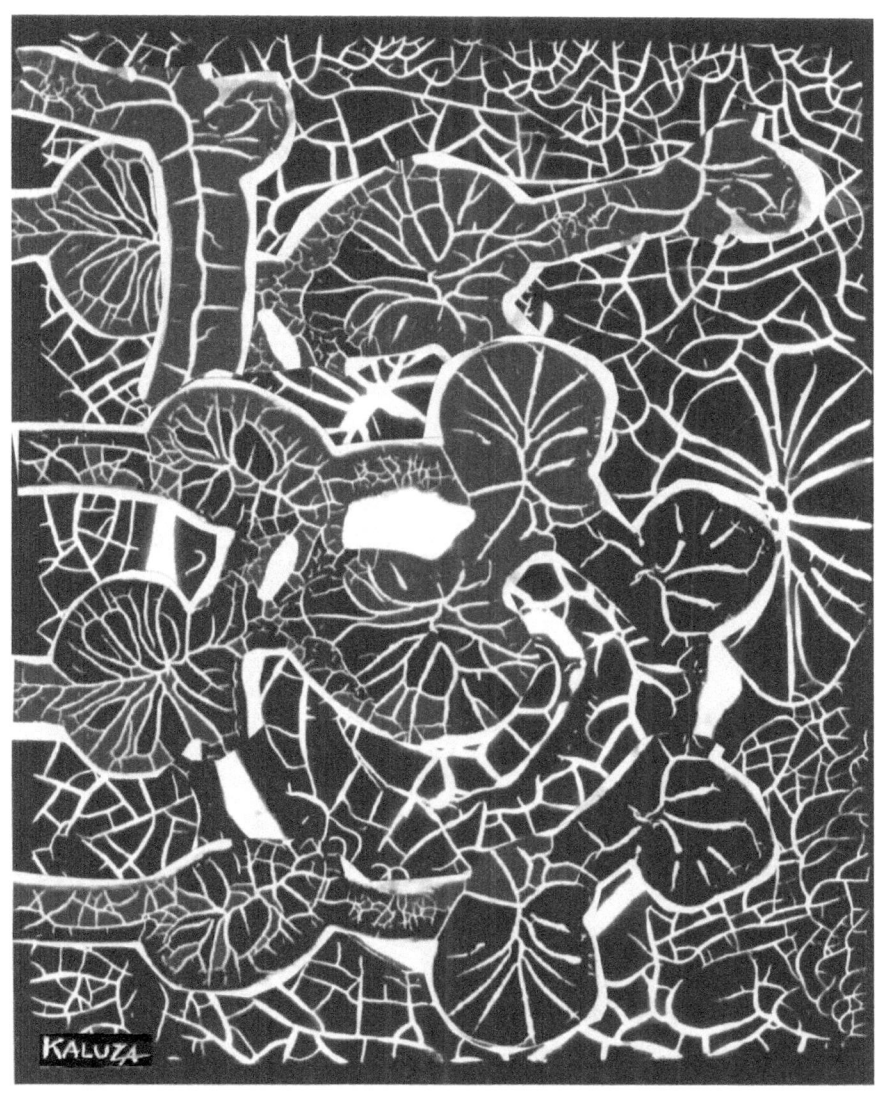

Microbes 5

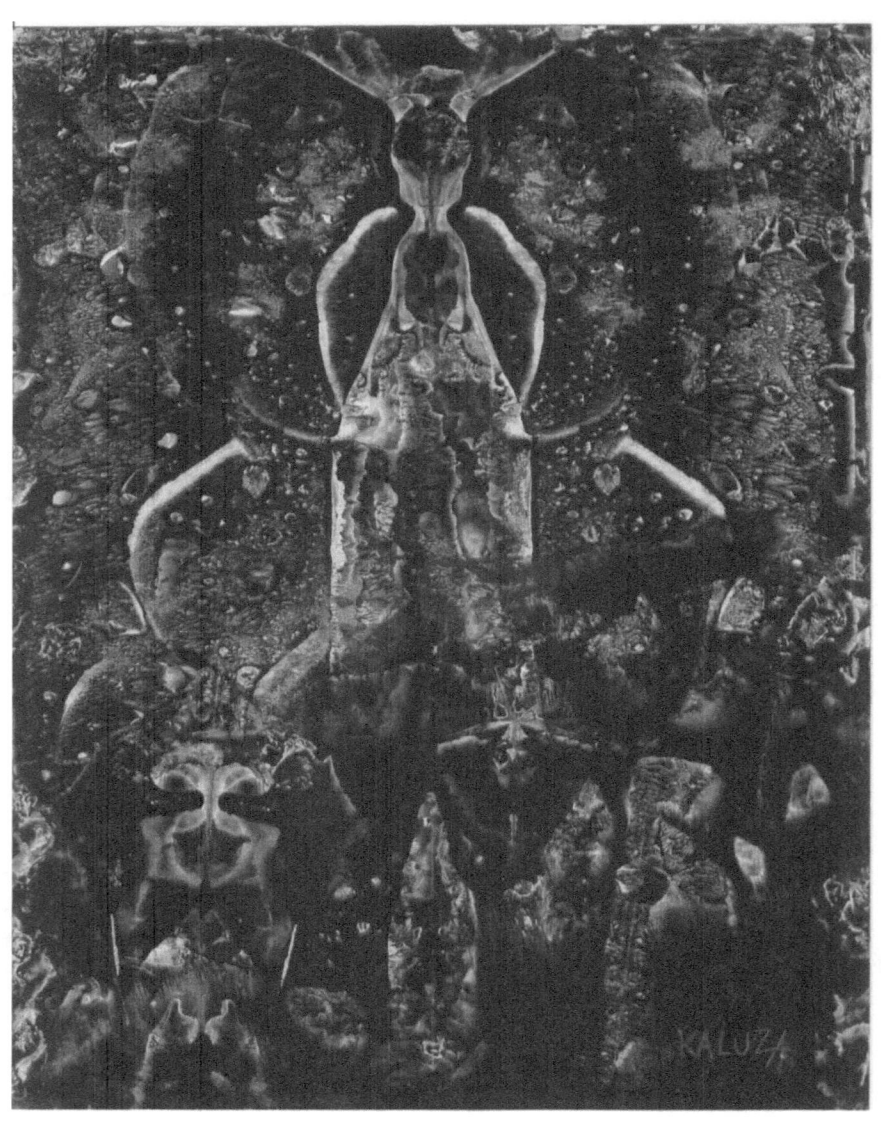

Apparition

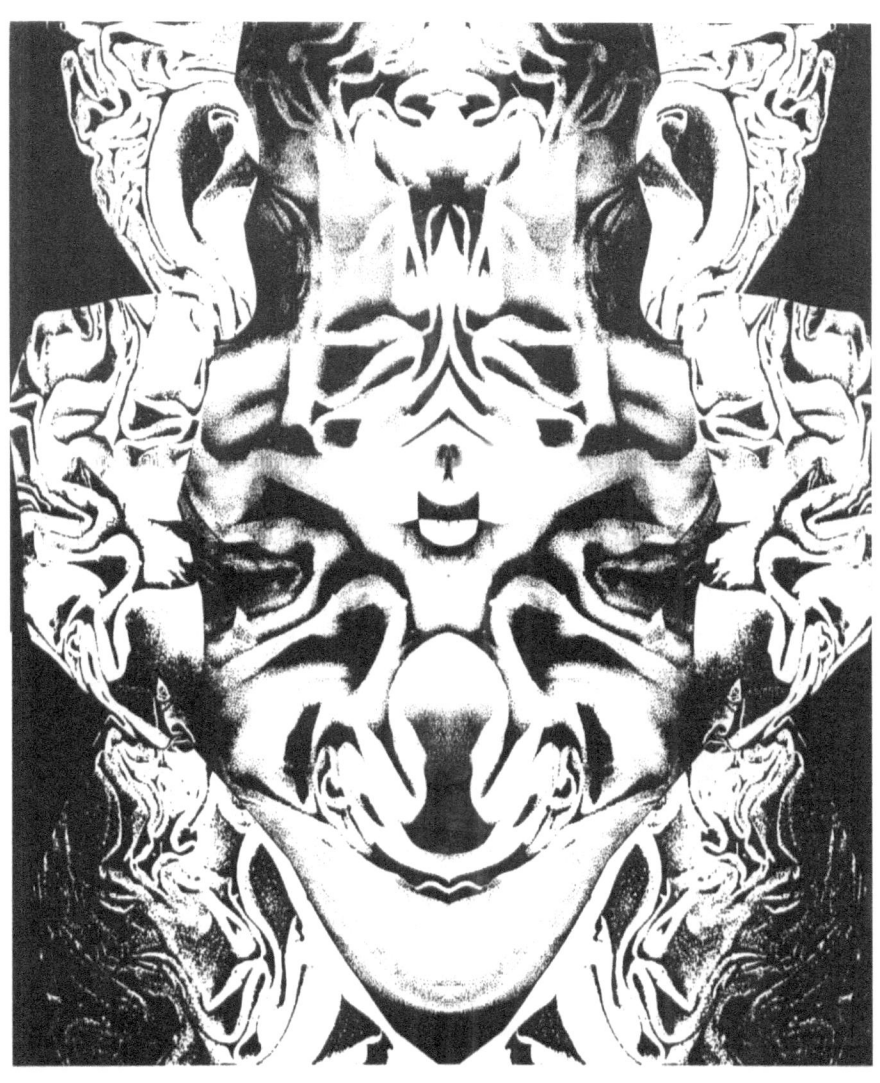

Funny Face

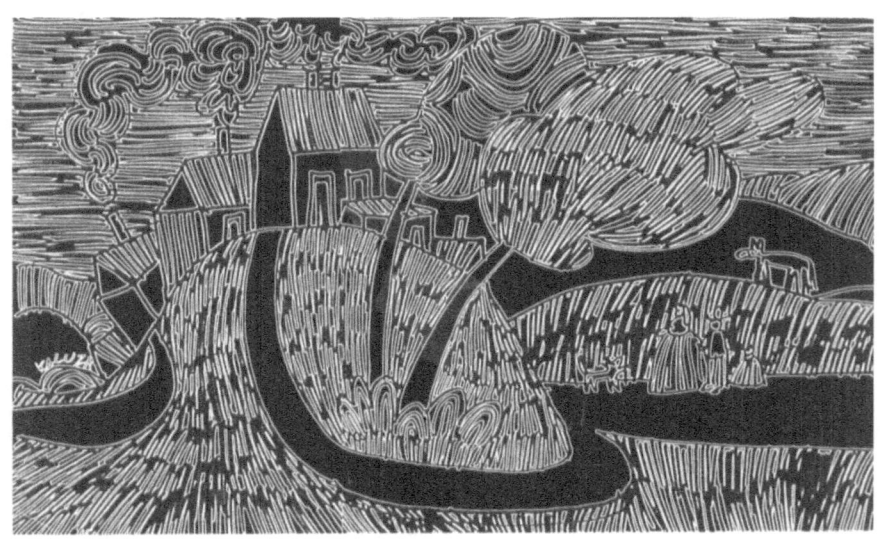

Village 4

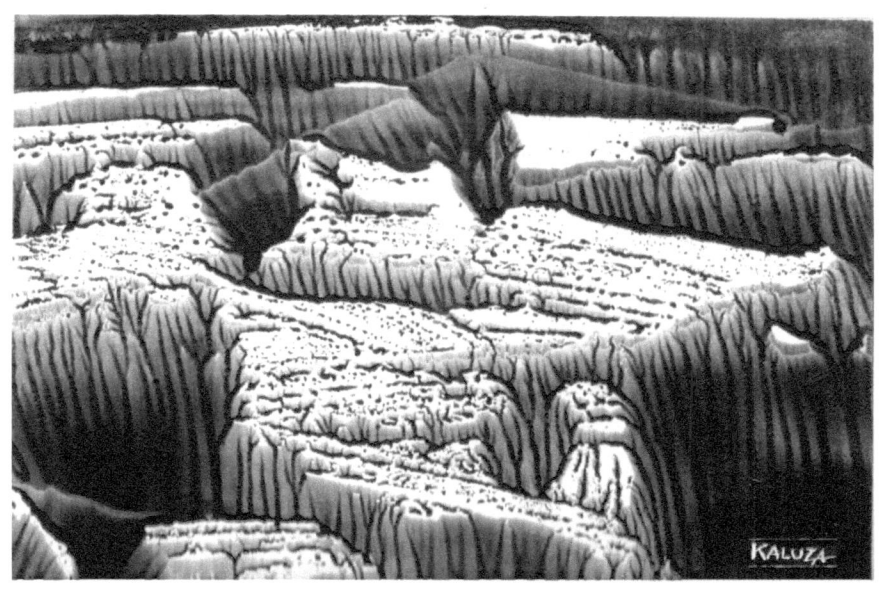

Landscape 4

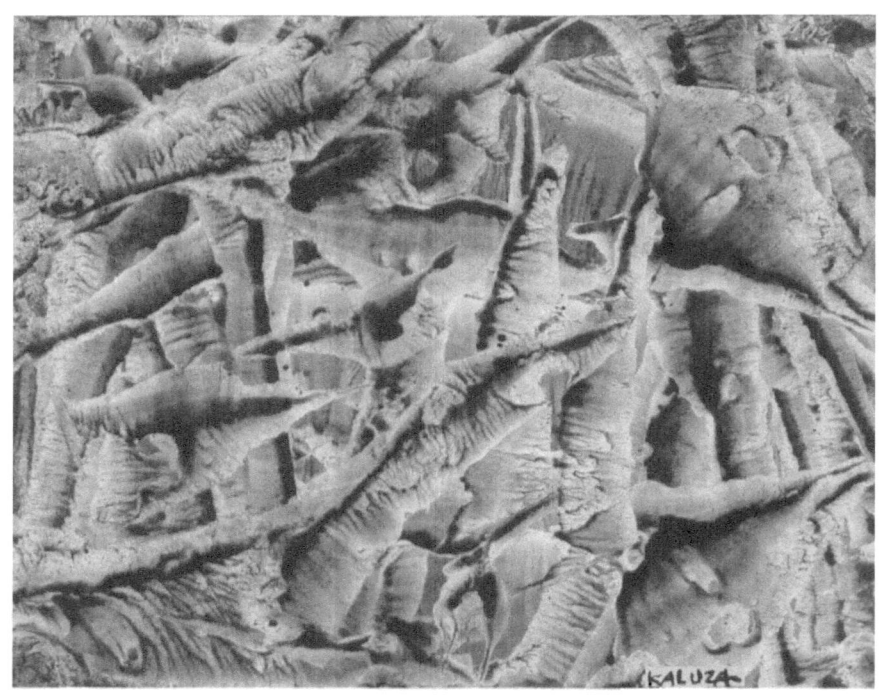

Cavern Interior

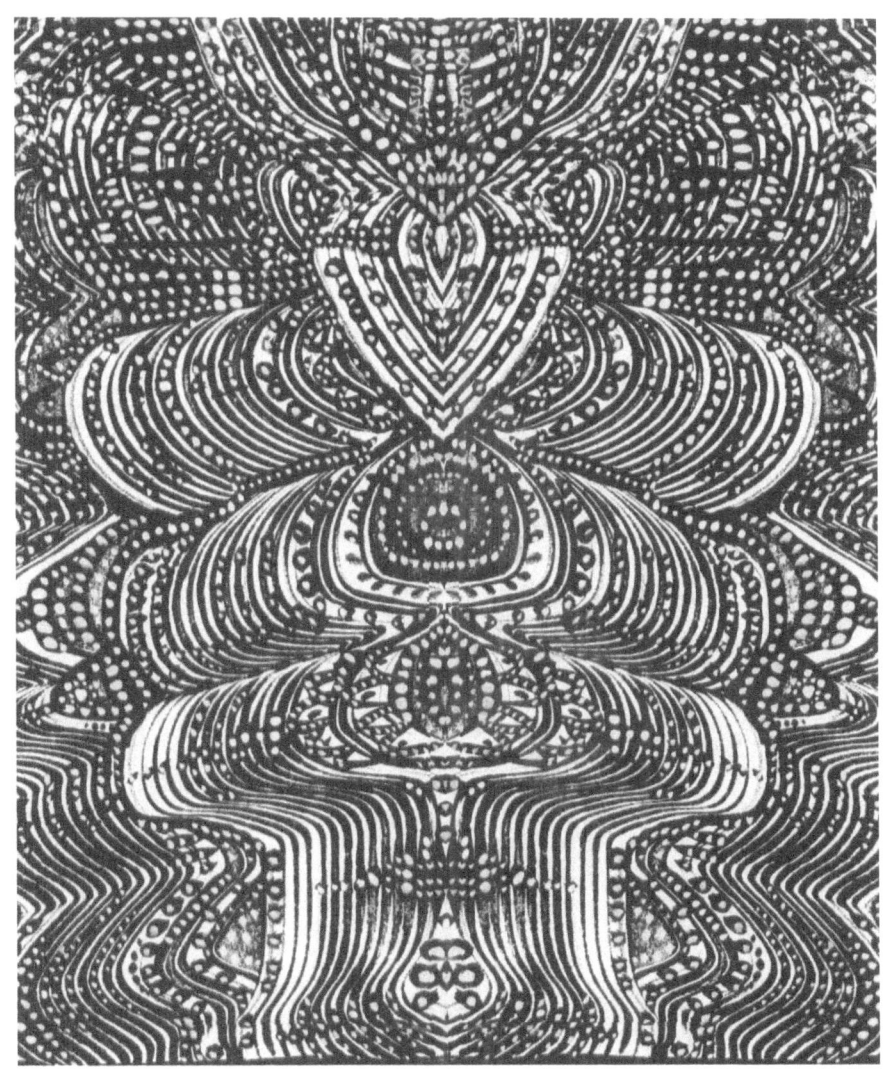

Dots and Lines

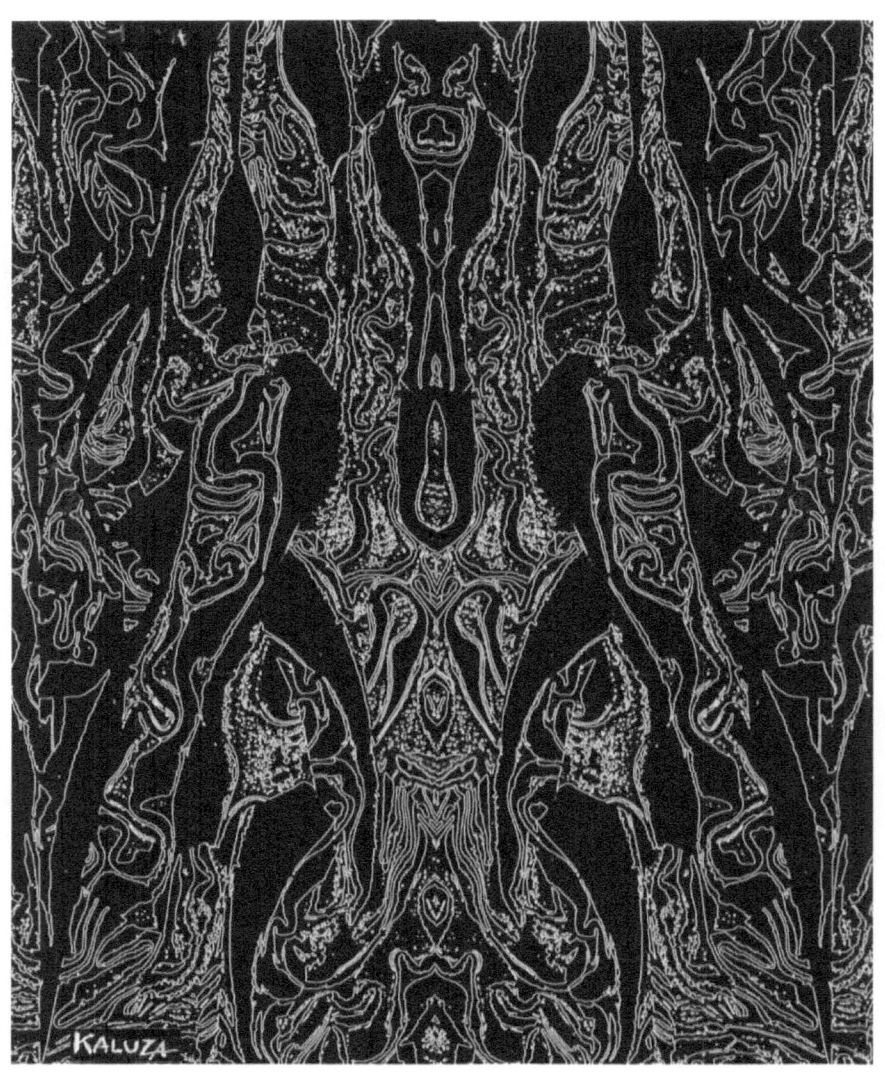

Design 30

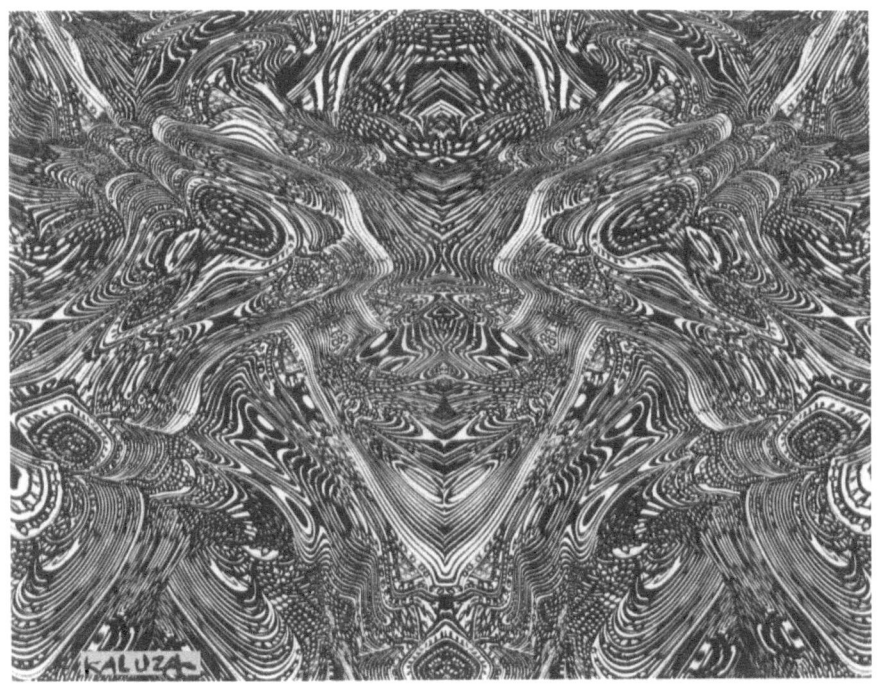

Alien Face 3

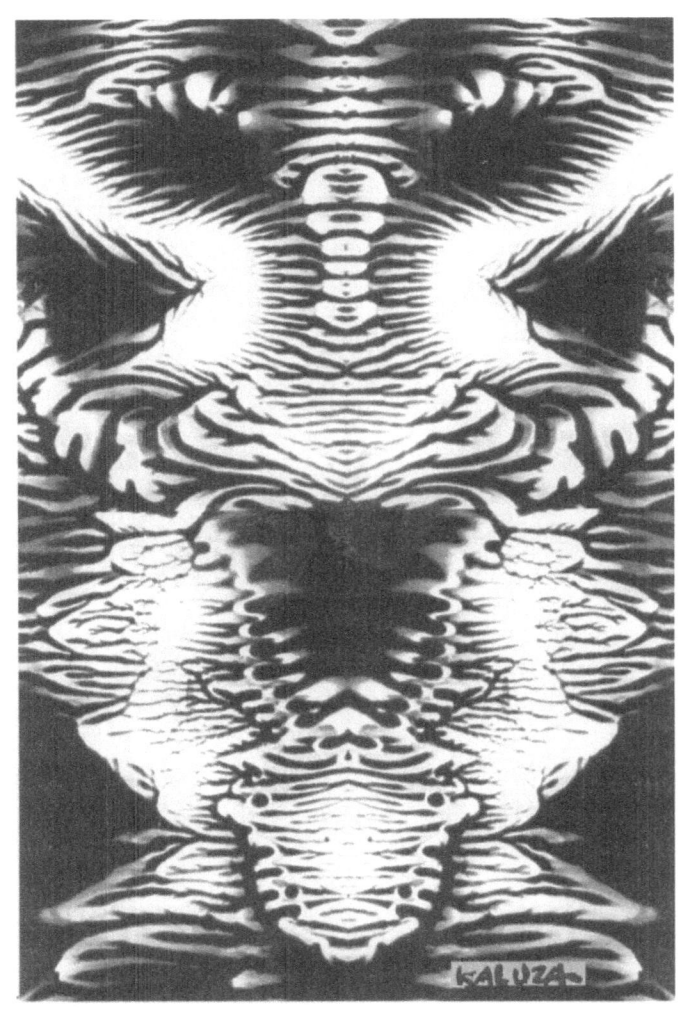

Alien Face

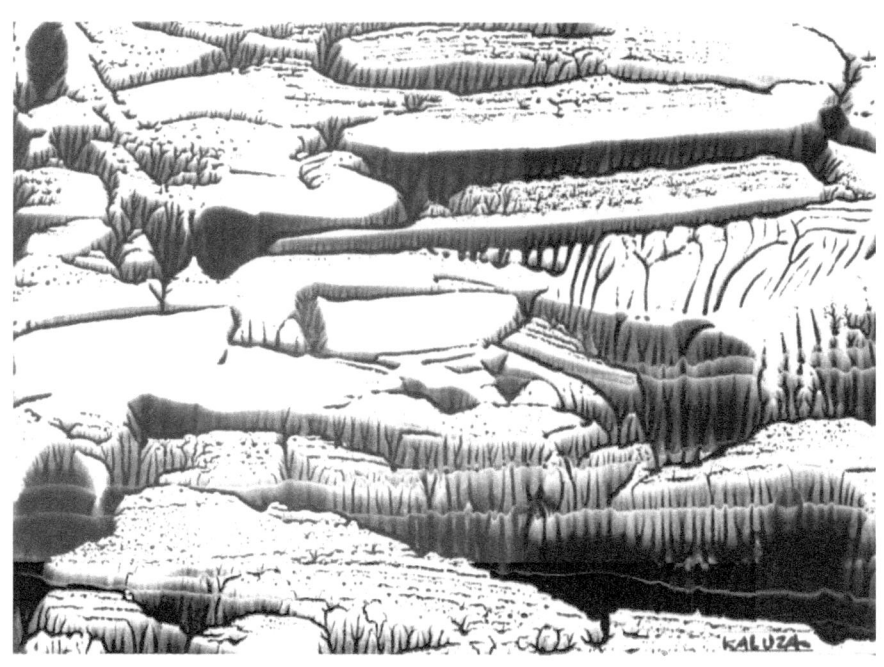

Winterscape

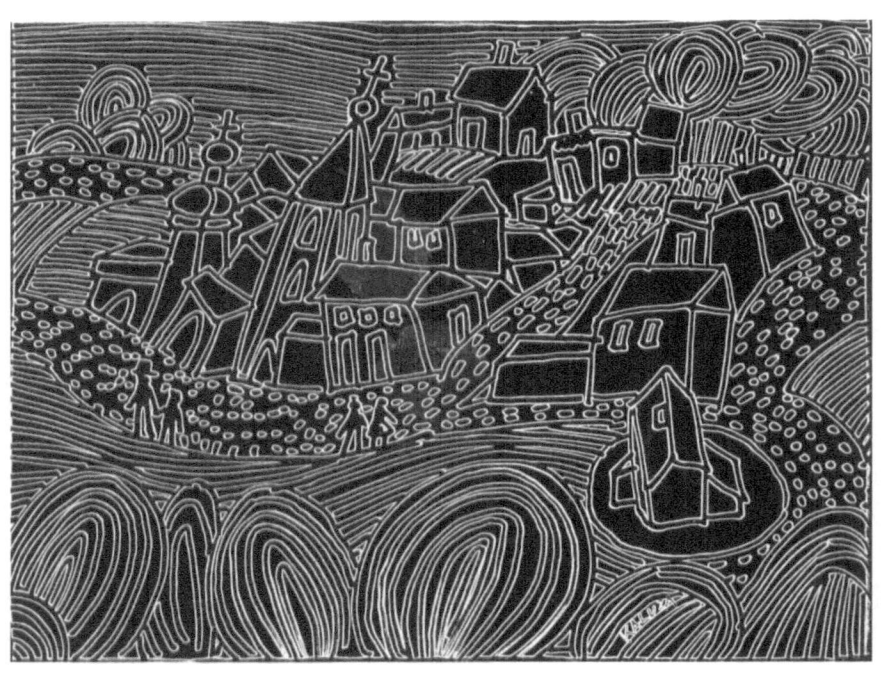

Village 3

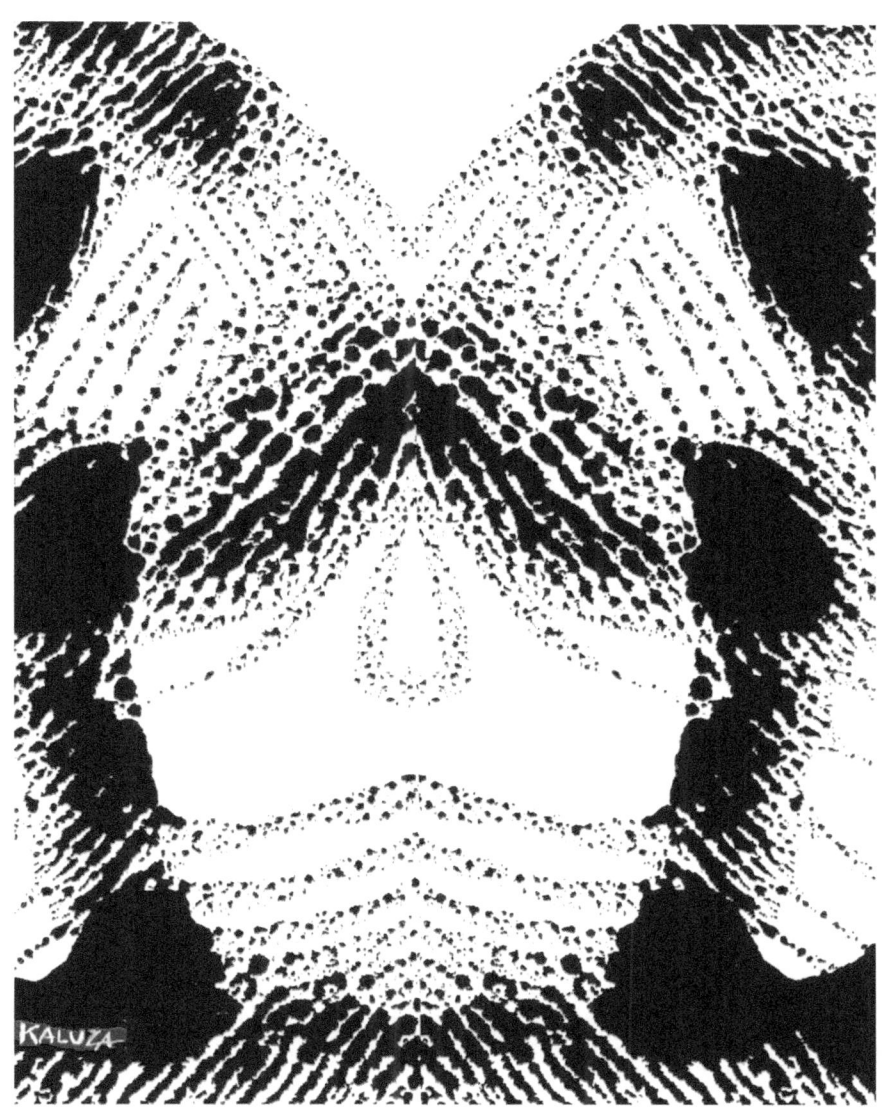

Face

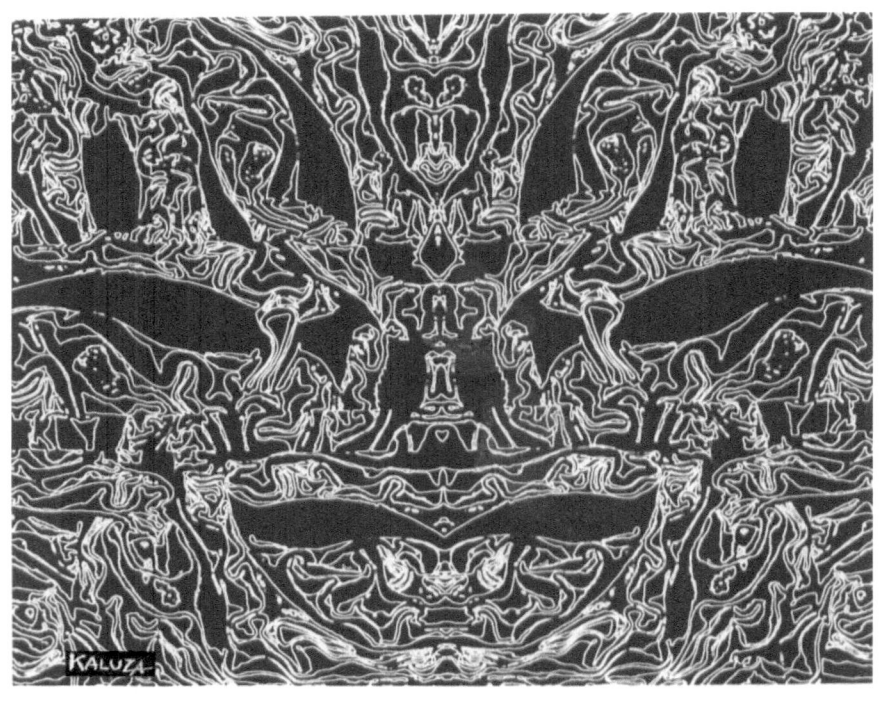

Design 40

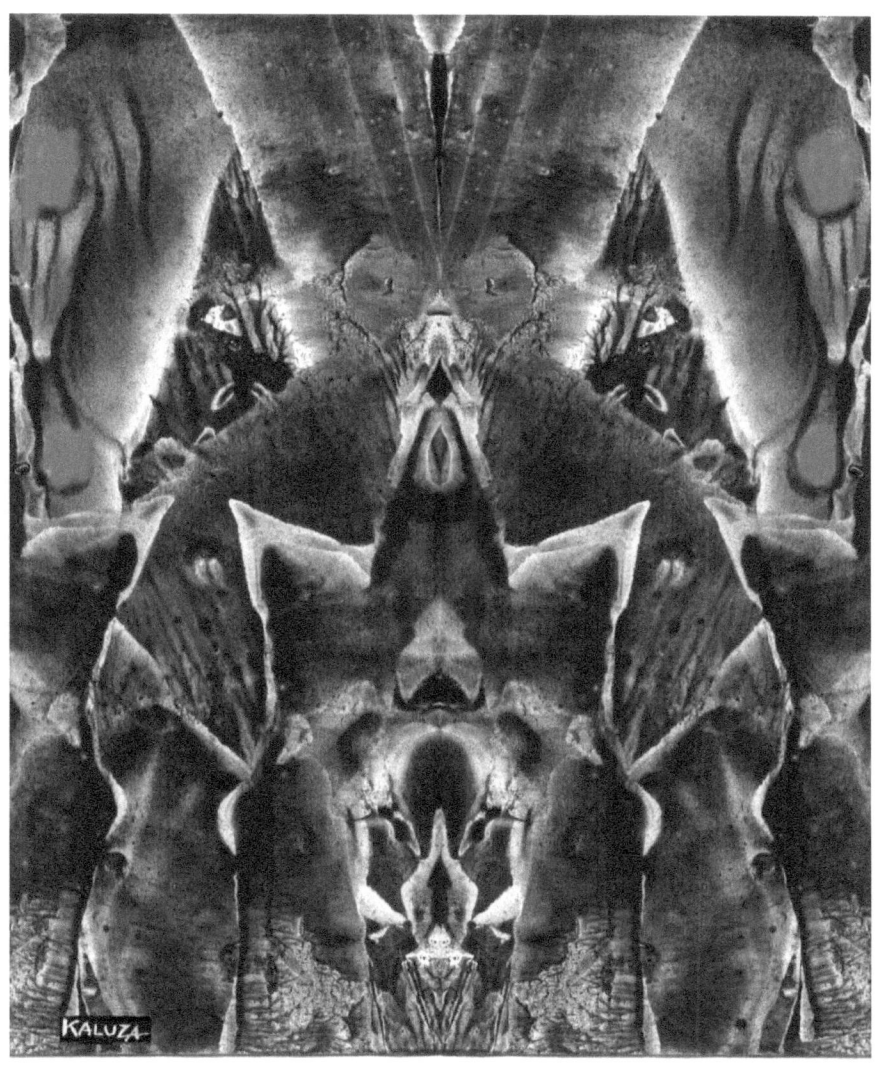

Mysterious Being

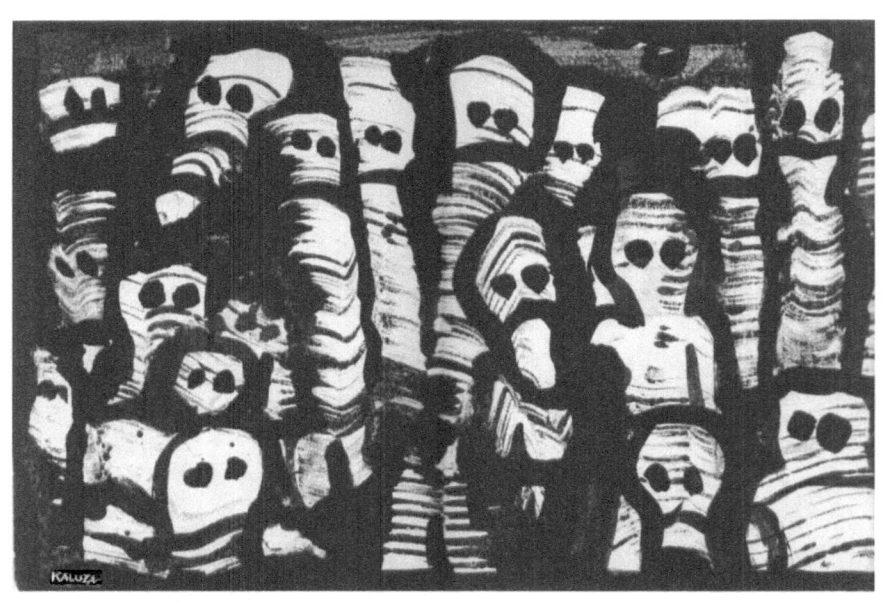

Creatures Watching

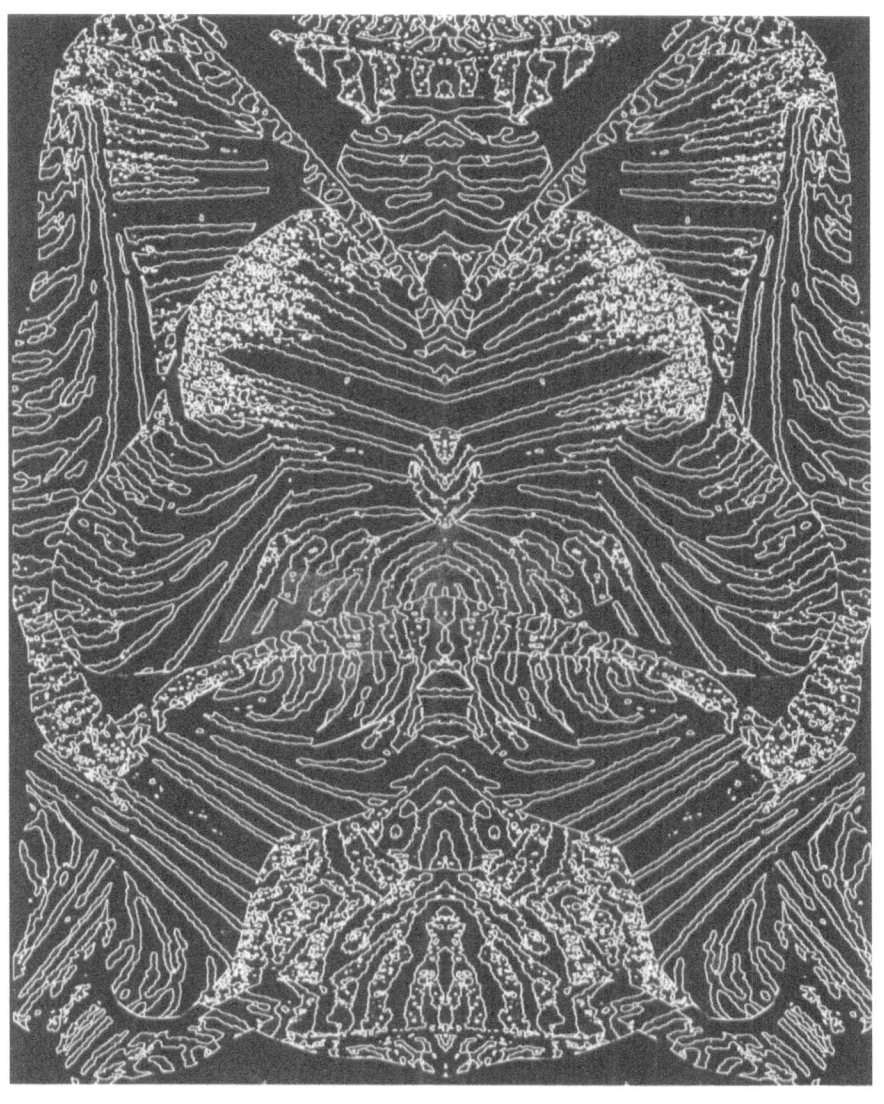

Design 44

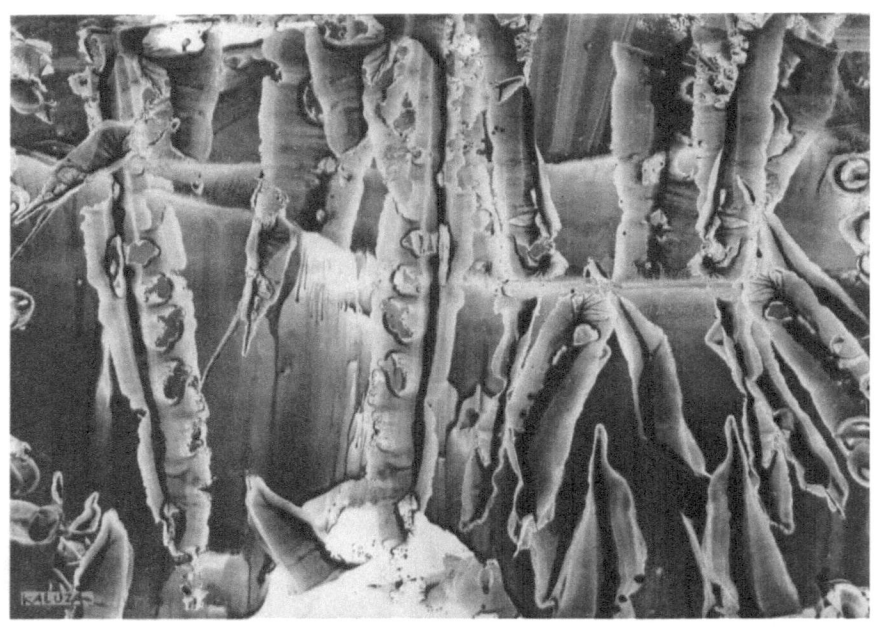

Inside a Cave

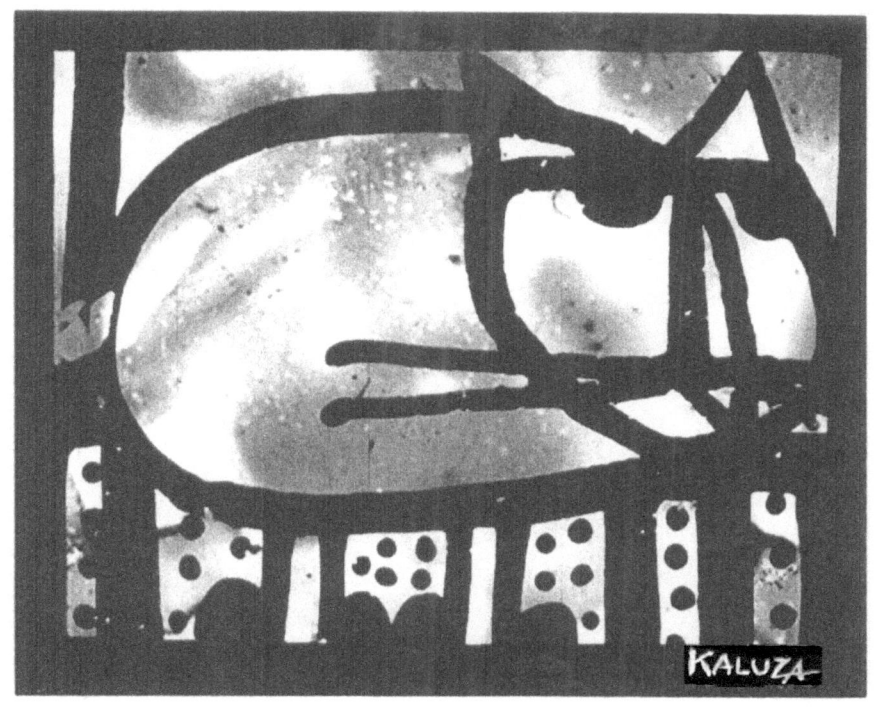

Cat 2

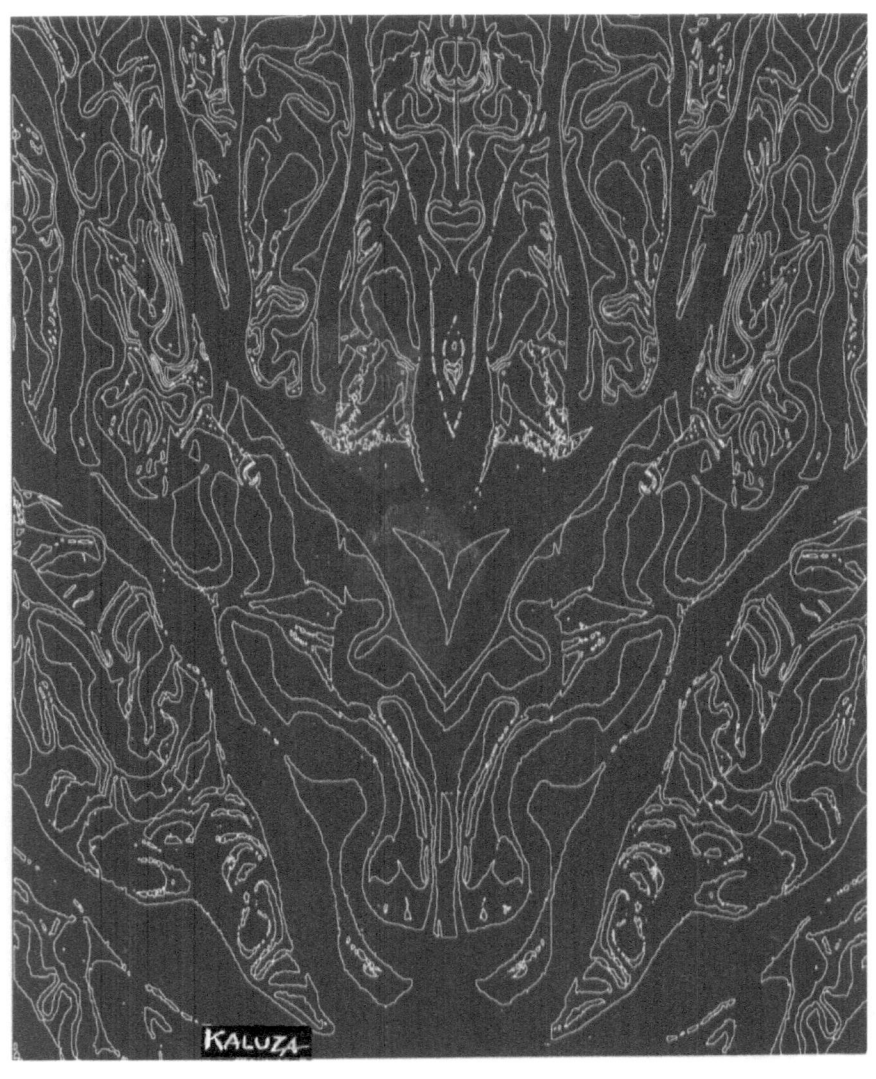

Design 43

Art In Black & White

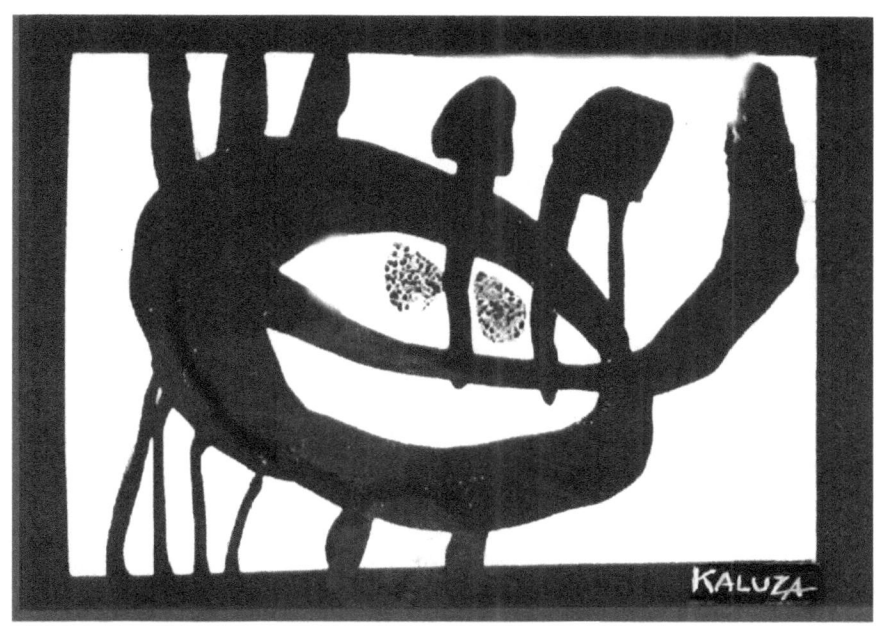

Crab

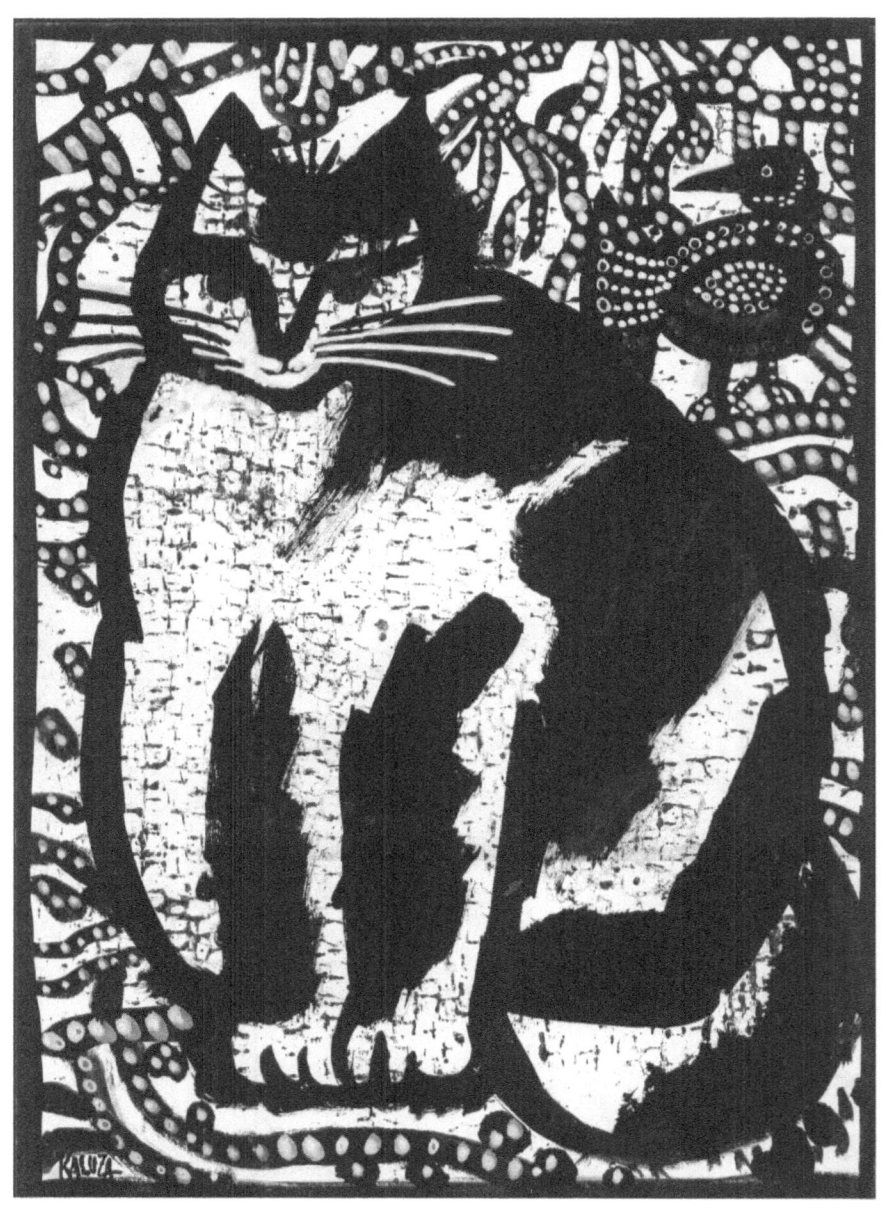

Cat 2

ART IN BLACK & WHITE

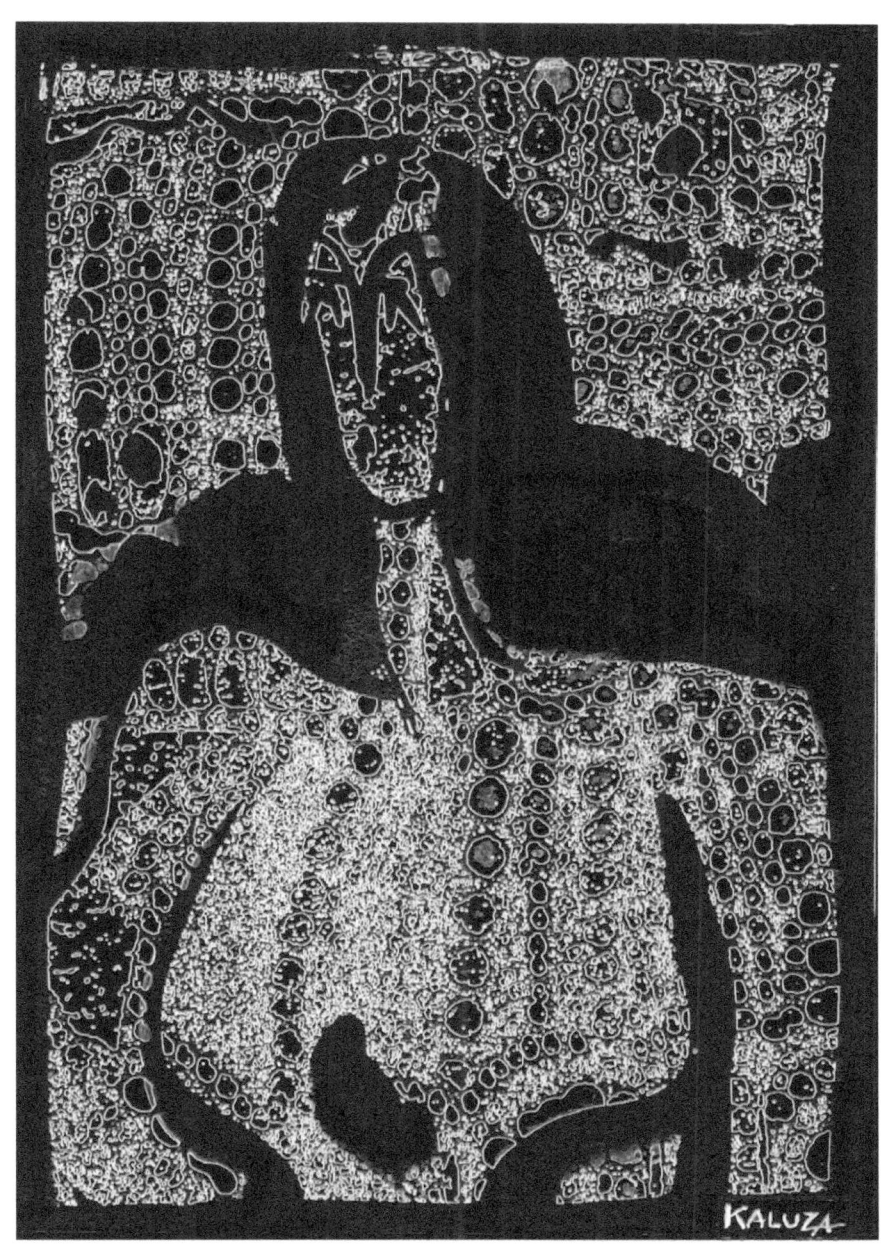

Woman

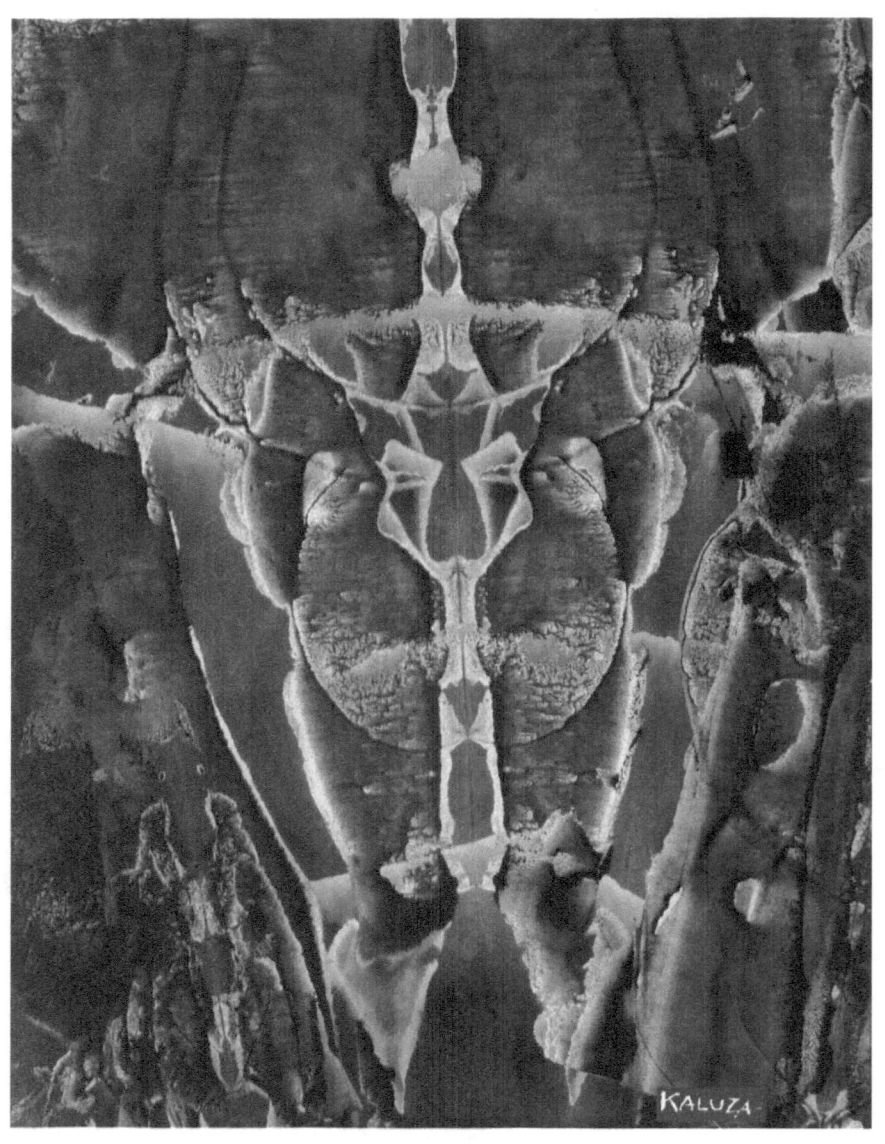

Dignitary

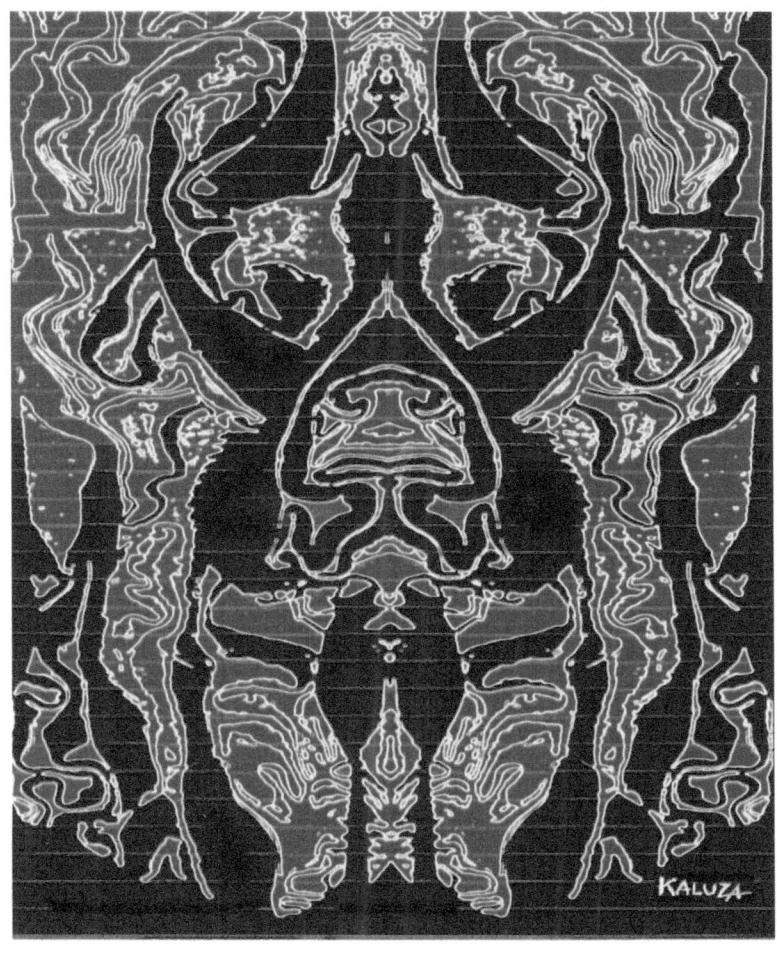

Design 6

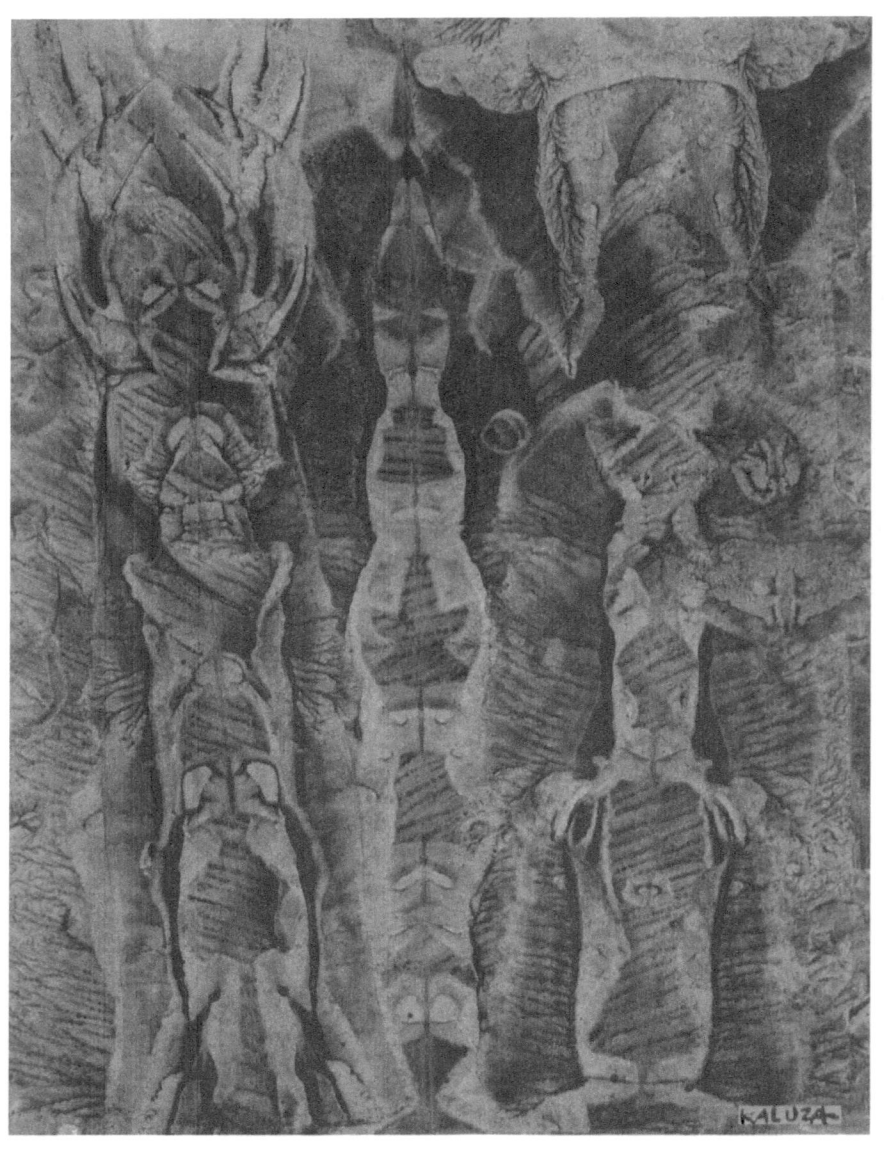

Three Extraterrestrials

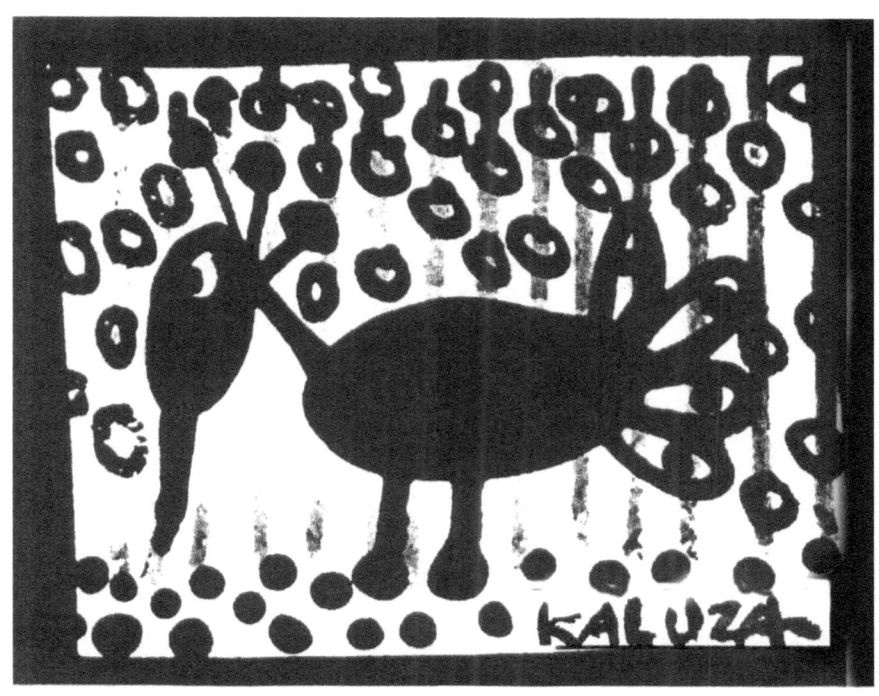

Bird 2

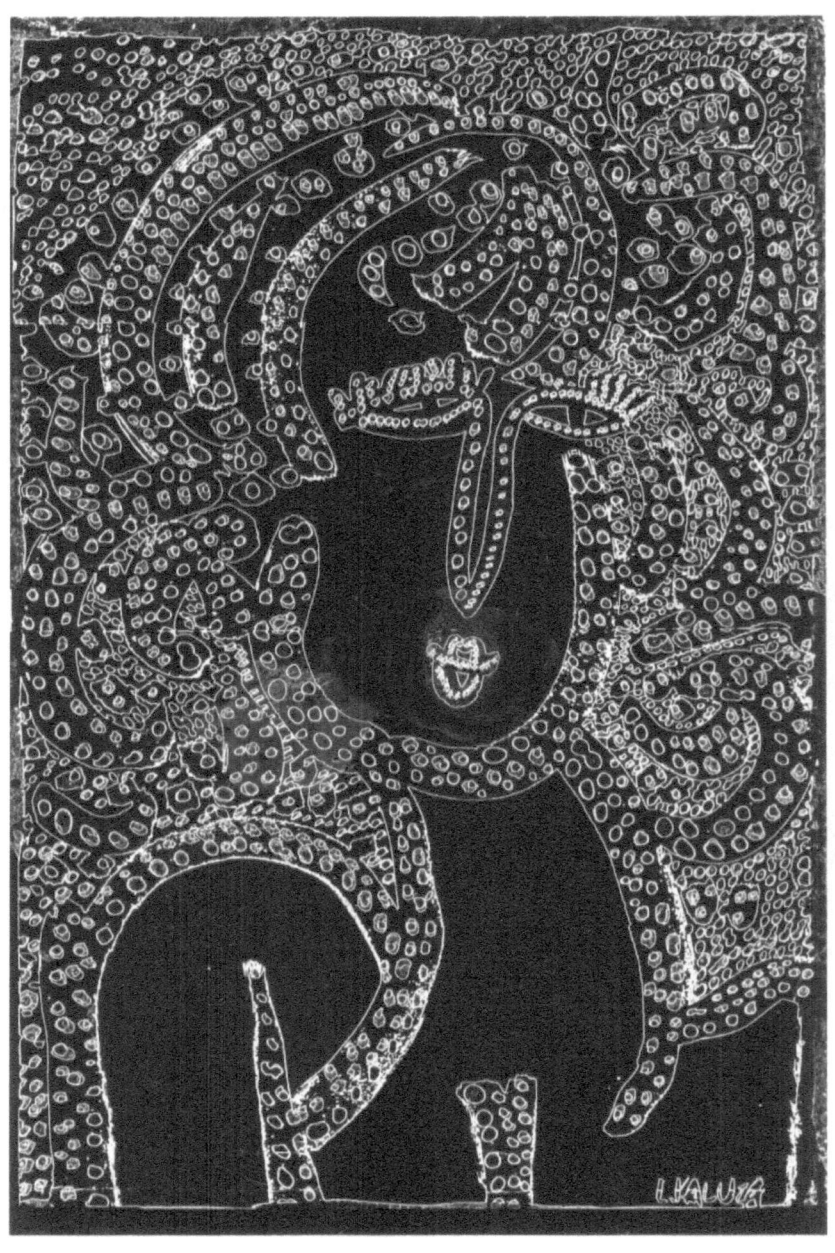

Woman

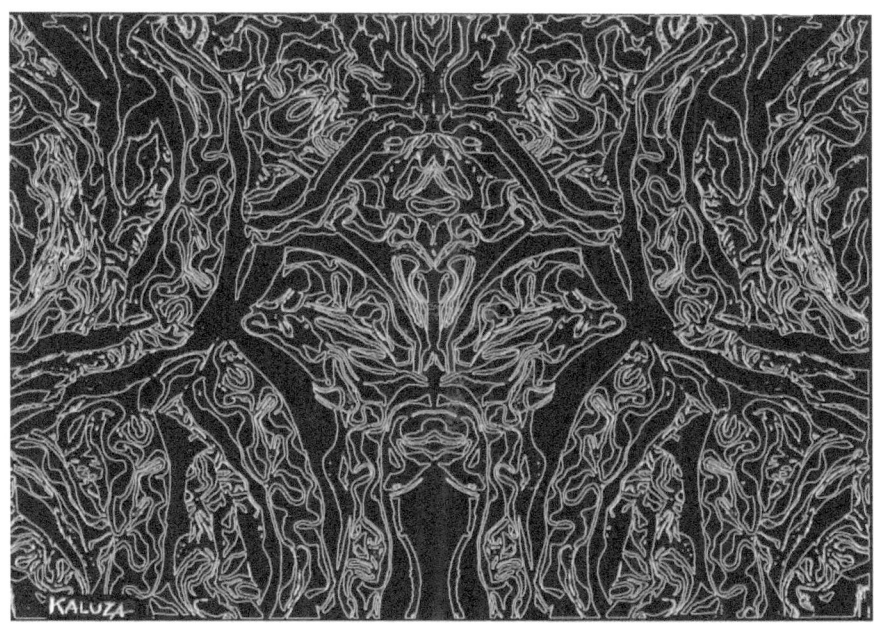

Design 13

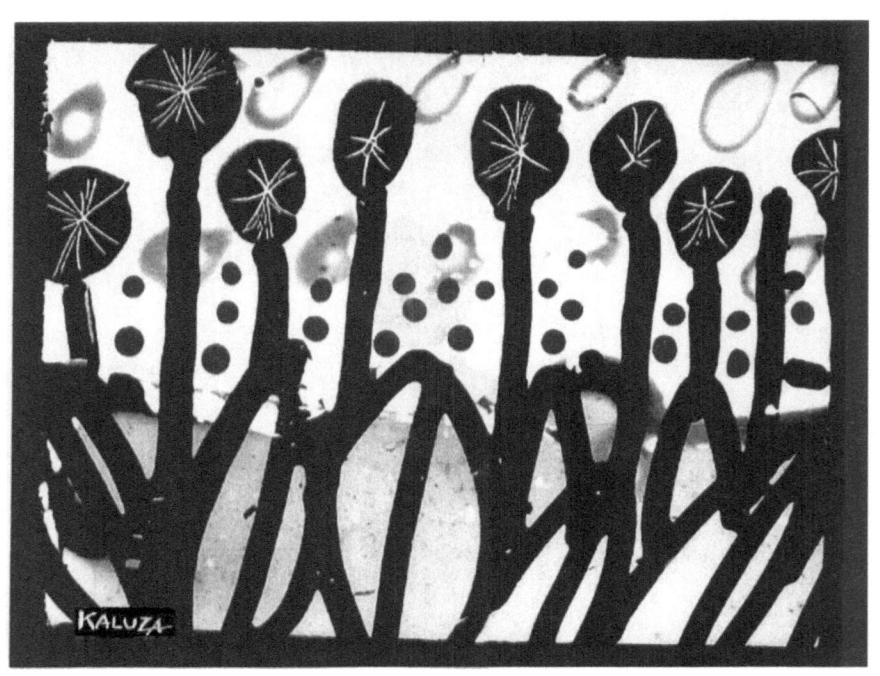

Flowers

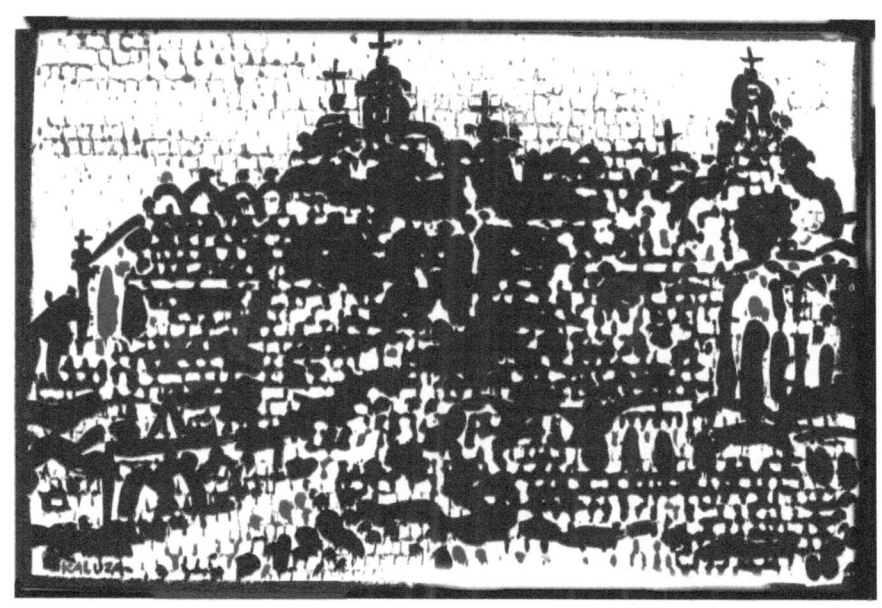

Churches

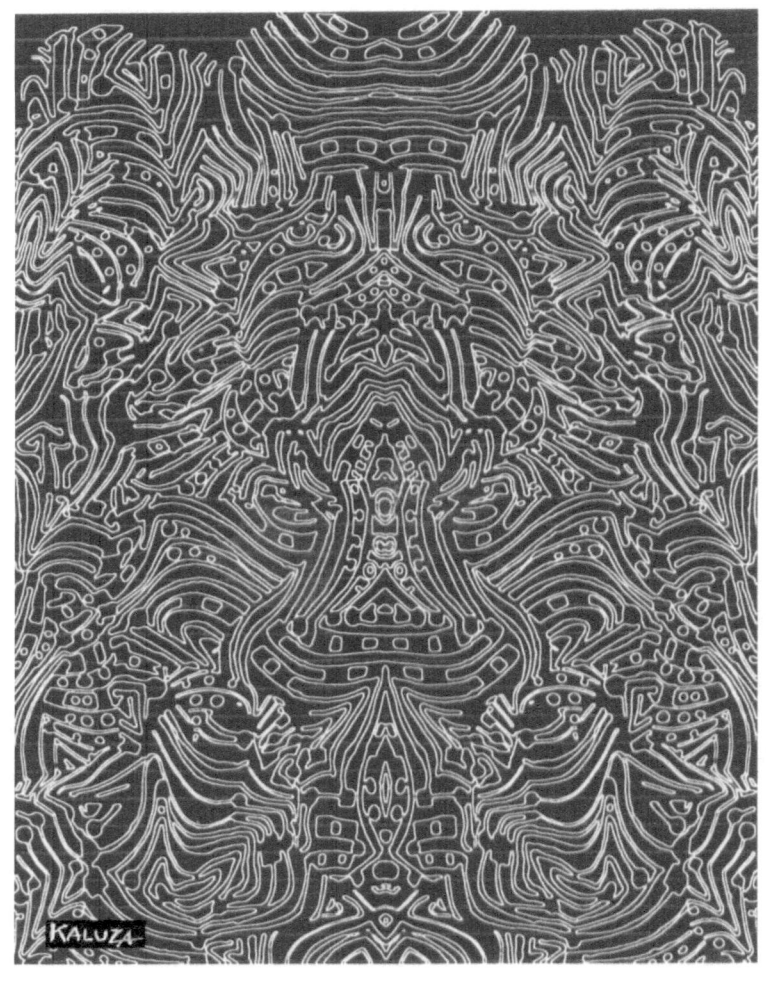

Design 3

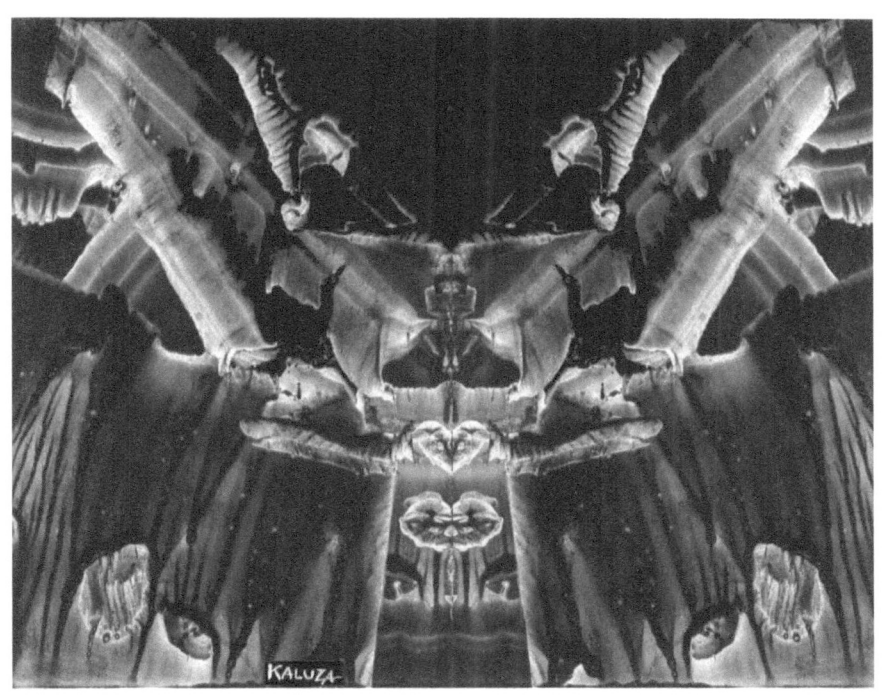

Thundercat

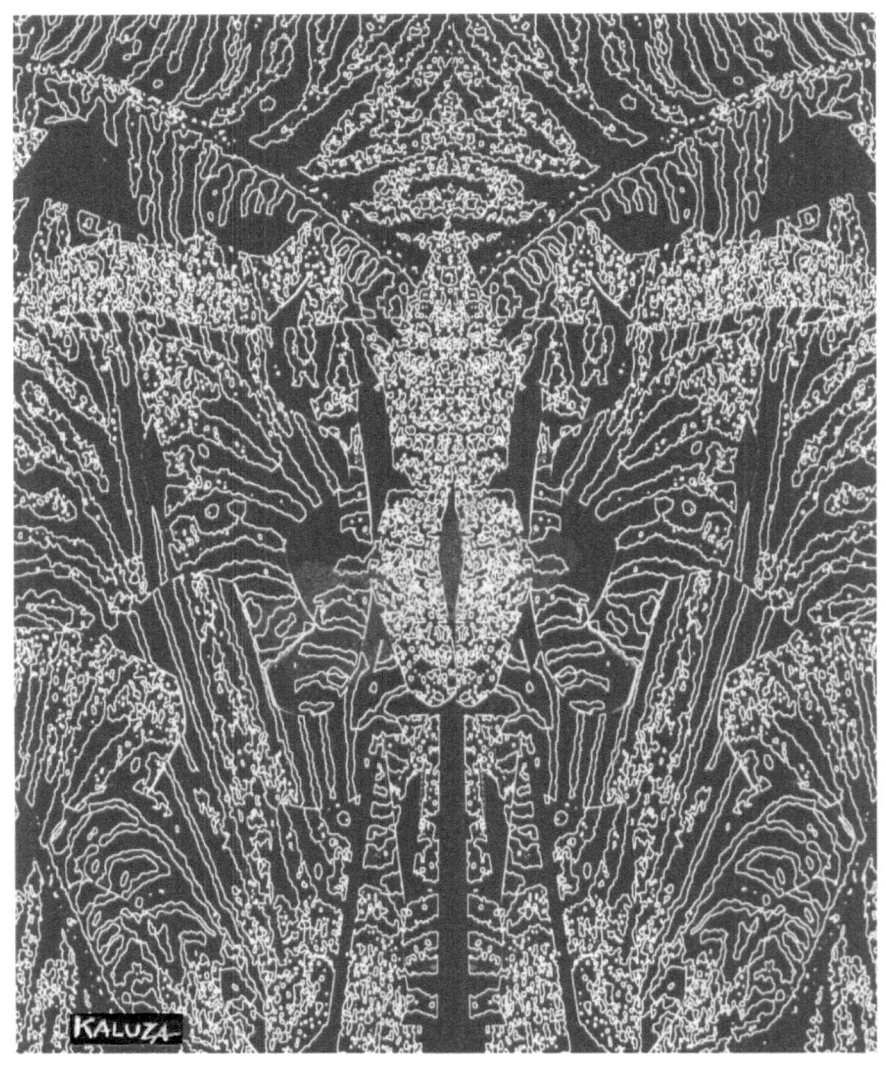

Design 41

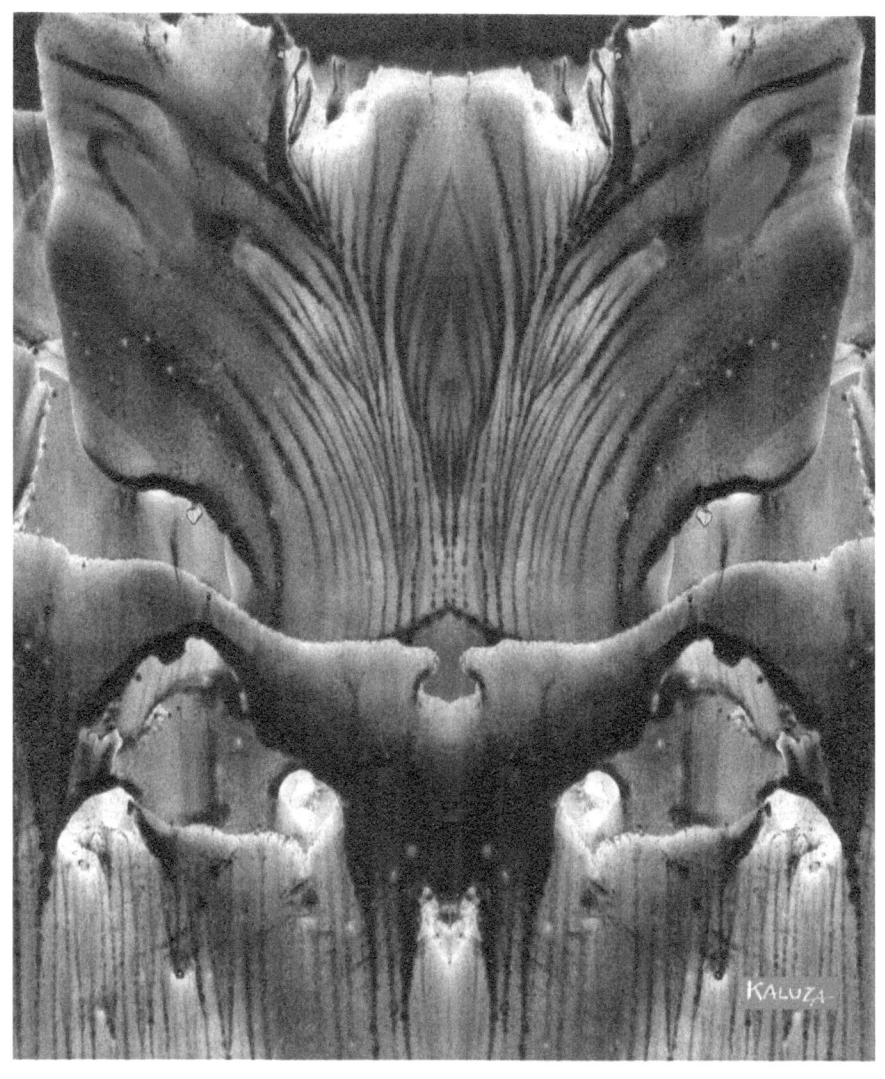

Kitten

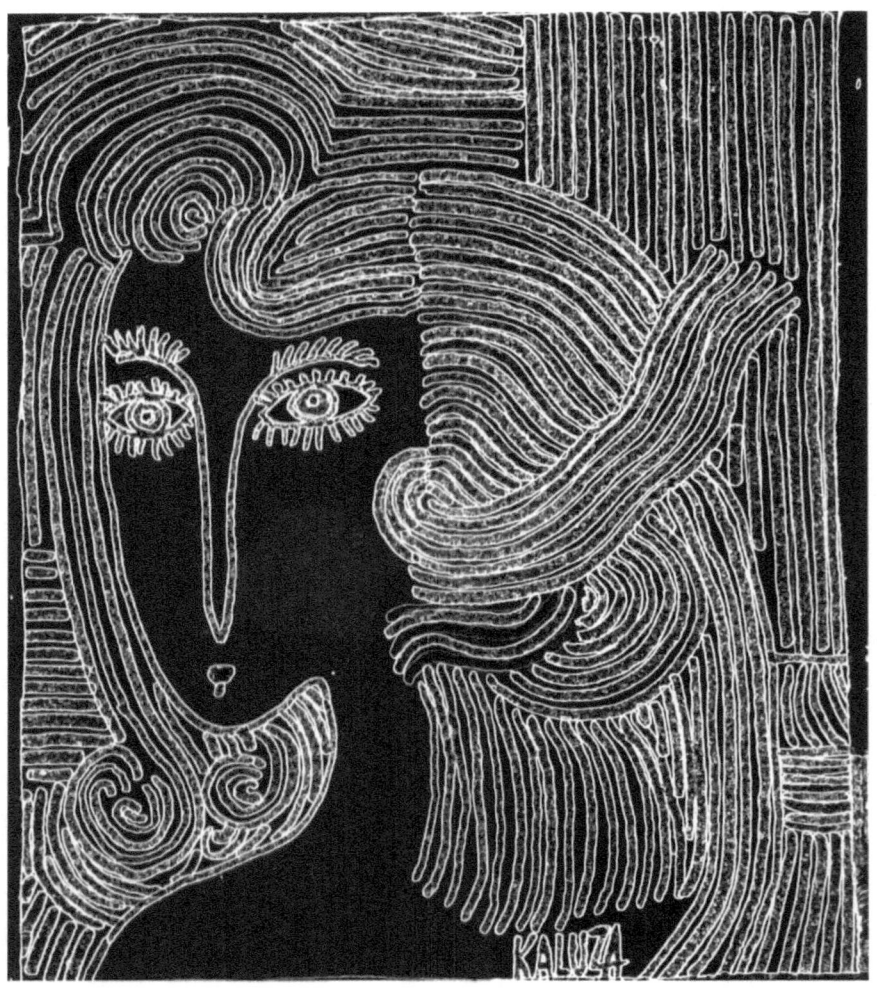

Face 2

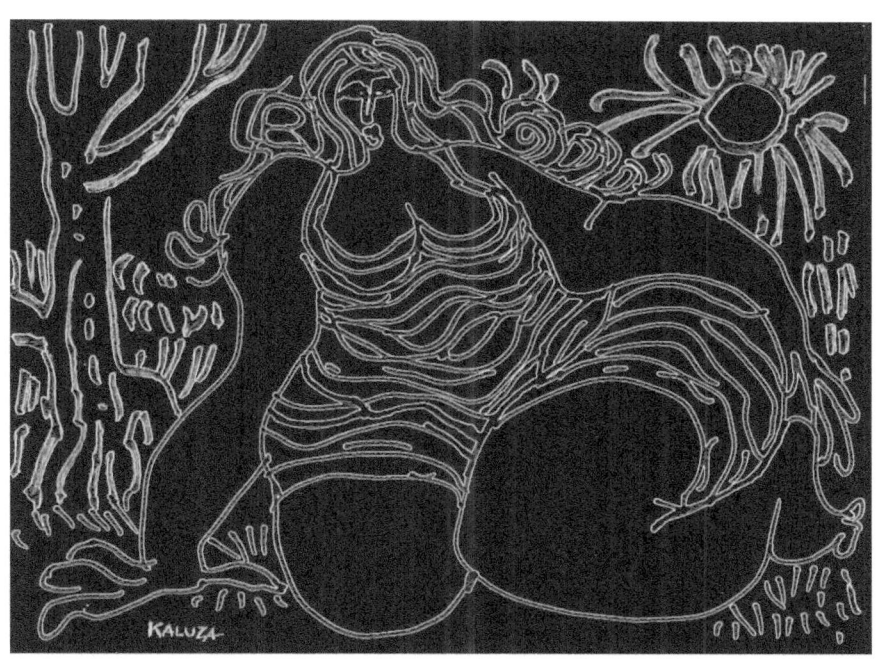

Woman with Sun

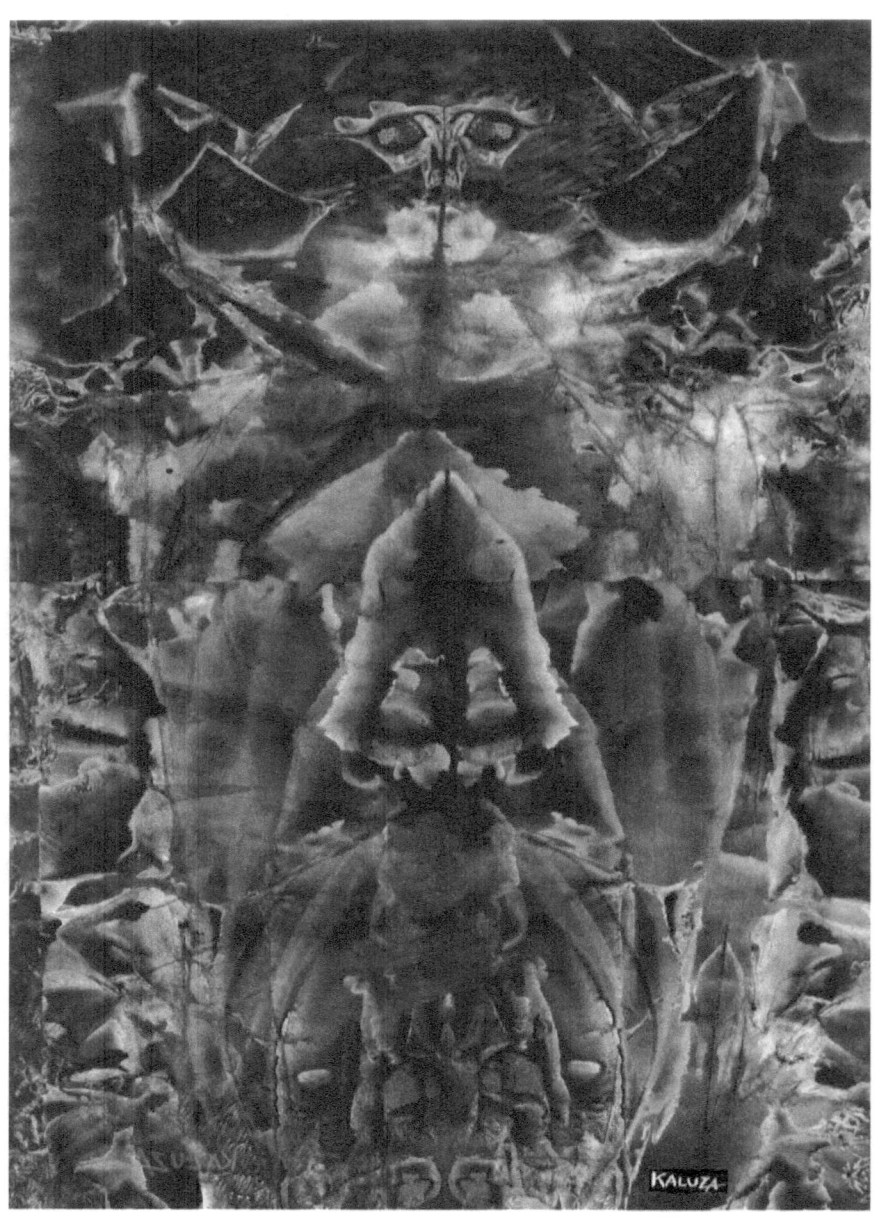

Spacemonkey

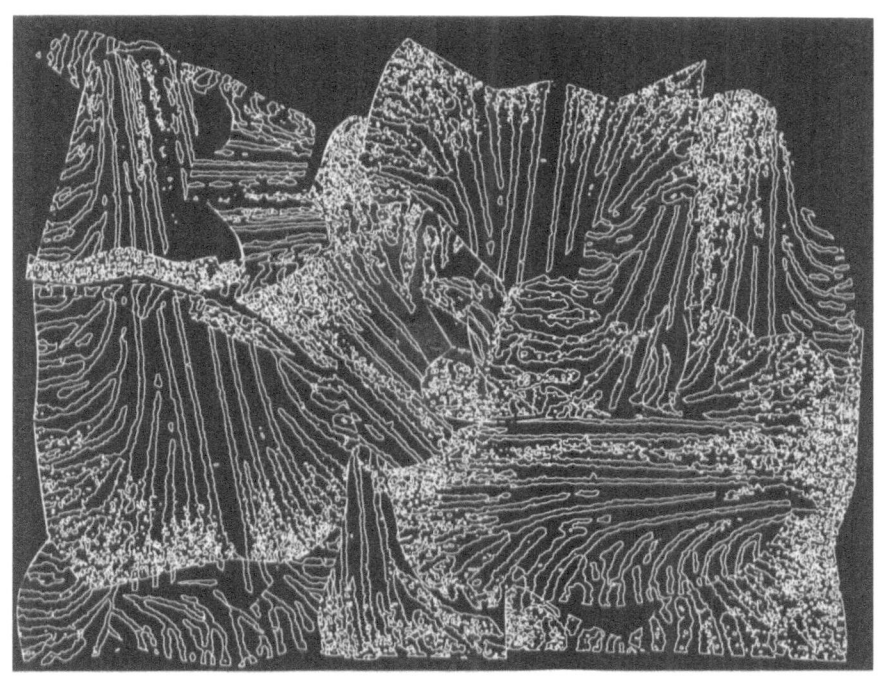

Camouflage Cat 2

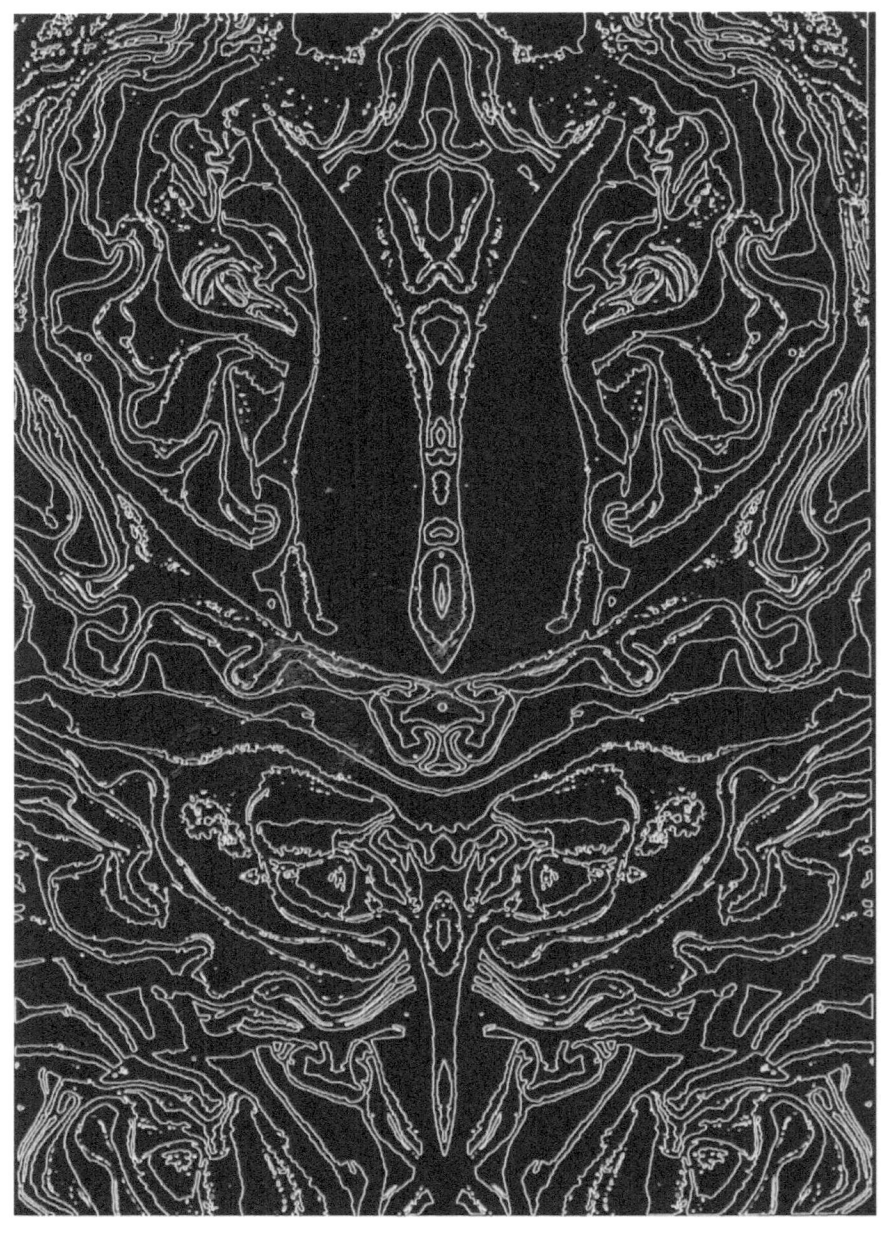

Design 29

ART IN BLACK & WHITE

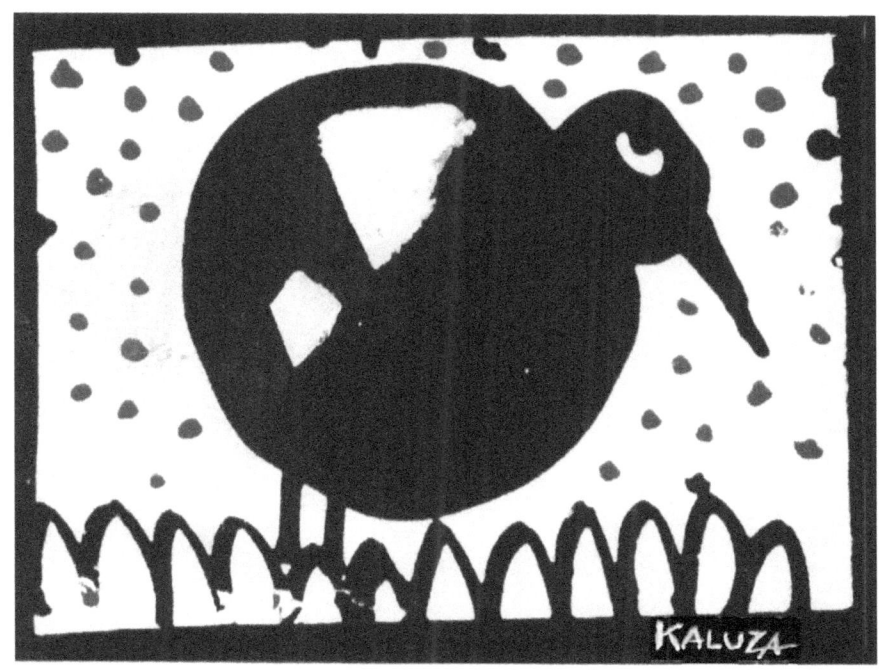

Kiwi

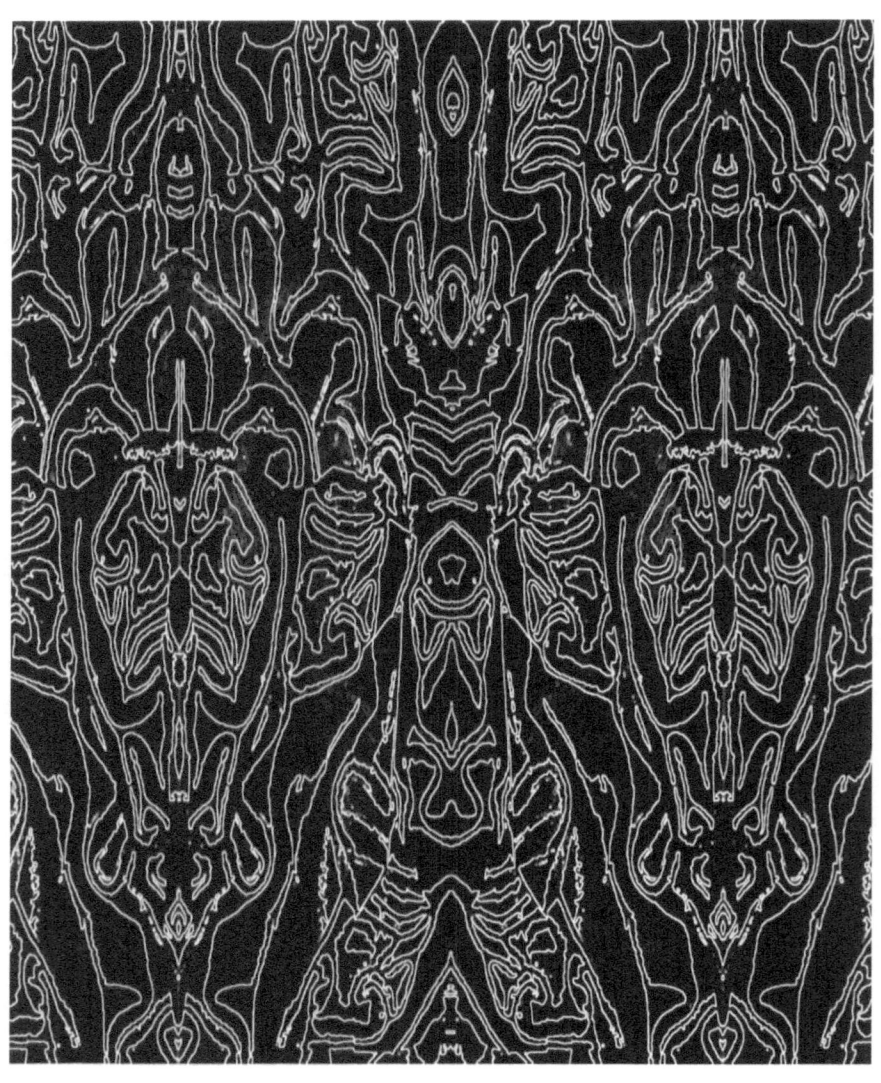

Guardians

ART IN BLACK & WHITE

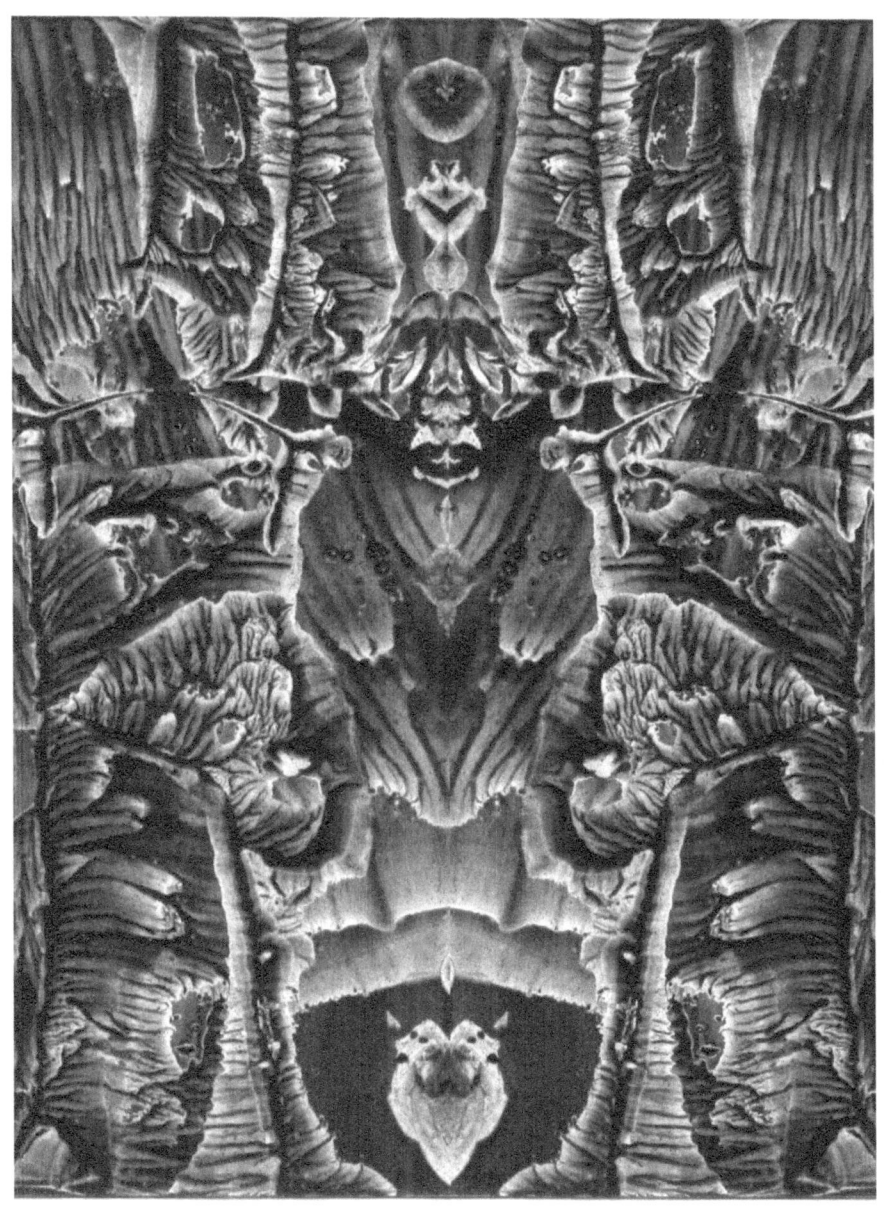

Monarch

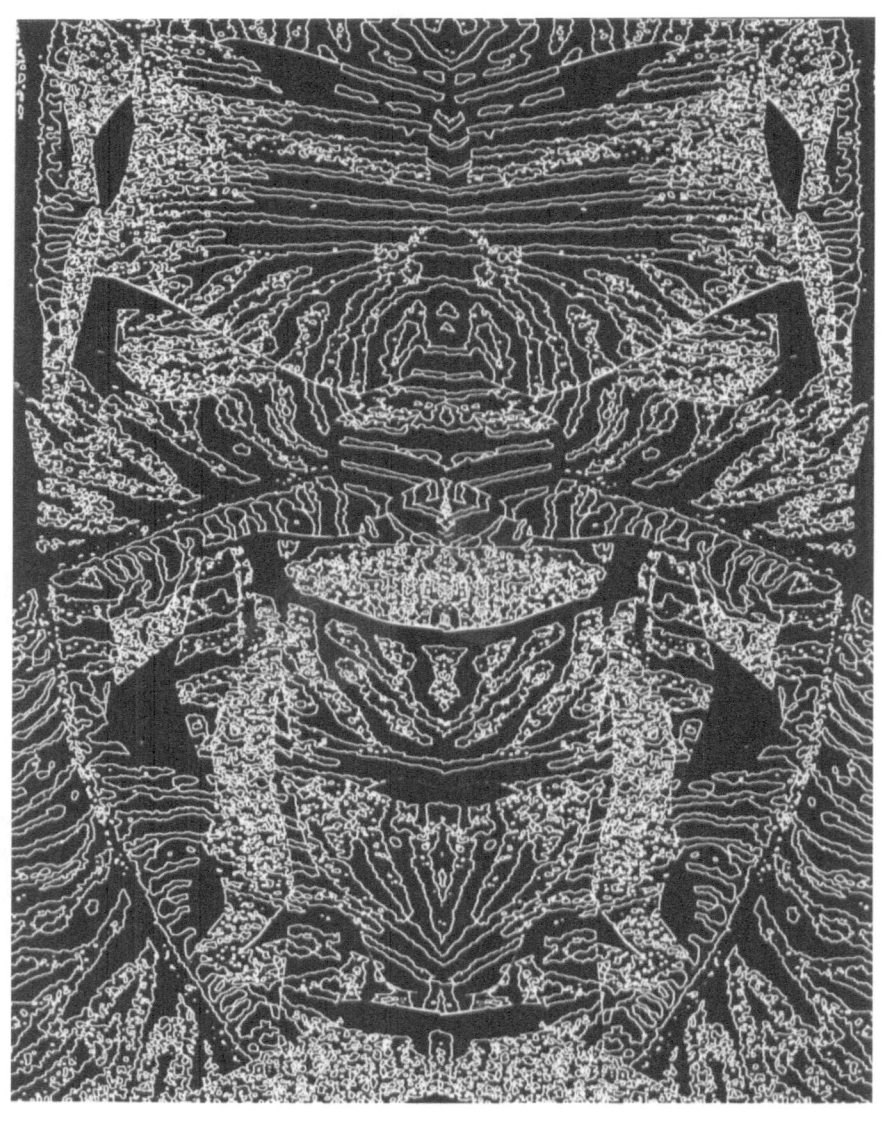

Design 42

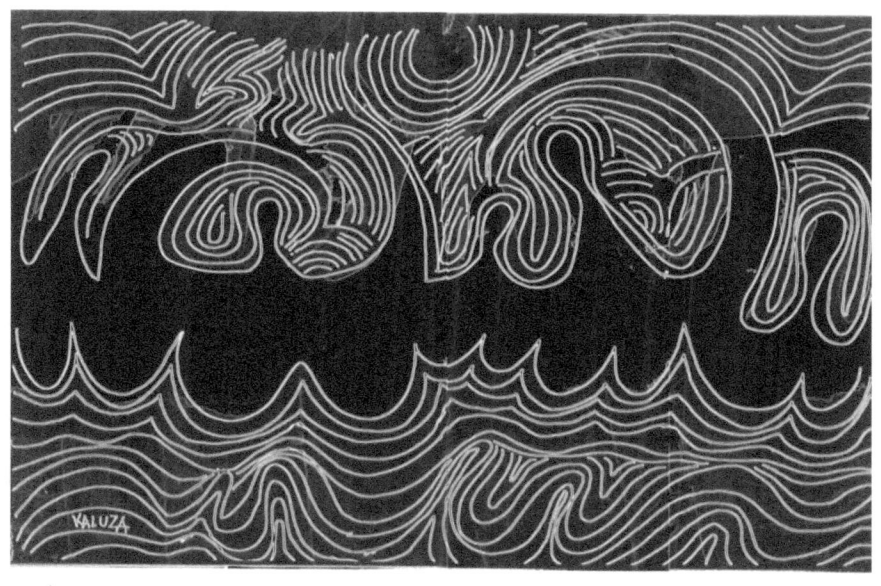

Nudes

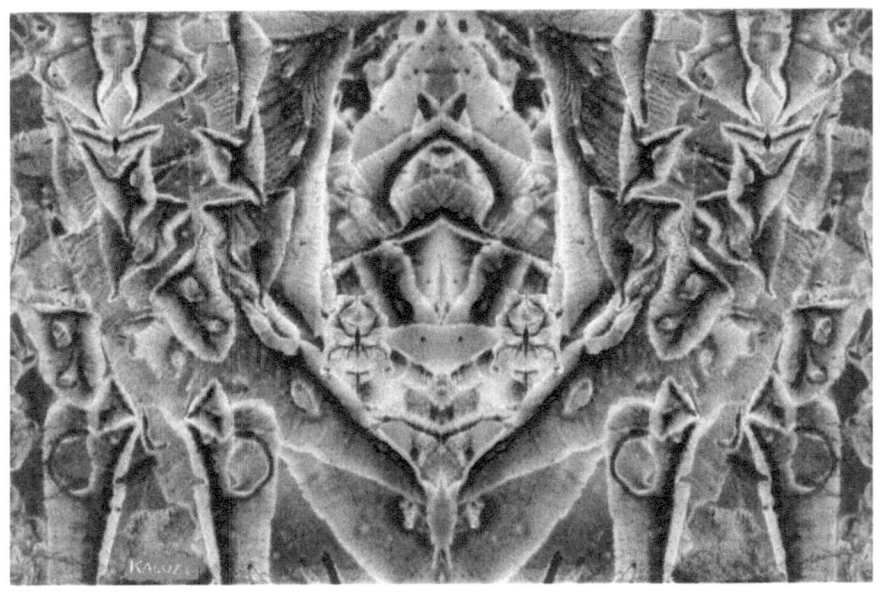

Benevolent Spirit

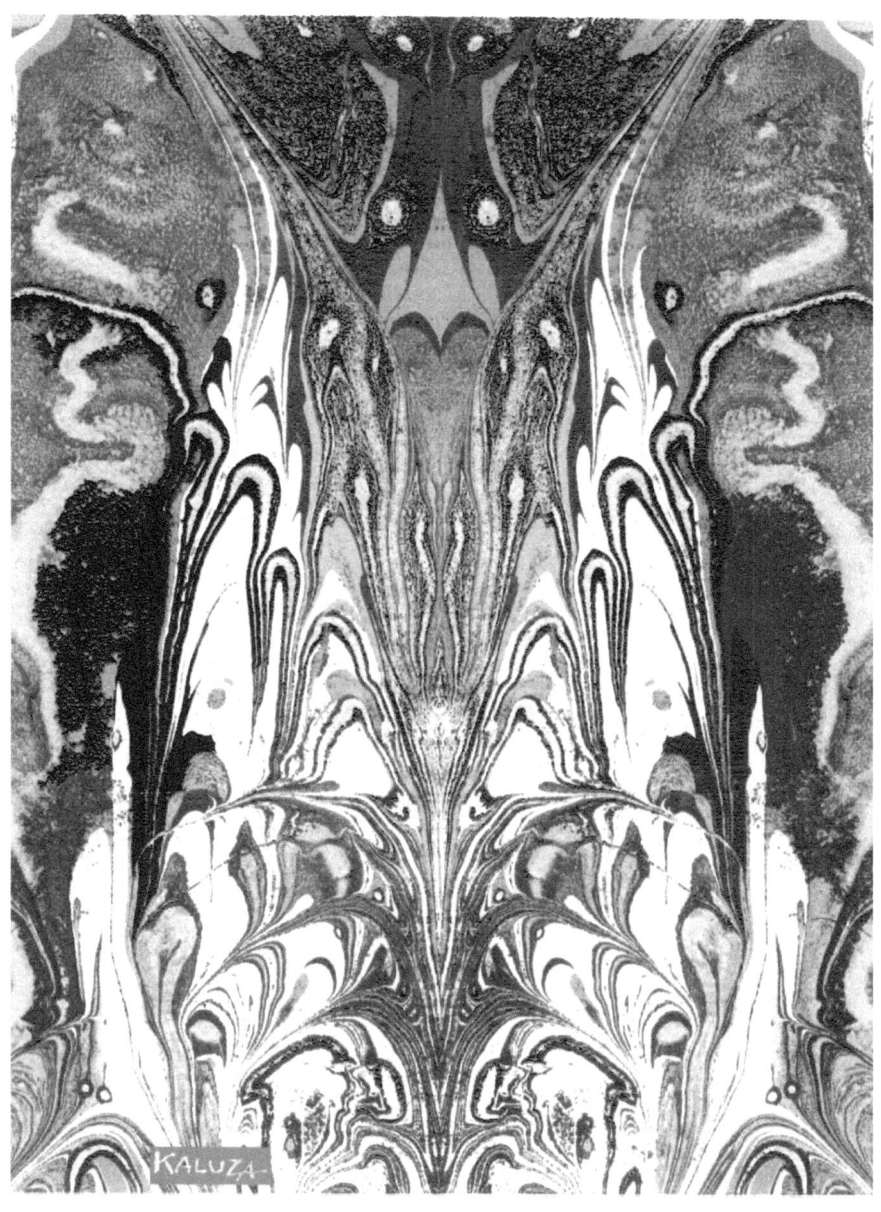

Design 51

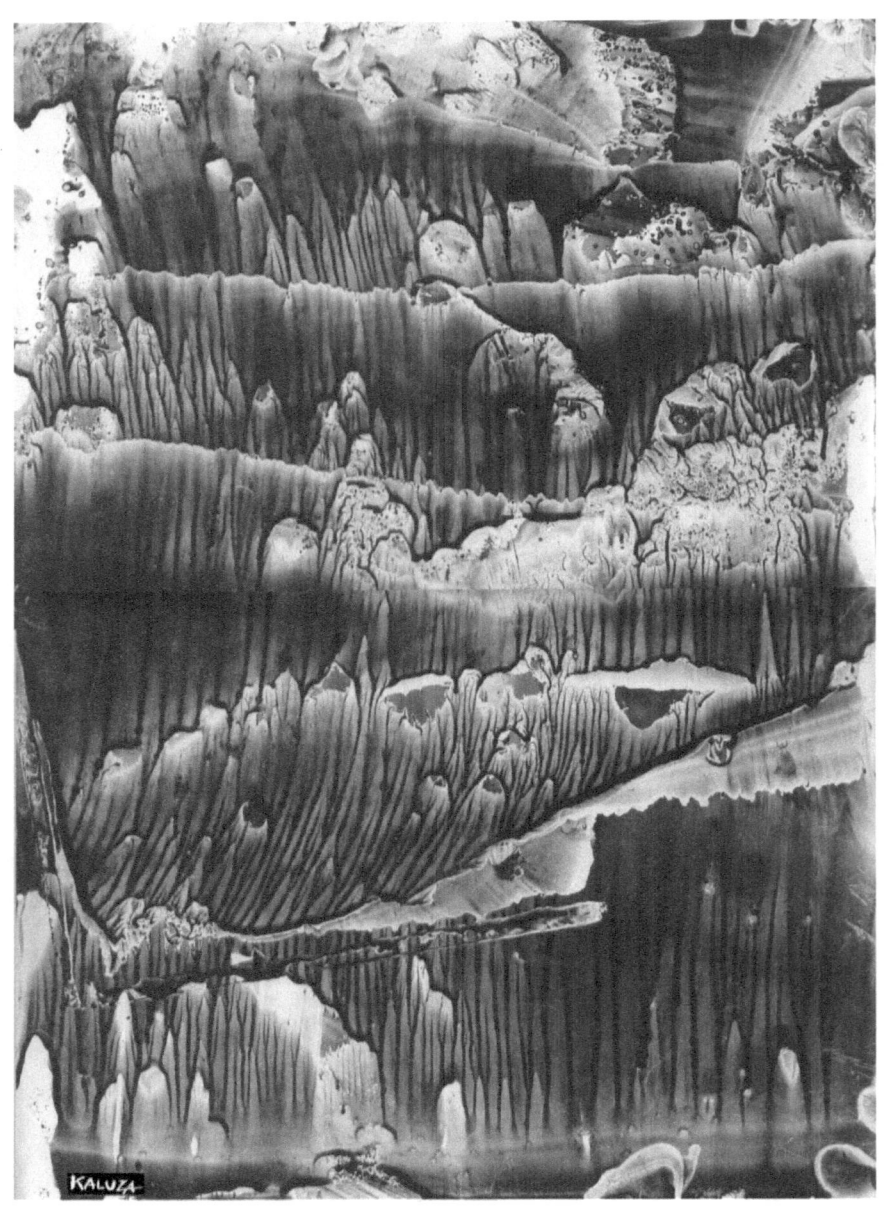

Fantastic Landscape

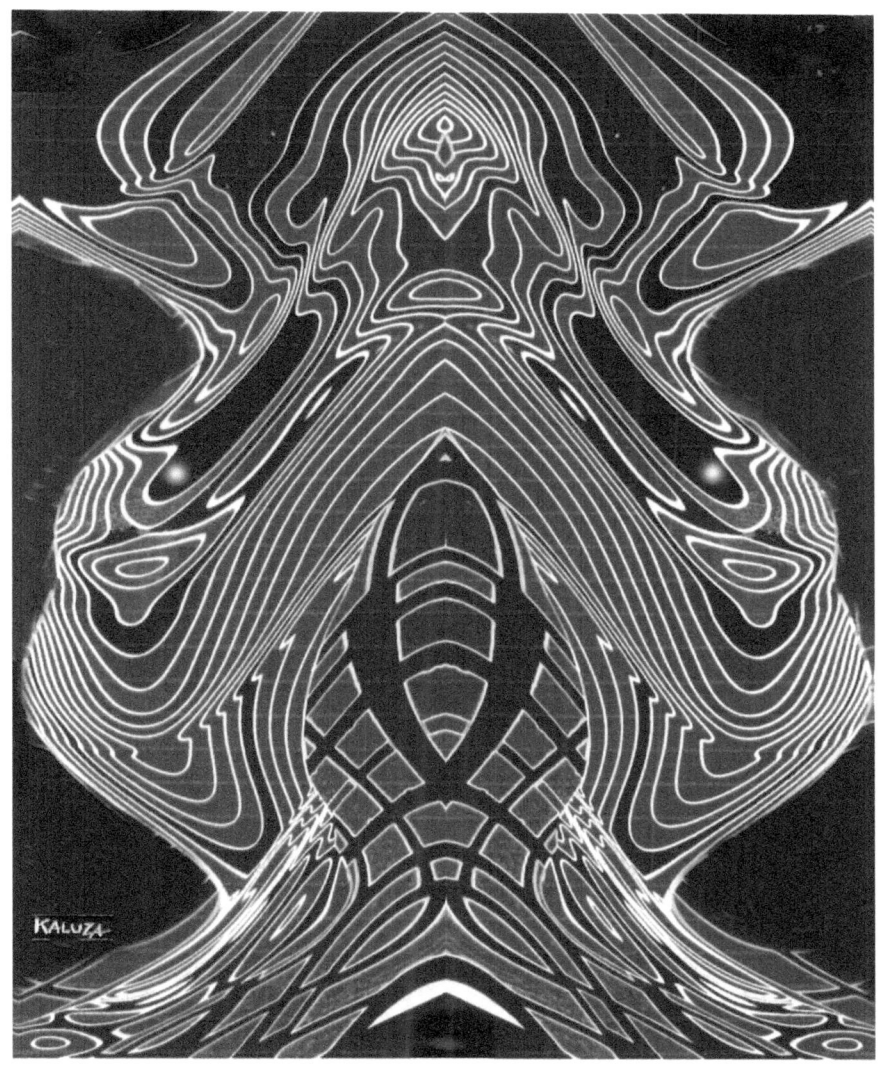

Design 53

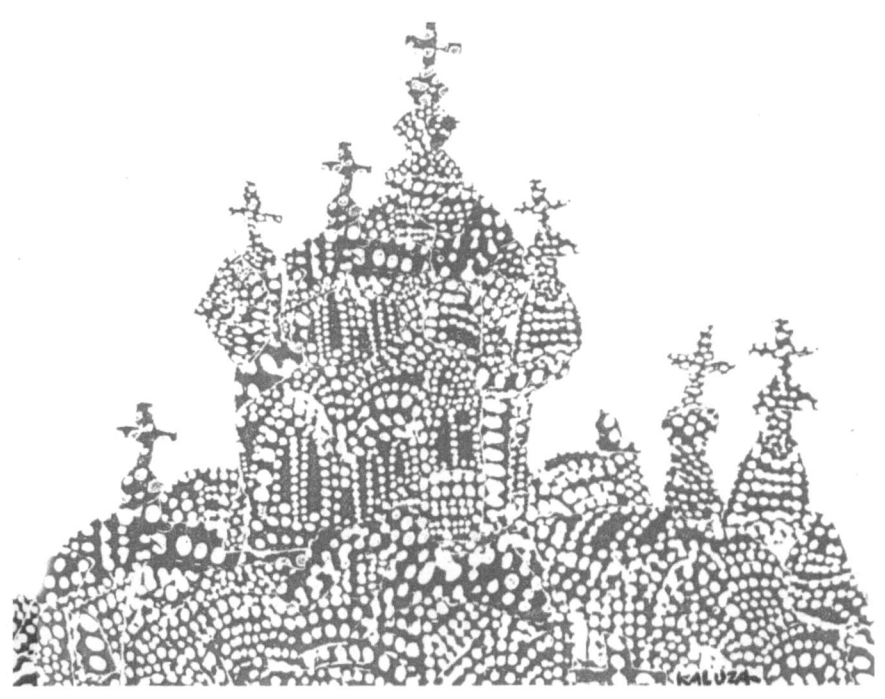

Elaborate Church

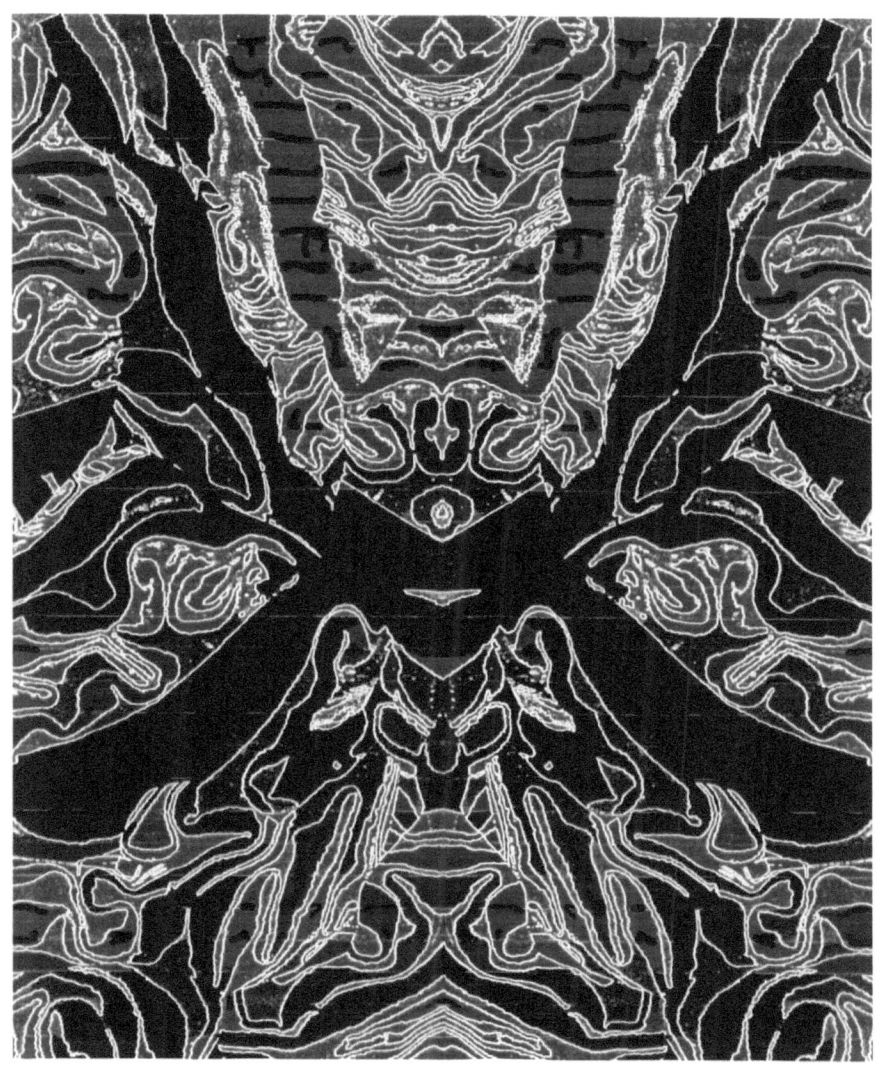

Design 47

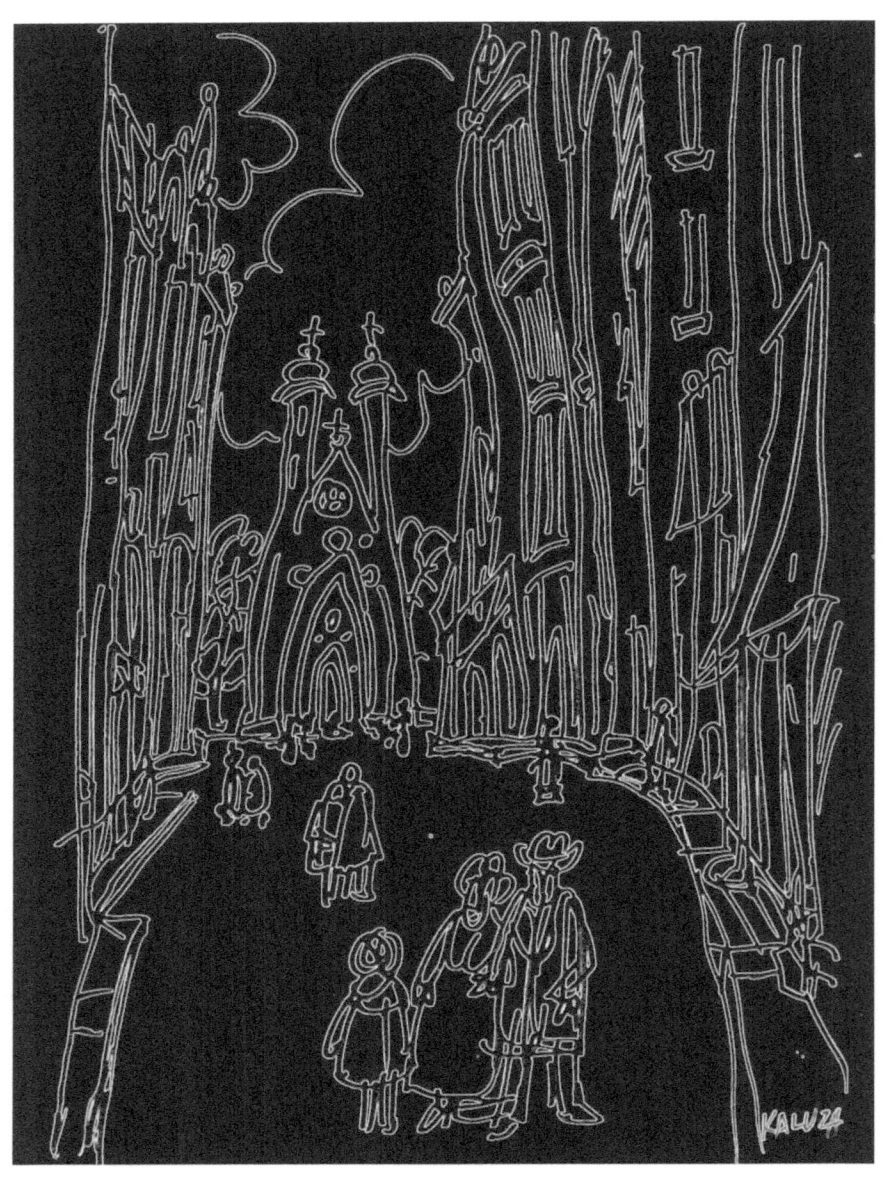

People Coming from Church

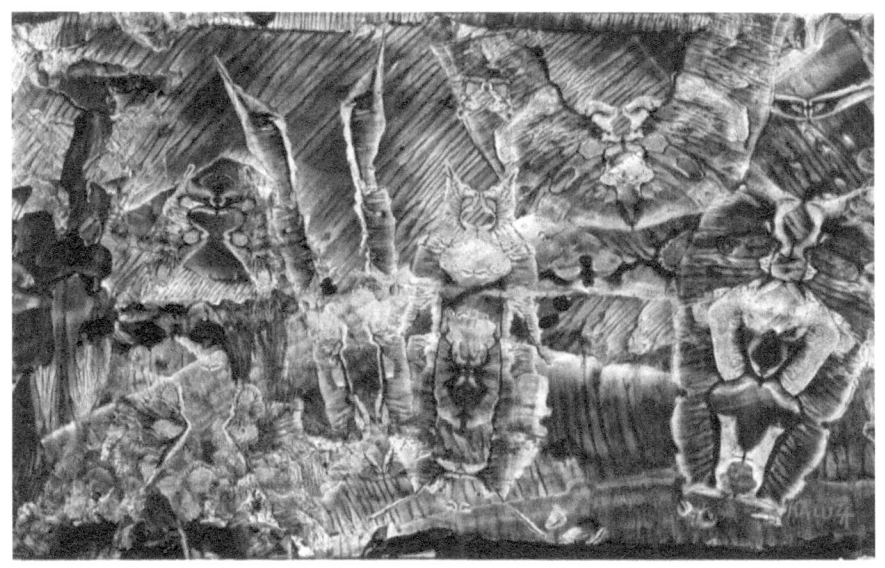

Cave Life

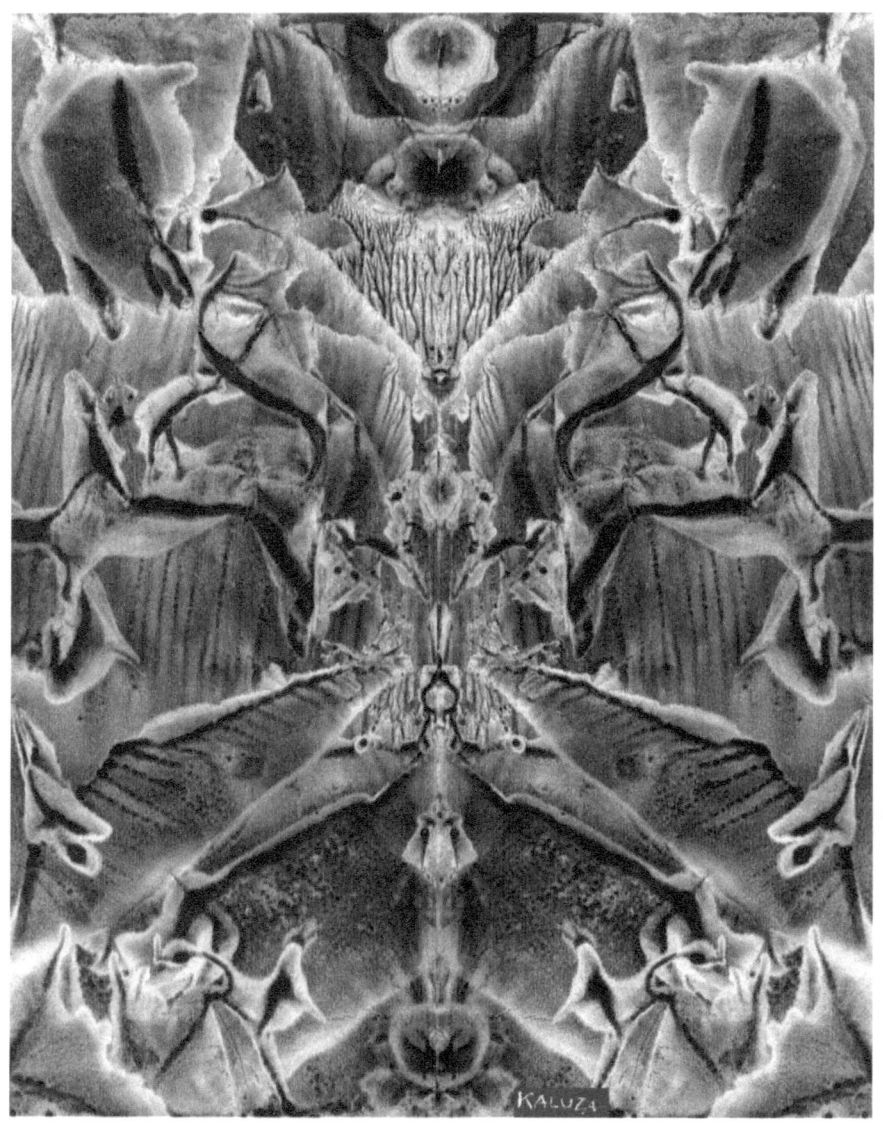

Unusual Creature

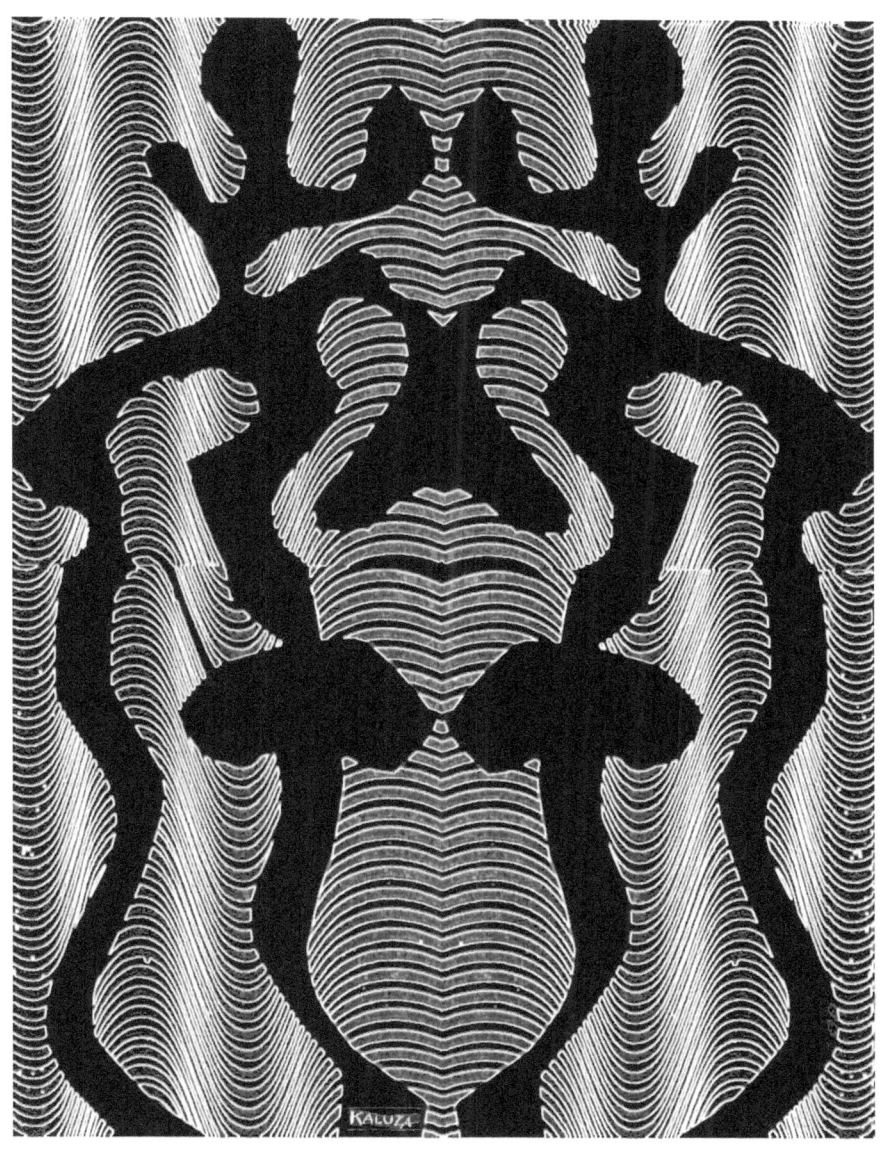

Dancing Figures

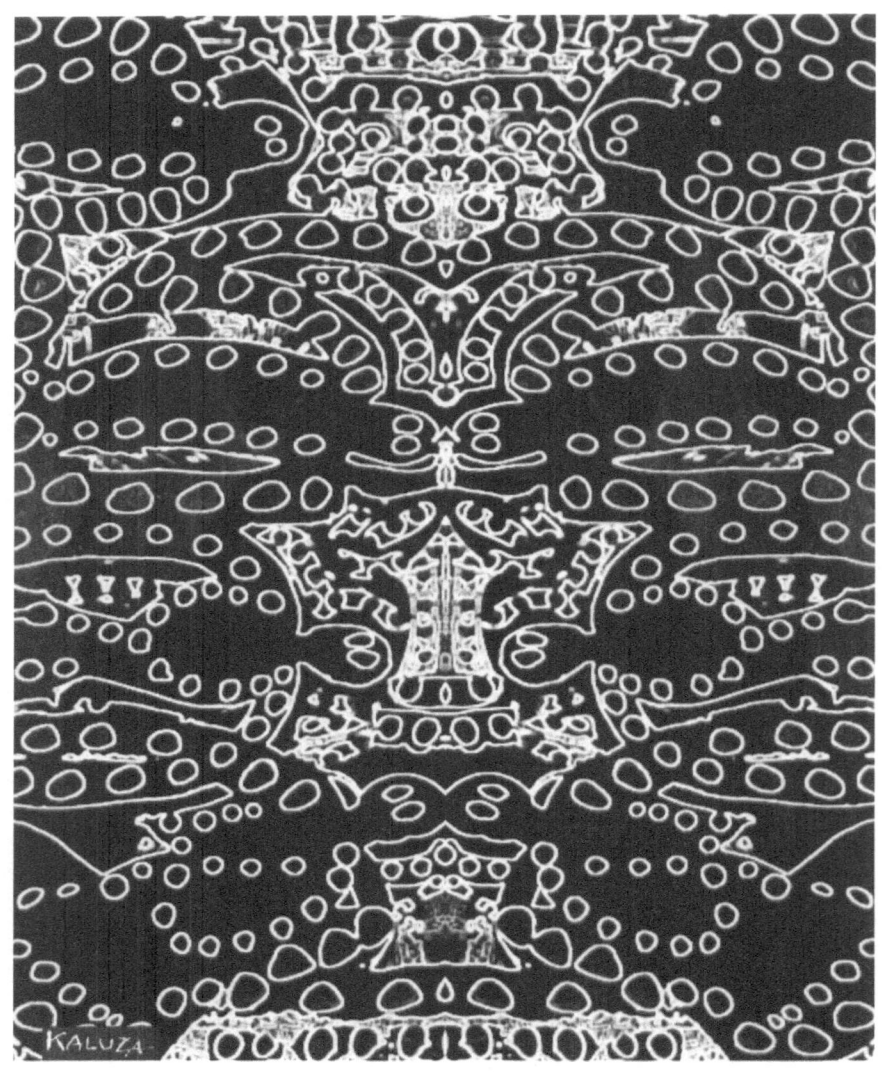

Emperess

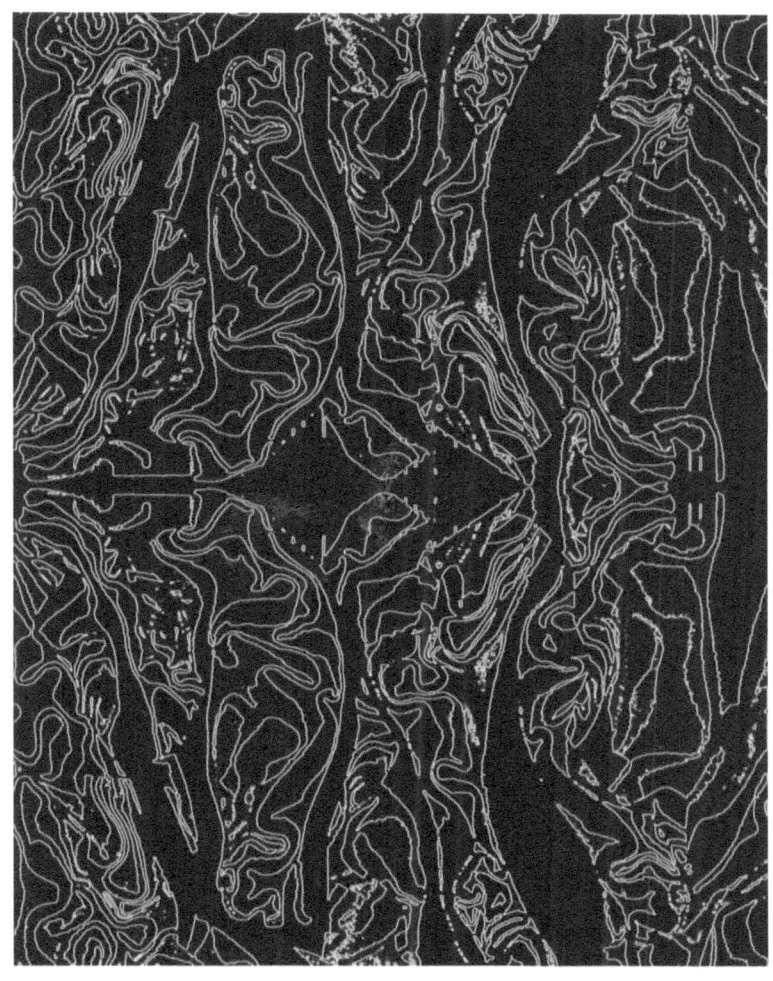

Design 28

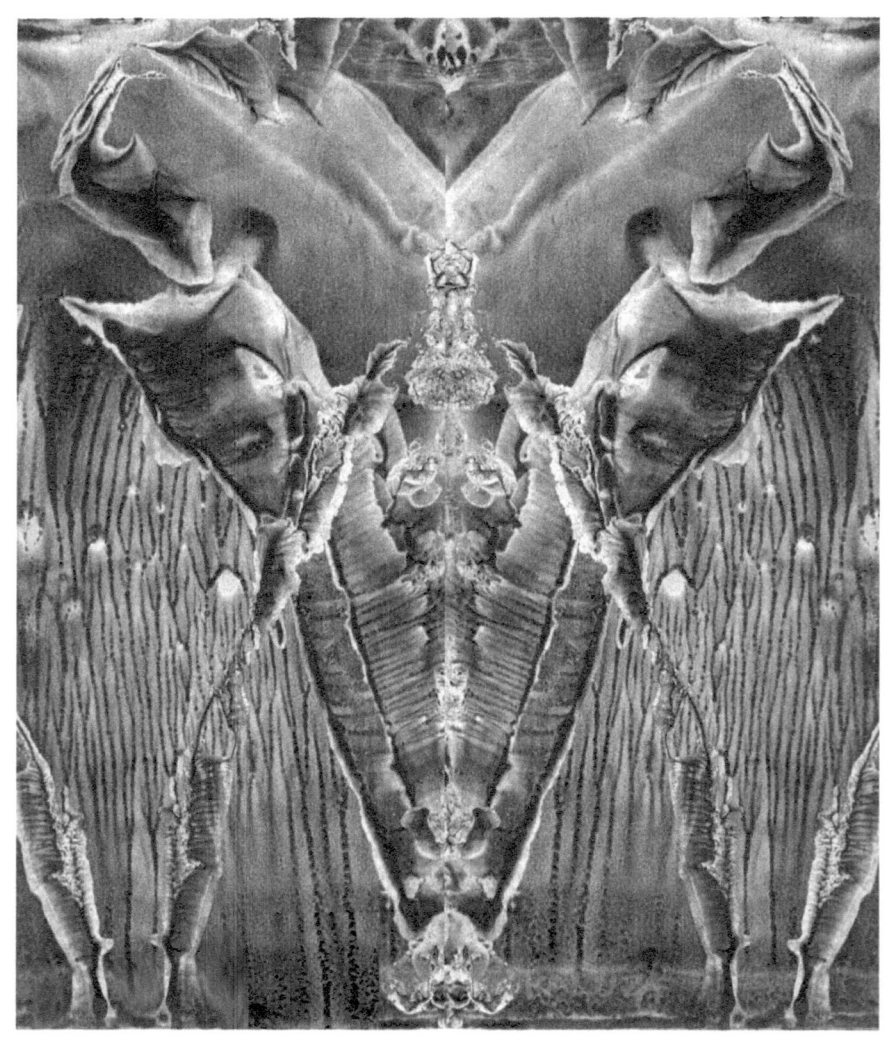

Demon

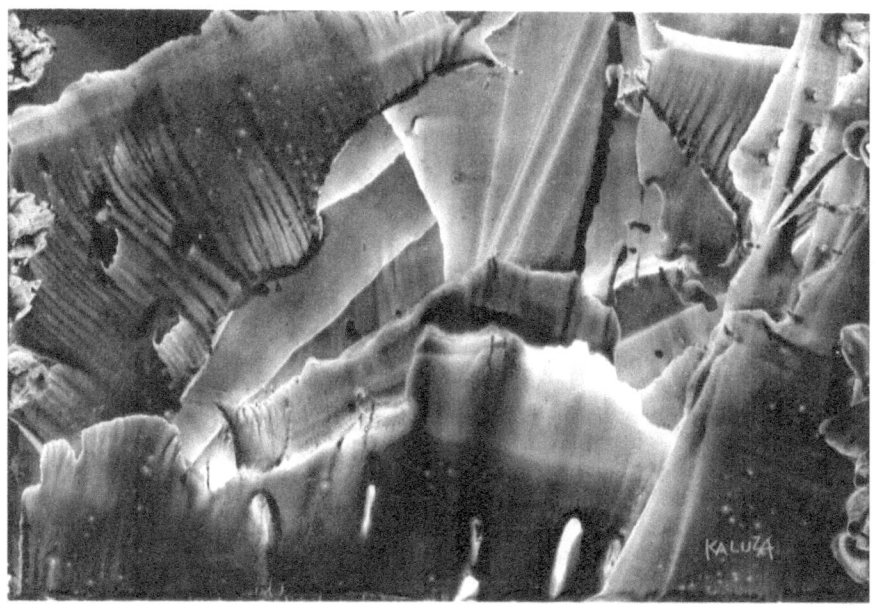

Unusual Landscape

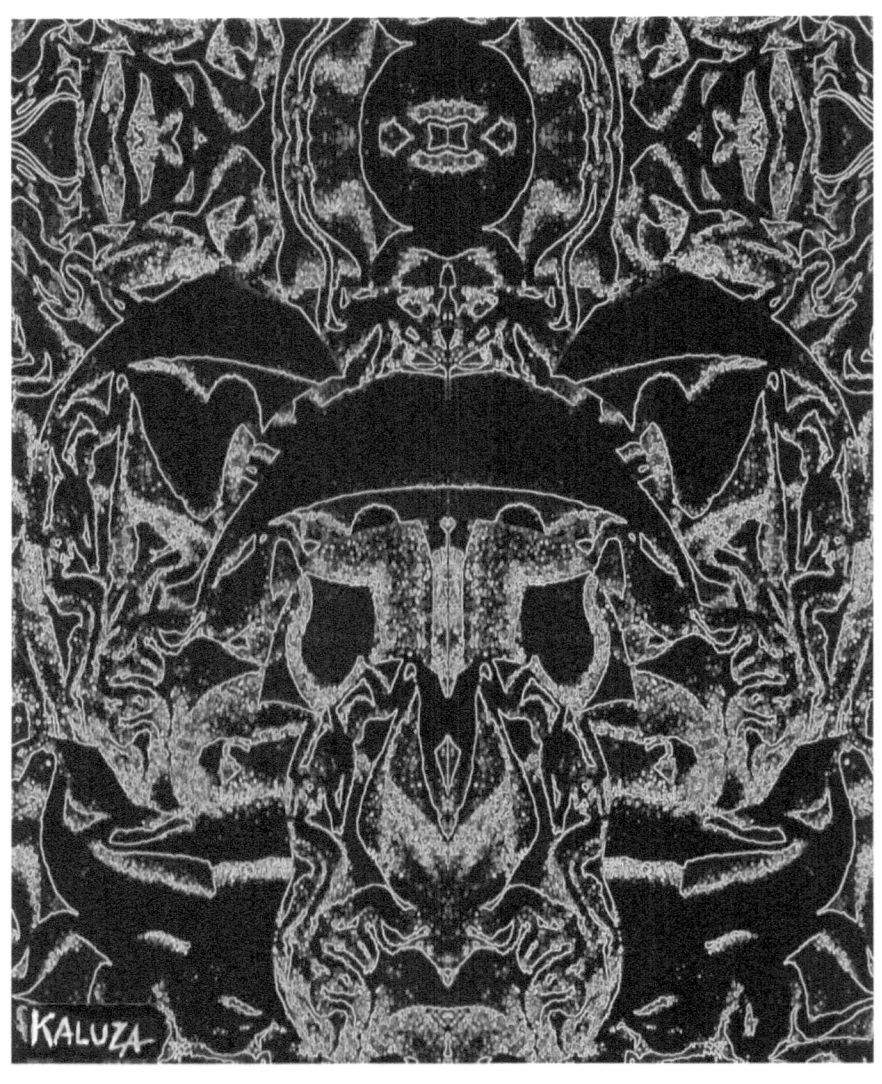

Design 50

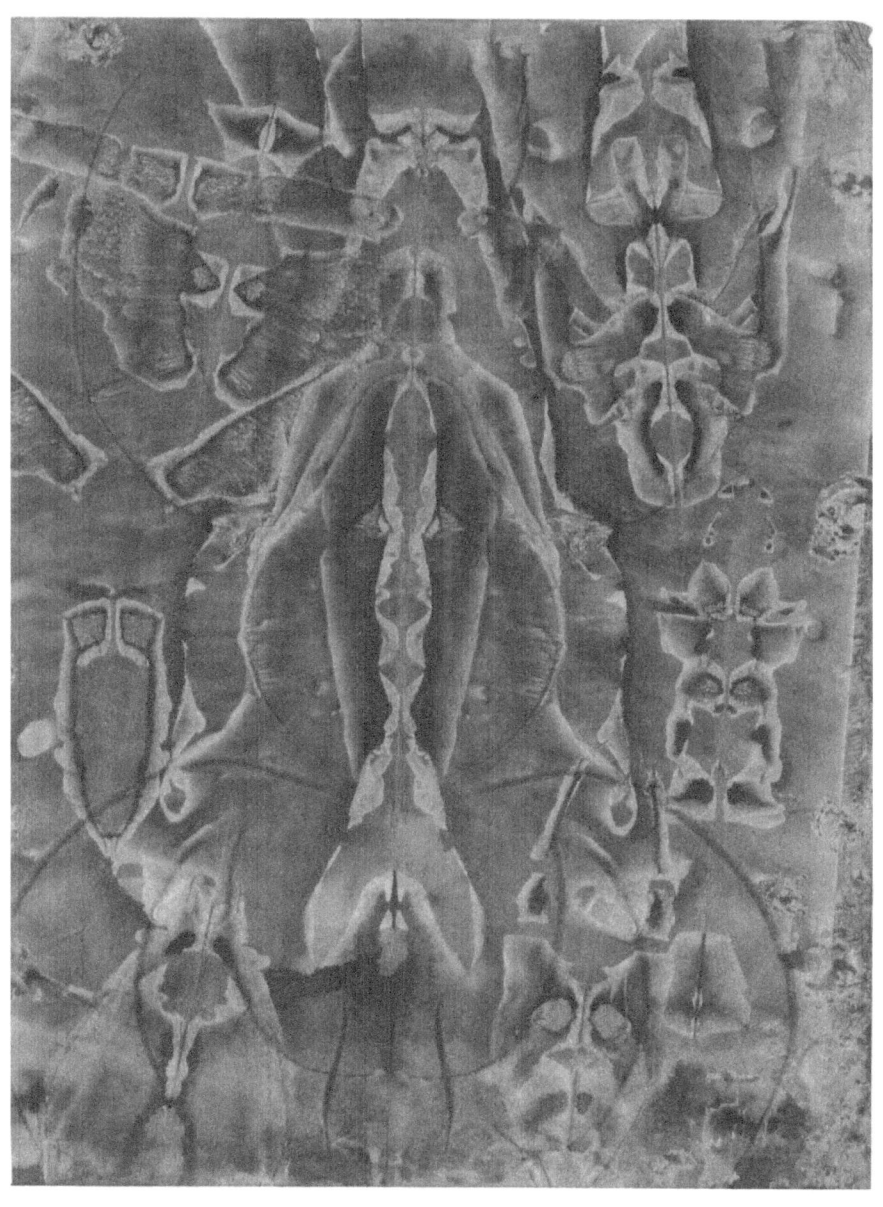

Alien Lady

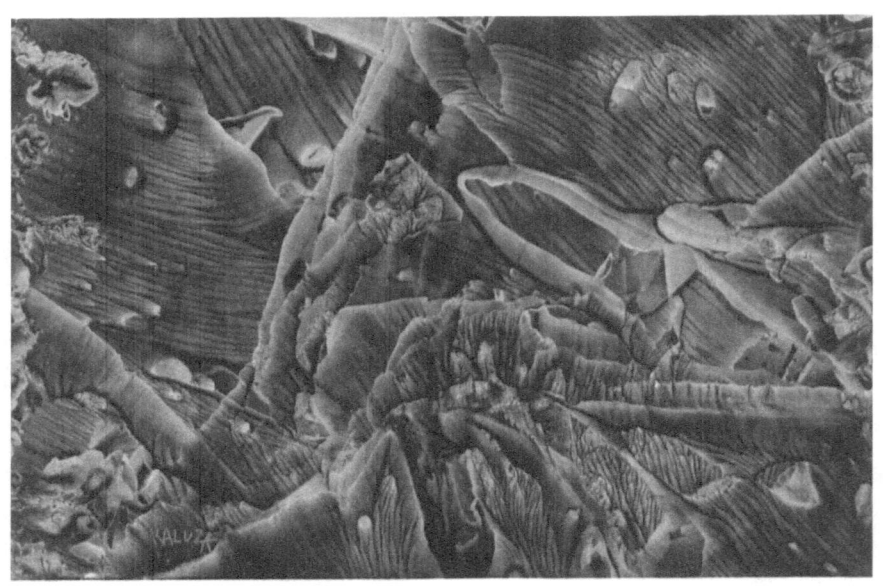

Weird Formation

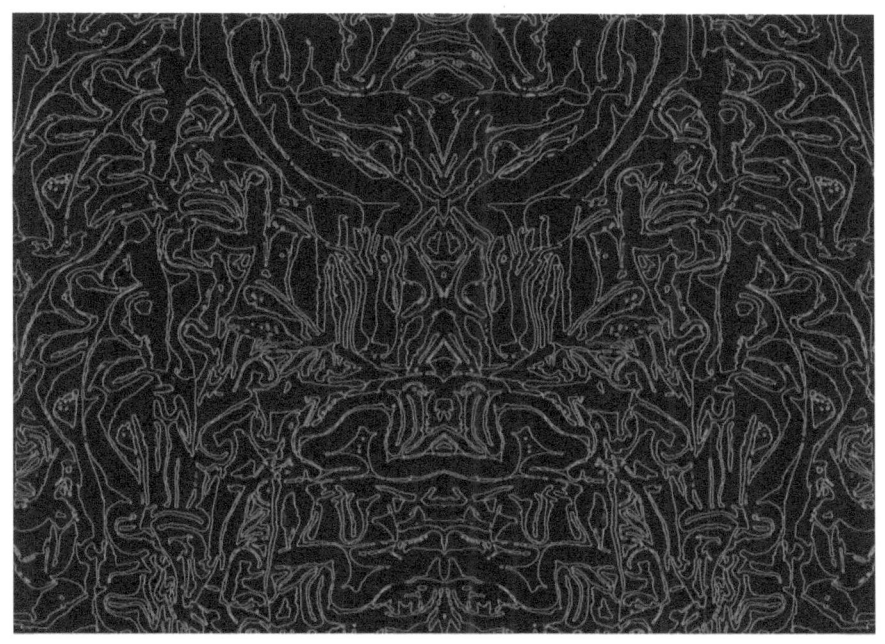

Design 48

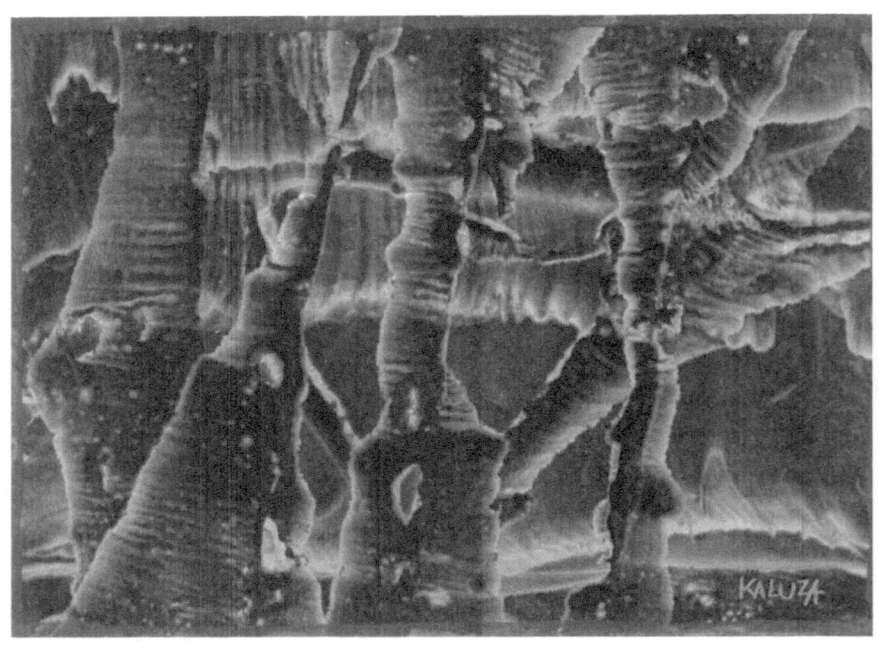

Stalactites and Columns

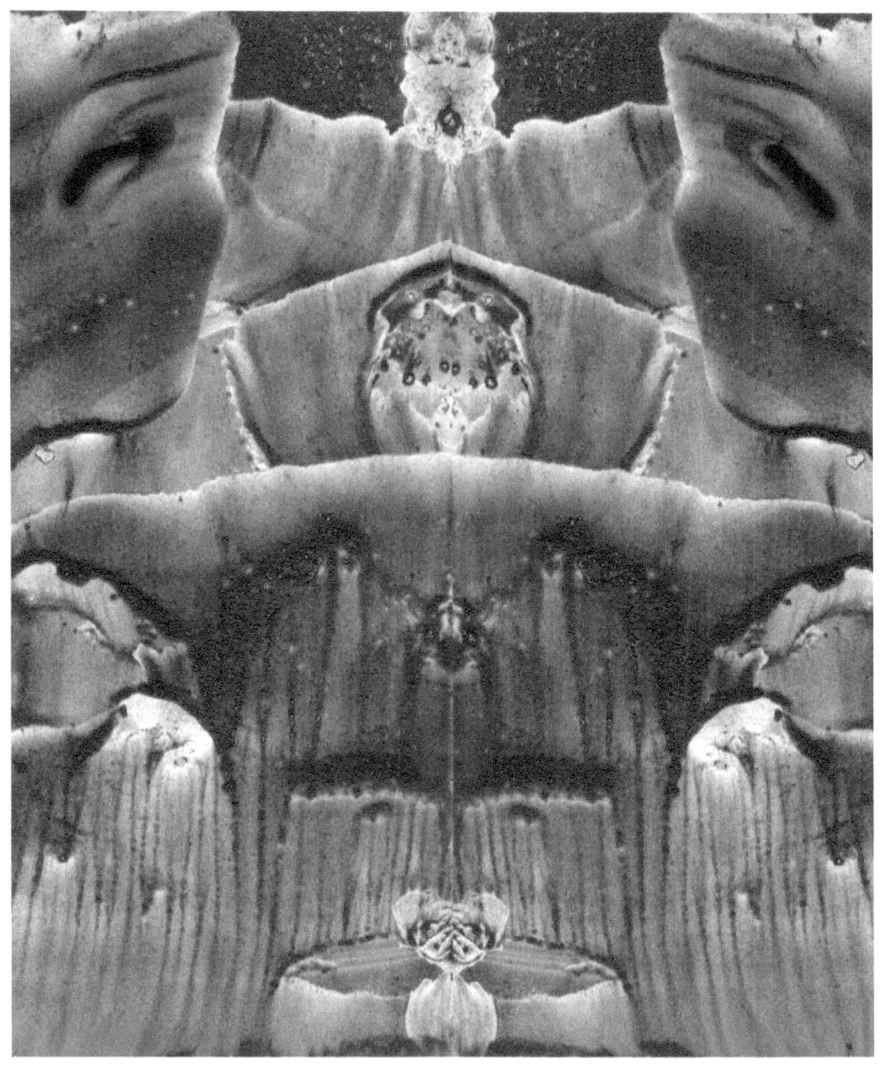

Zeus

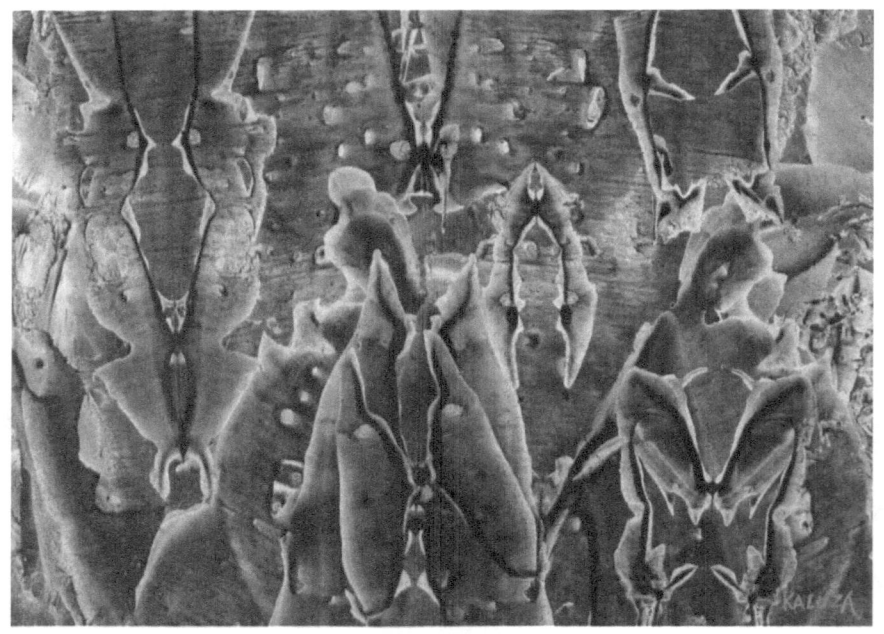

Trick or Treat

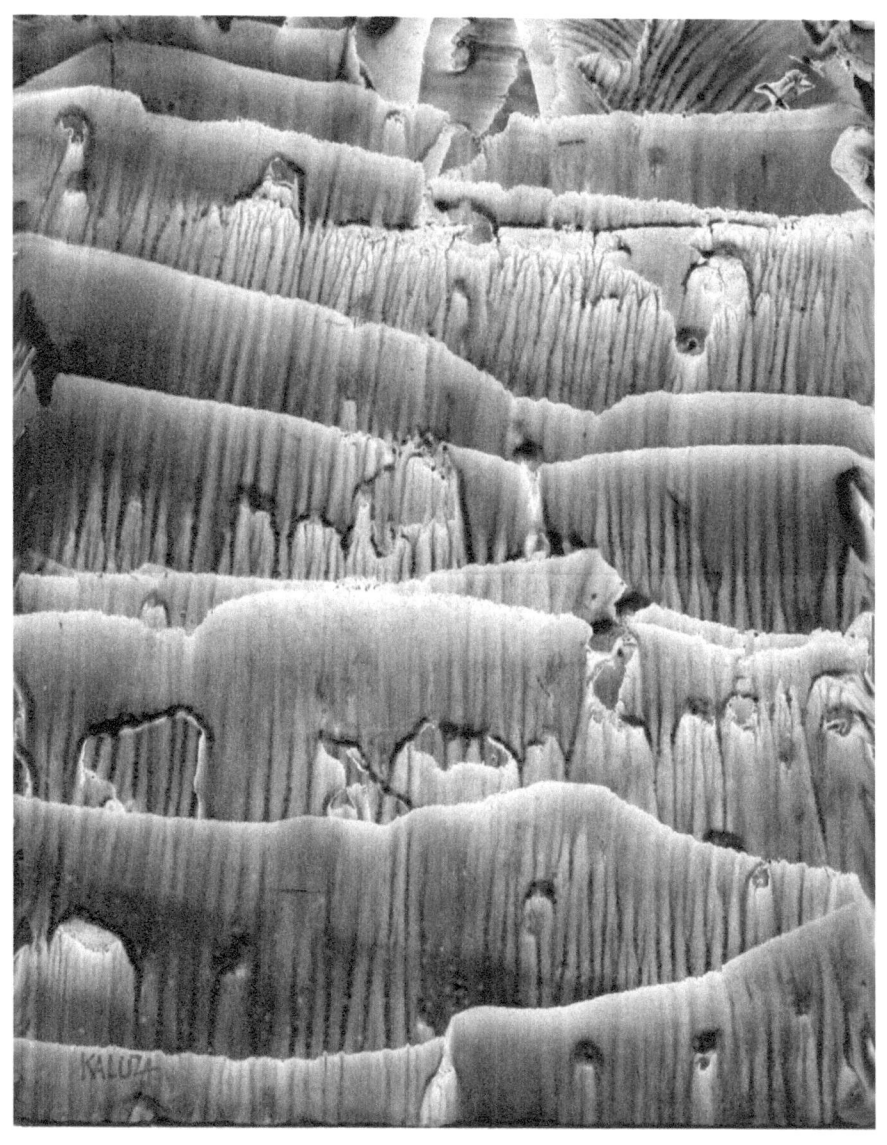

Steps

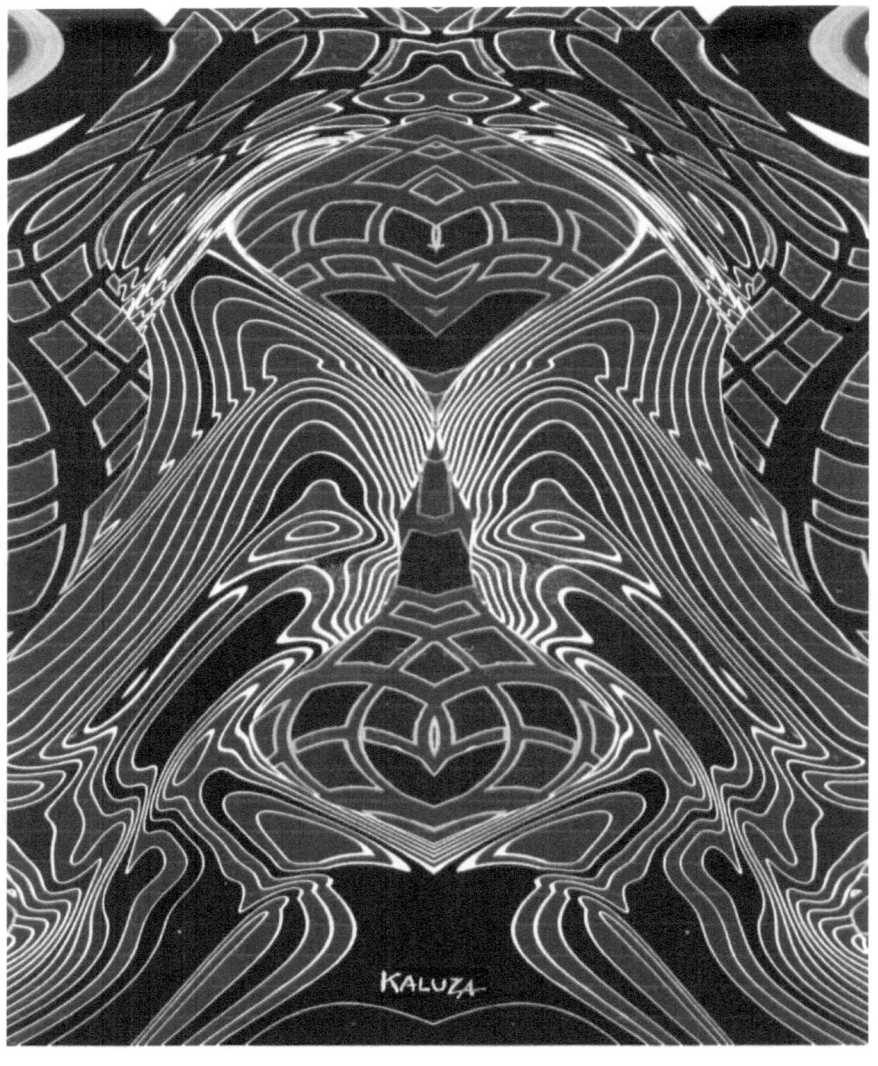

Design 52

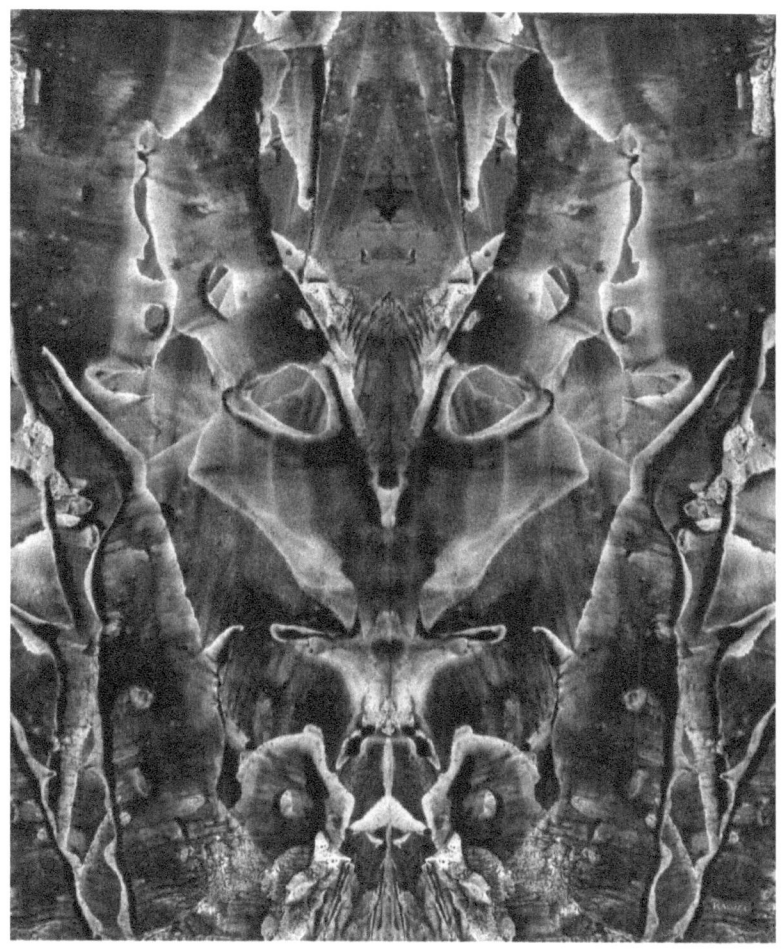

Alien Woman

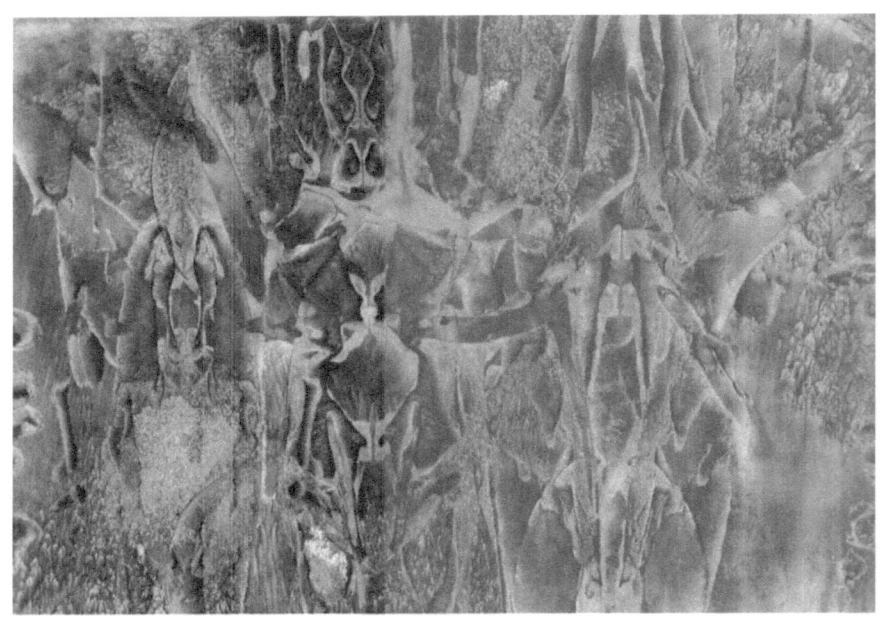

Witches

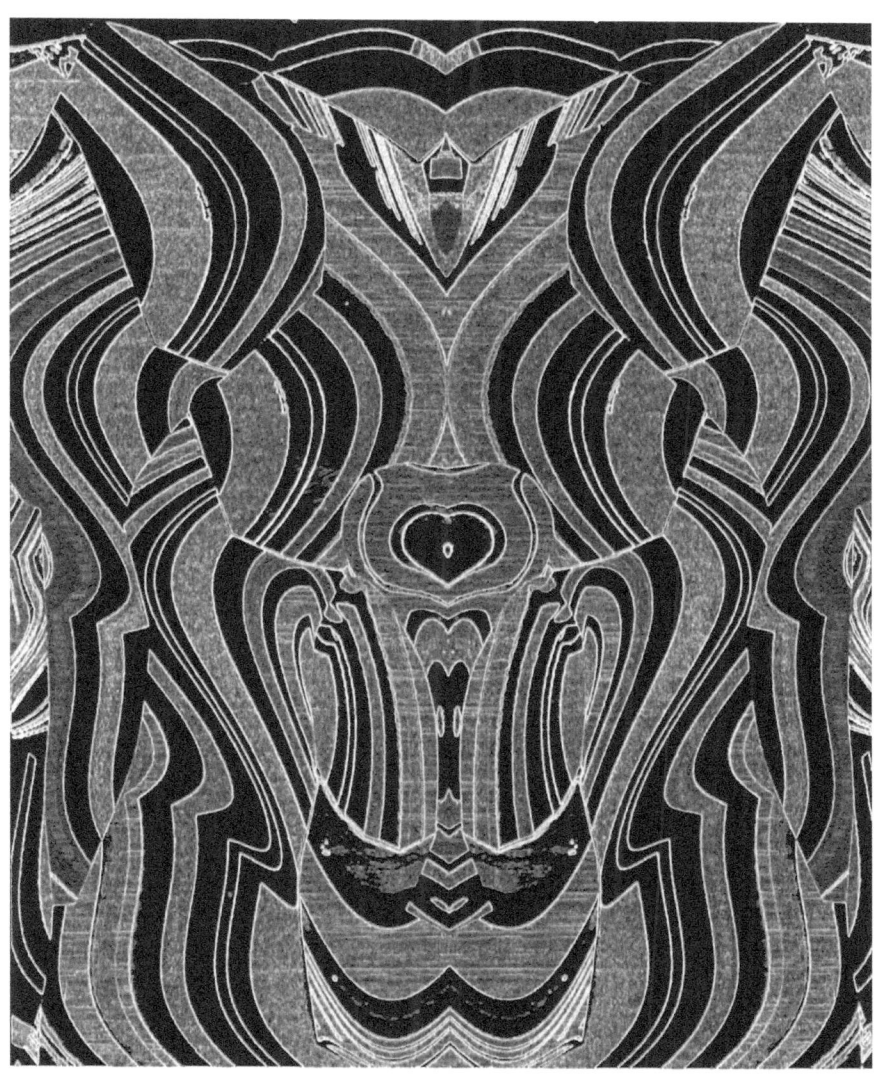

Face

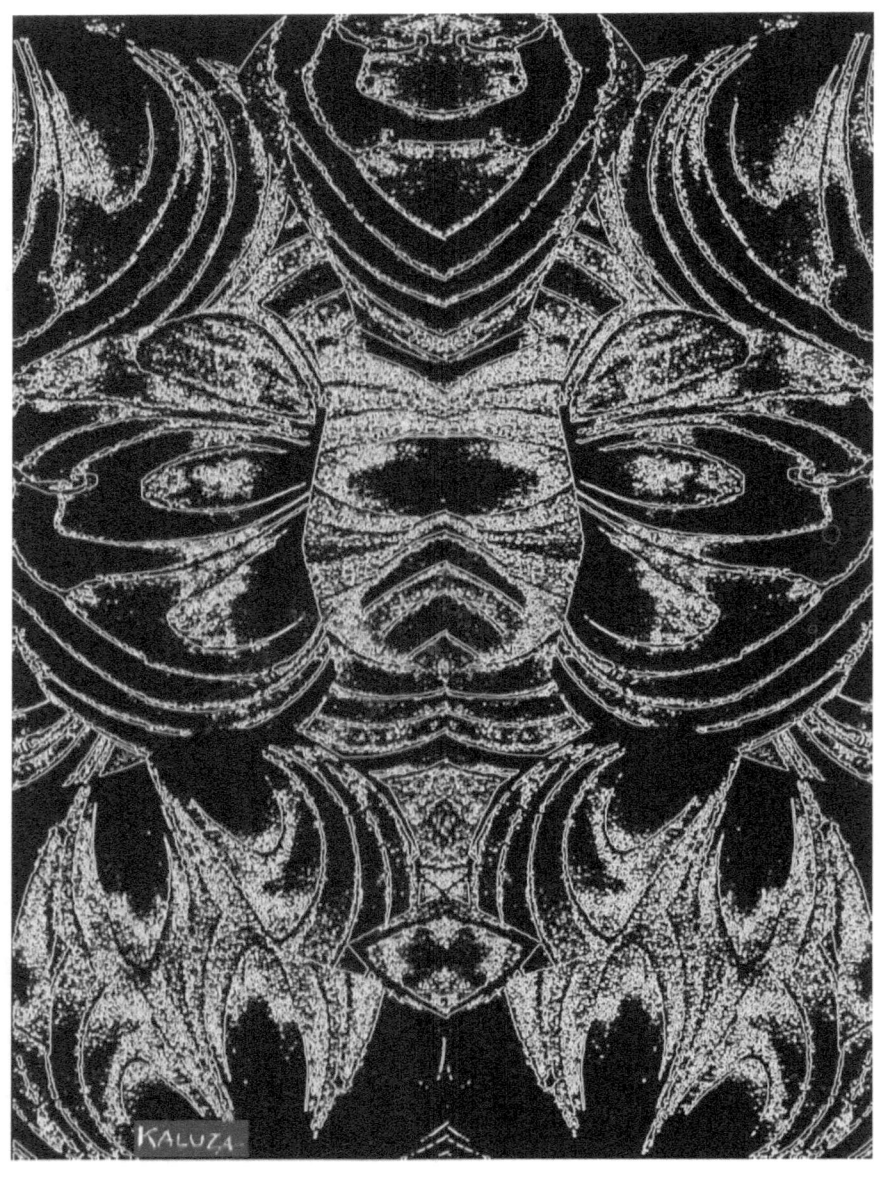

Design 56

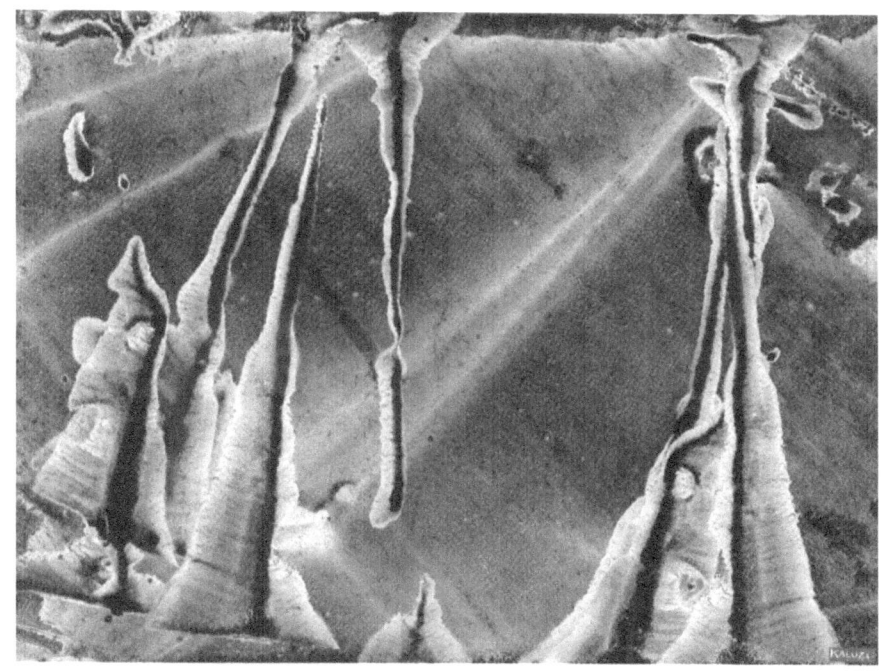

Stalagmites and Stalactites

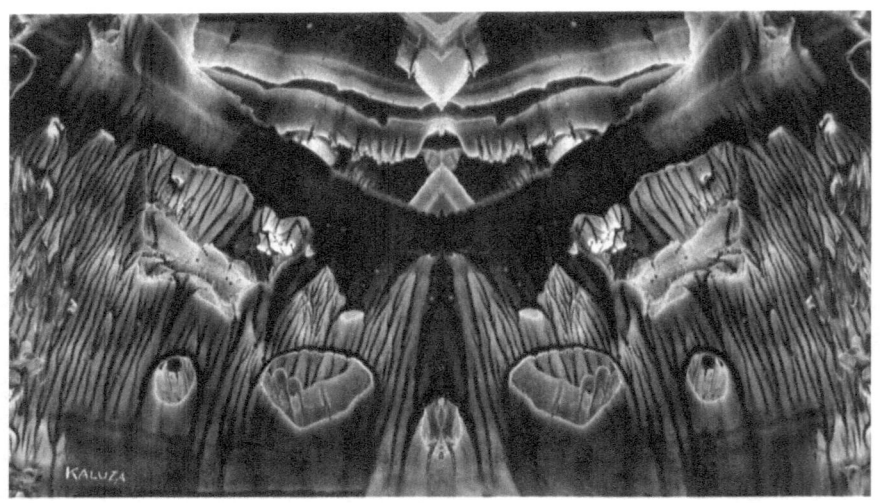

The Eagle

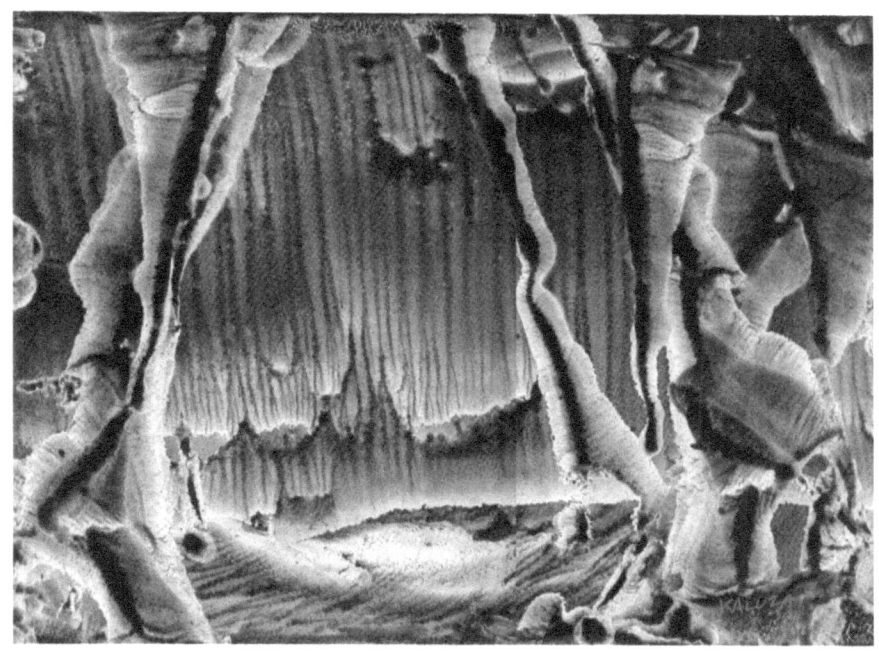

Stone Age Landscape

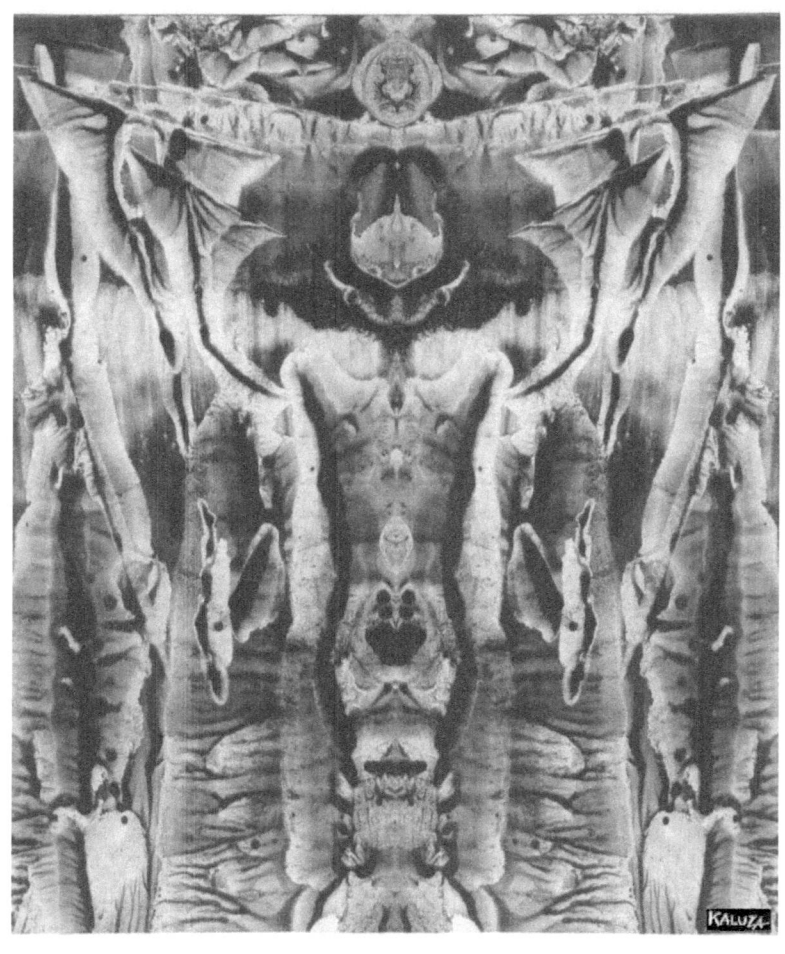

Apparition 2

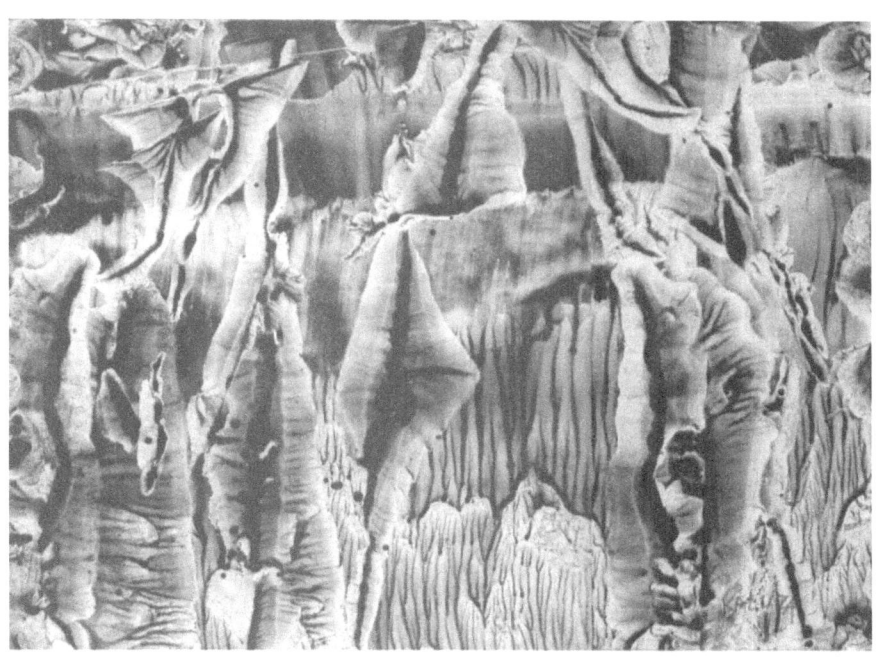

Entrance to a Cave

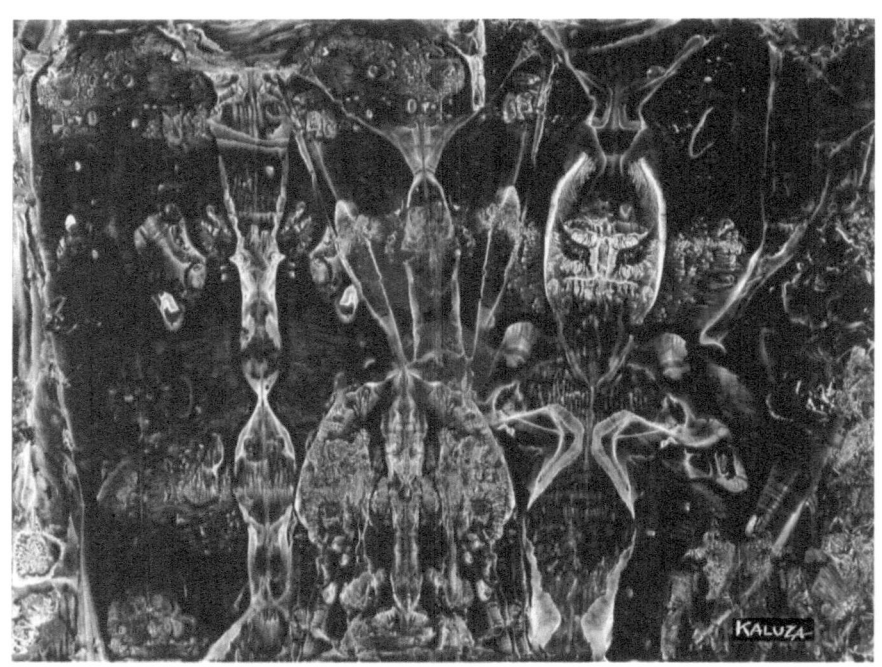

Alien Threesome

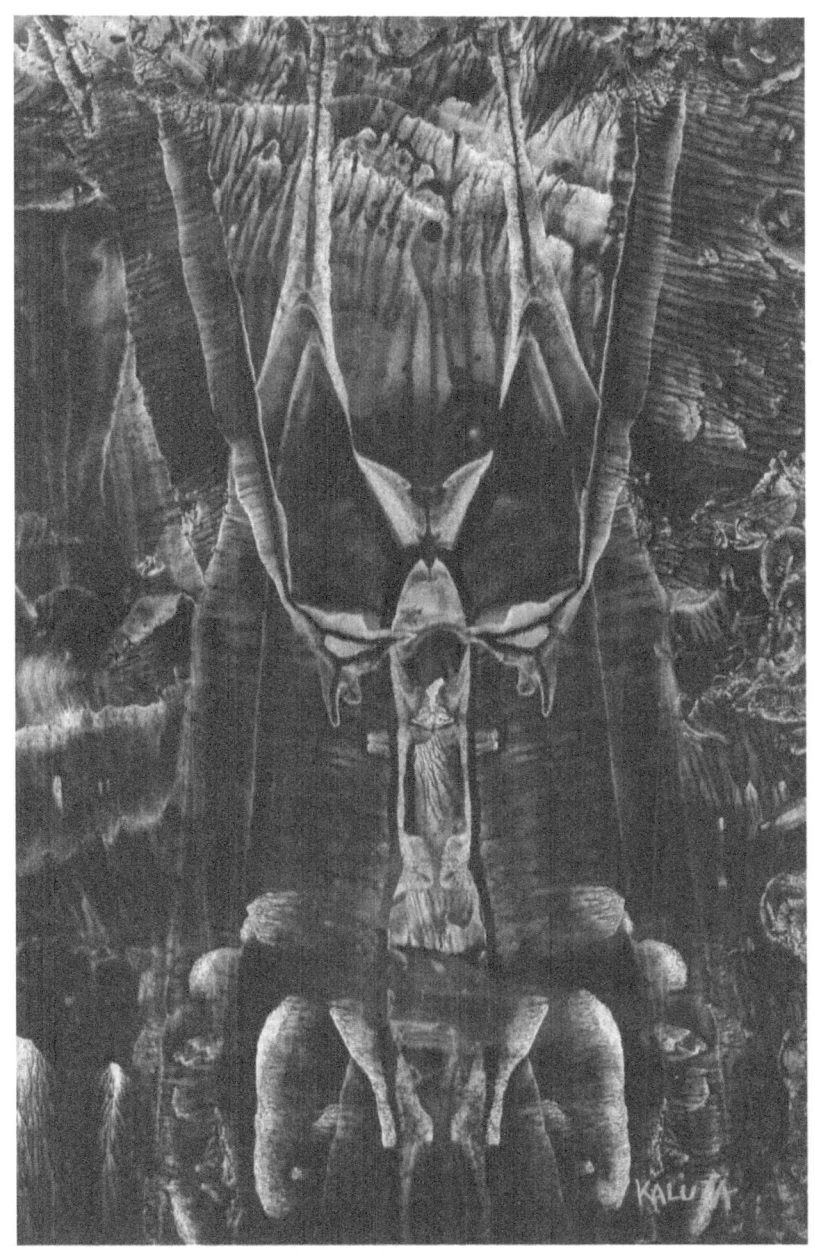

Bug

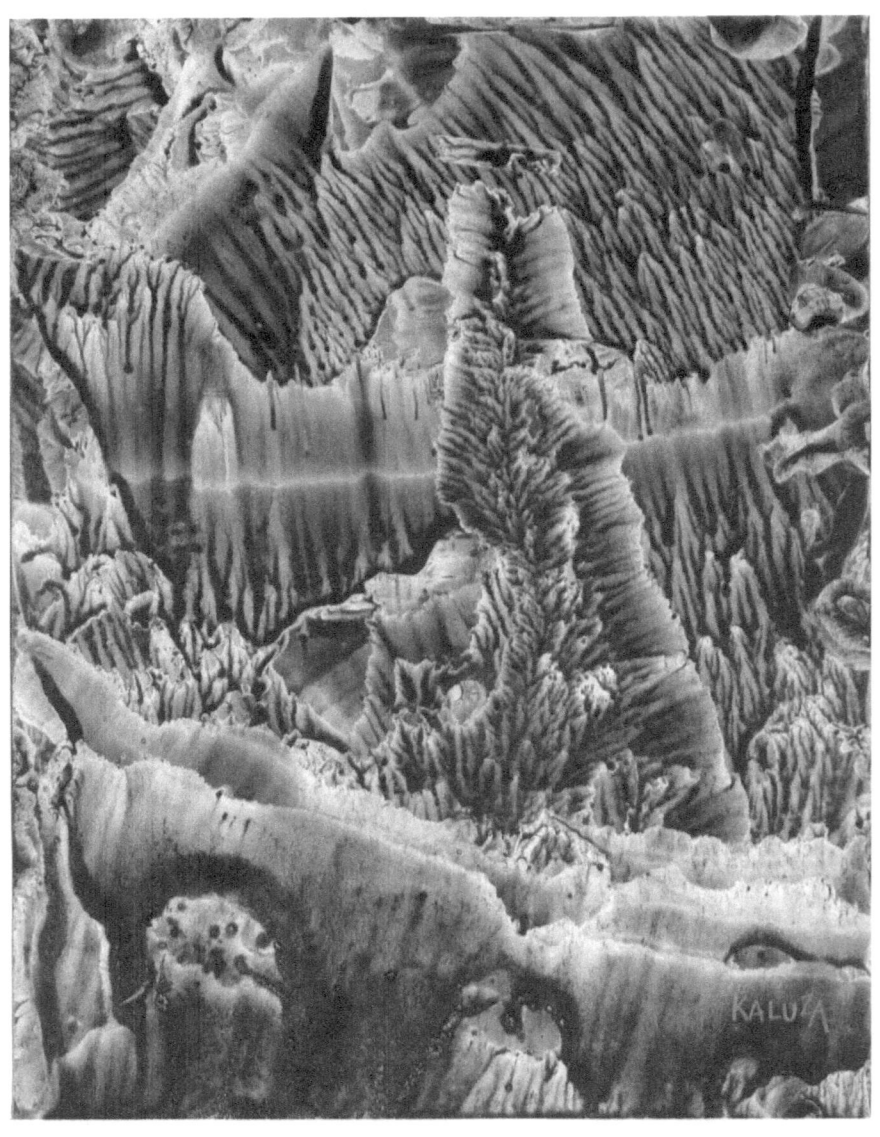

Enchanted Landscape

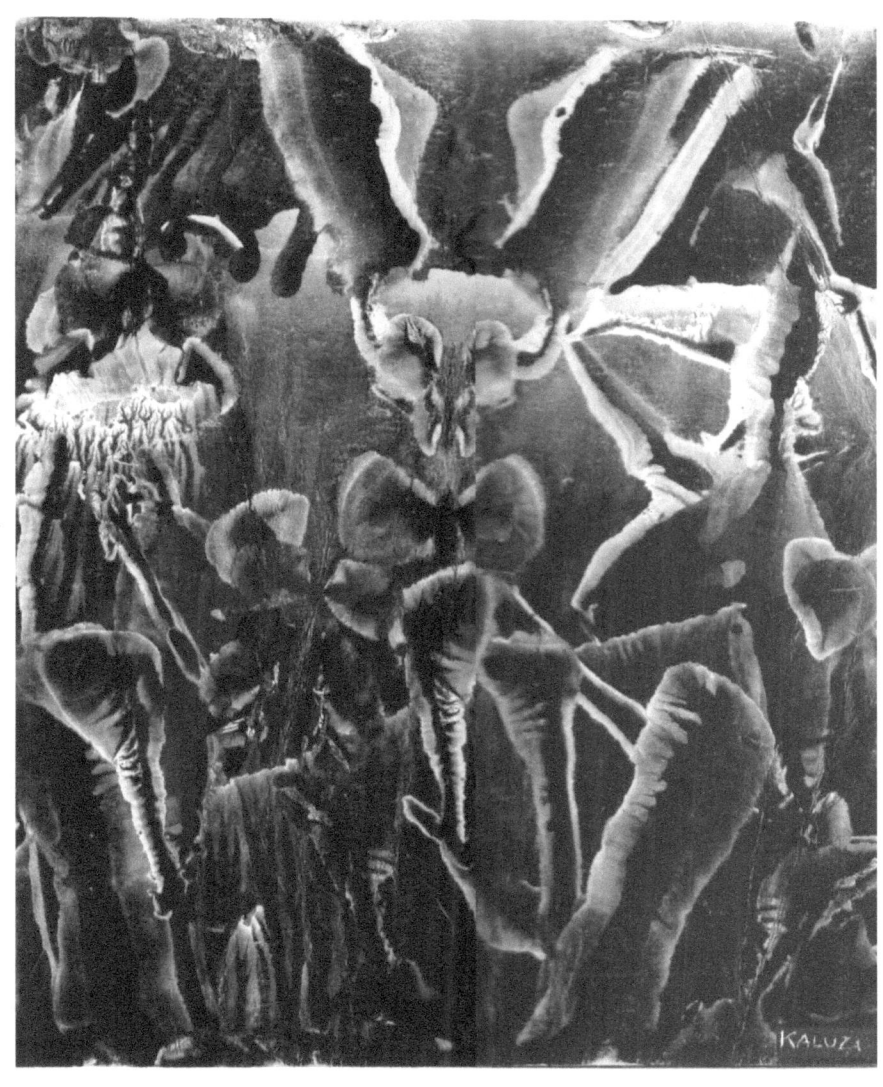

Rabbit

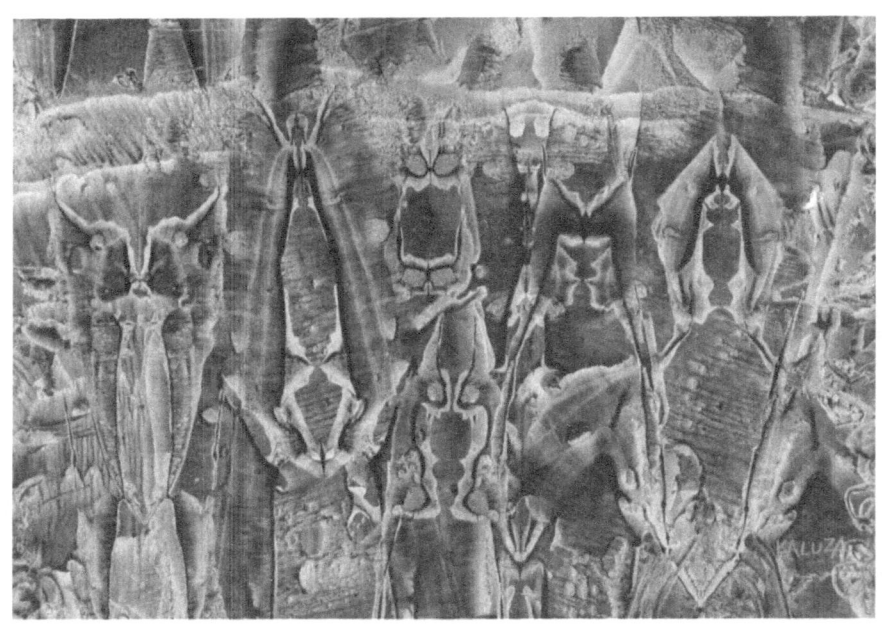

Chieftains

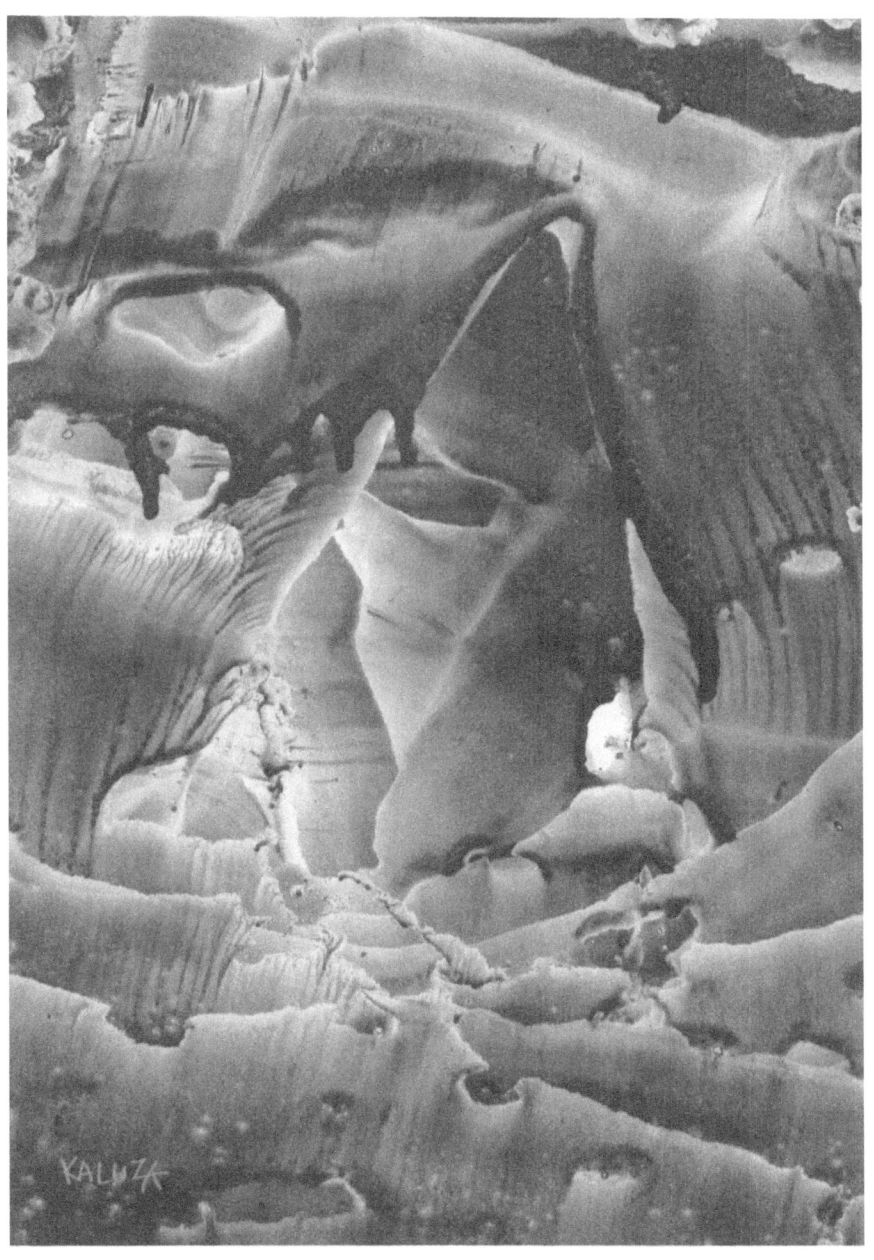

Strange Landscape

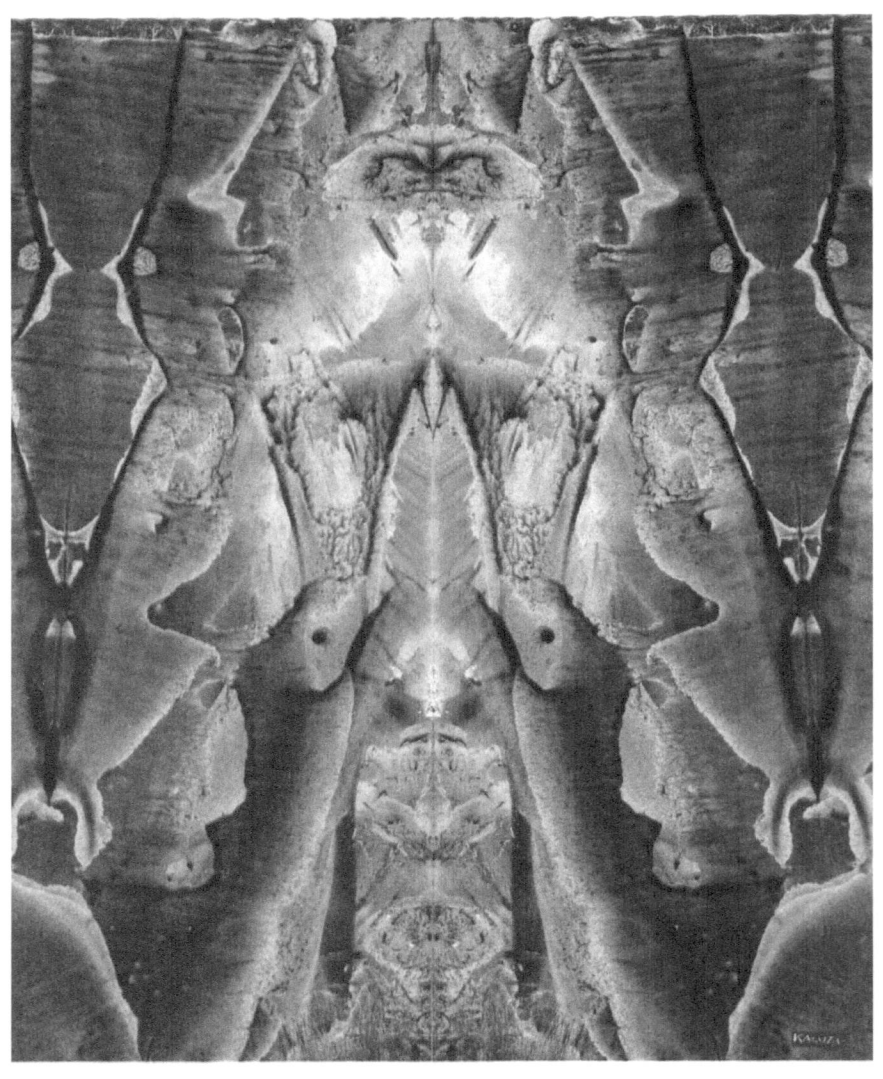

Mysterious Figure

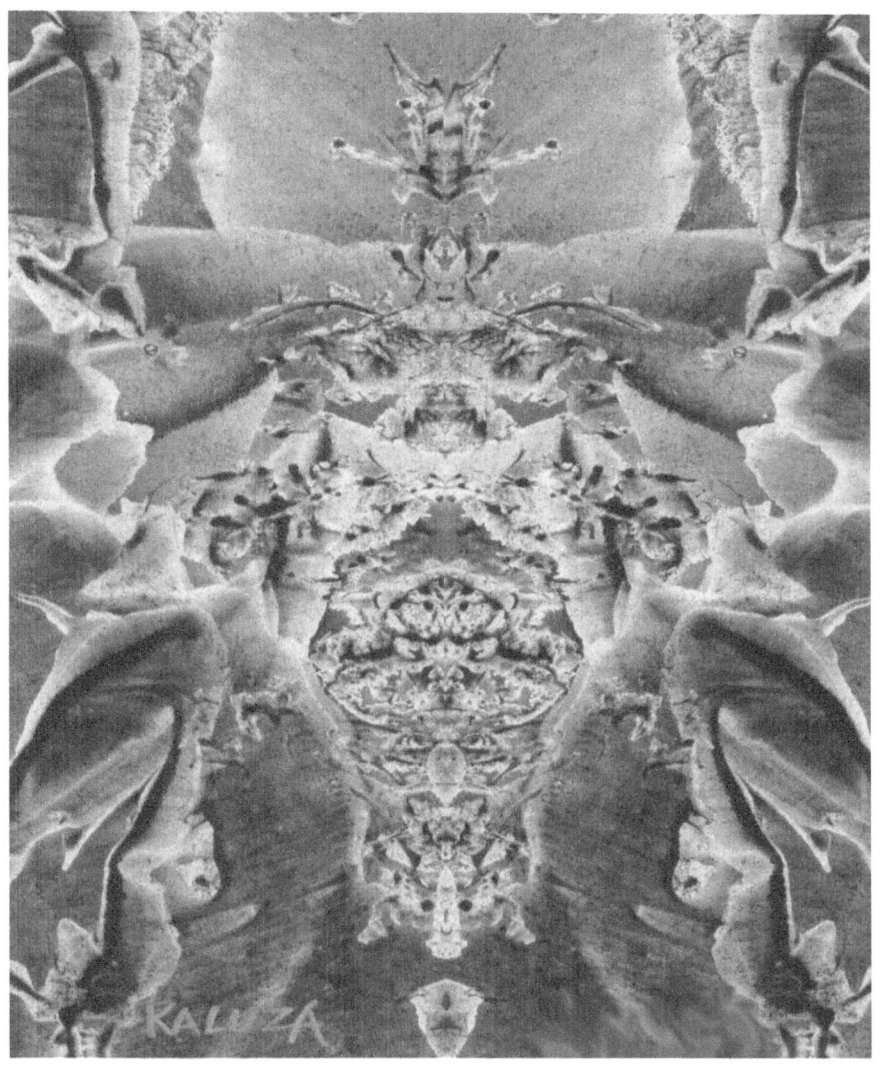

Face 3

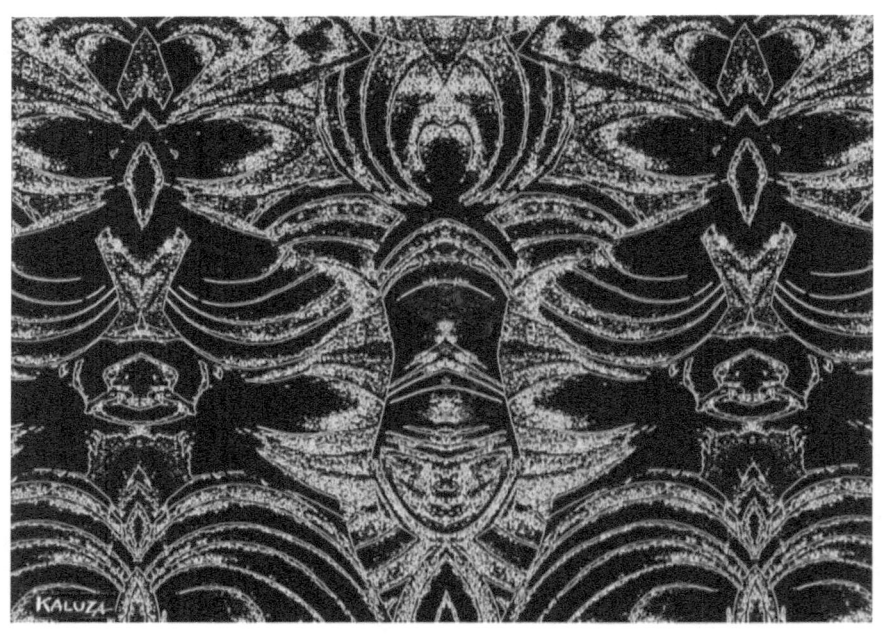

Design 54

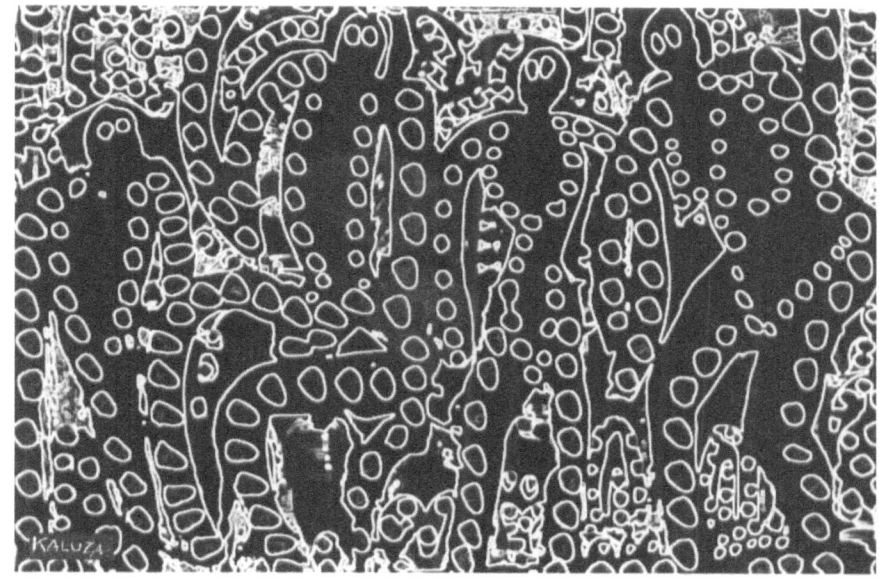

Four Friends

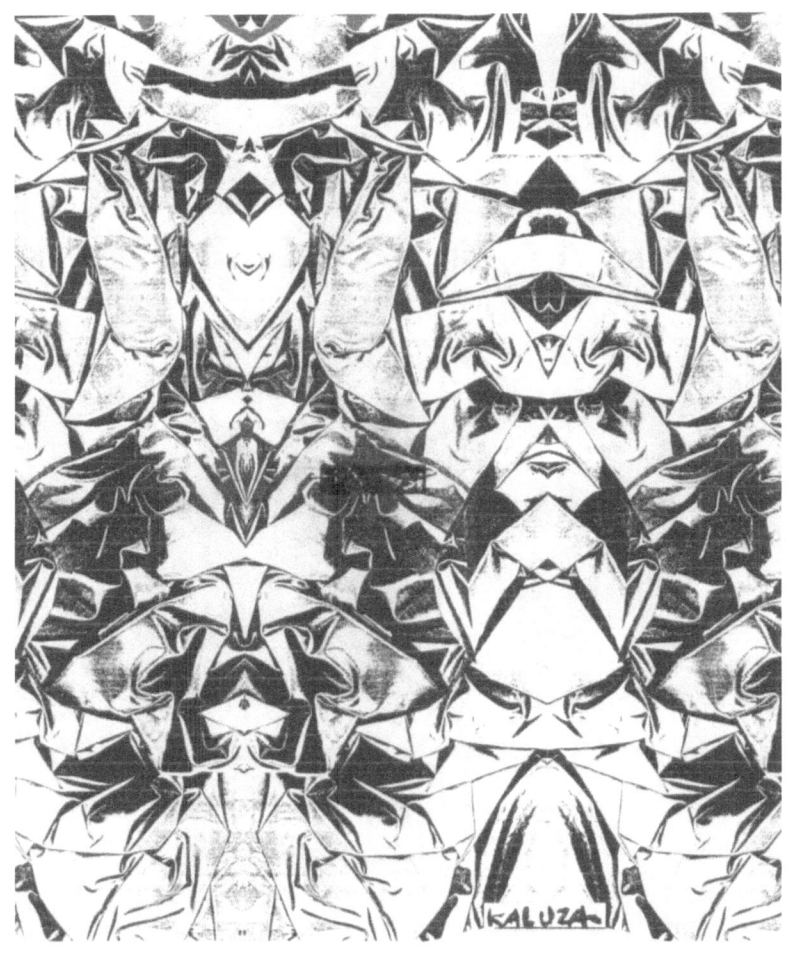

Alien Beings

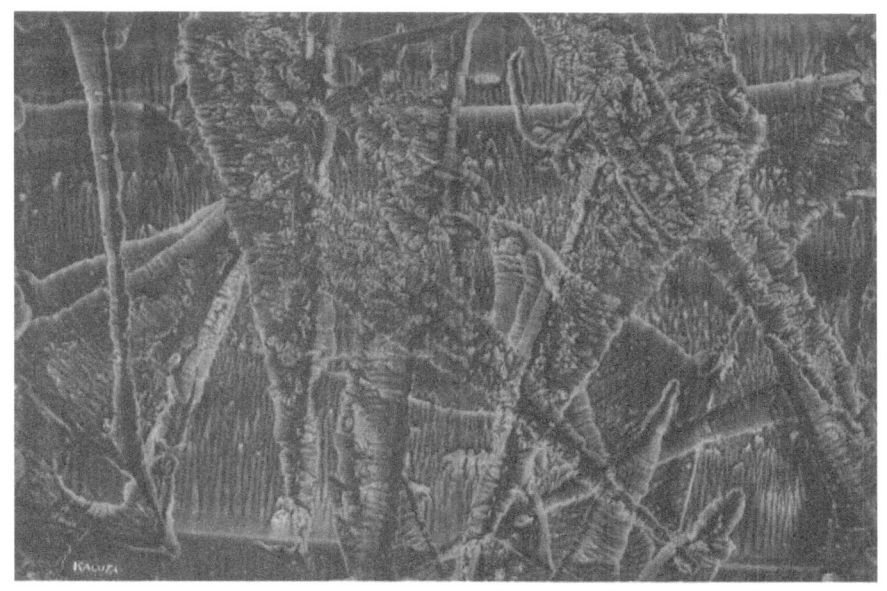

Cave Interior

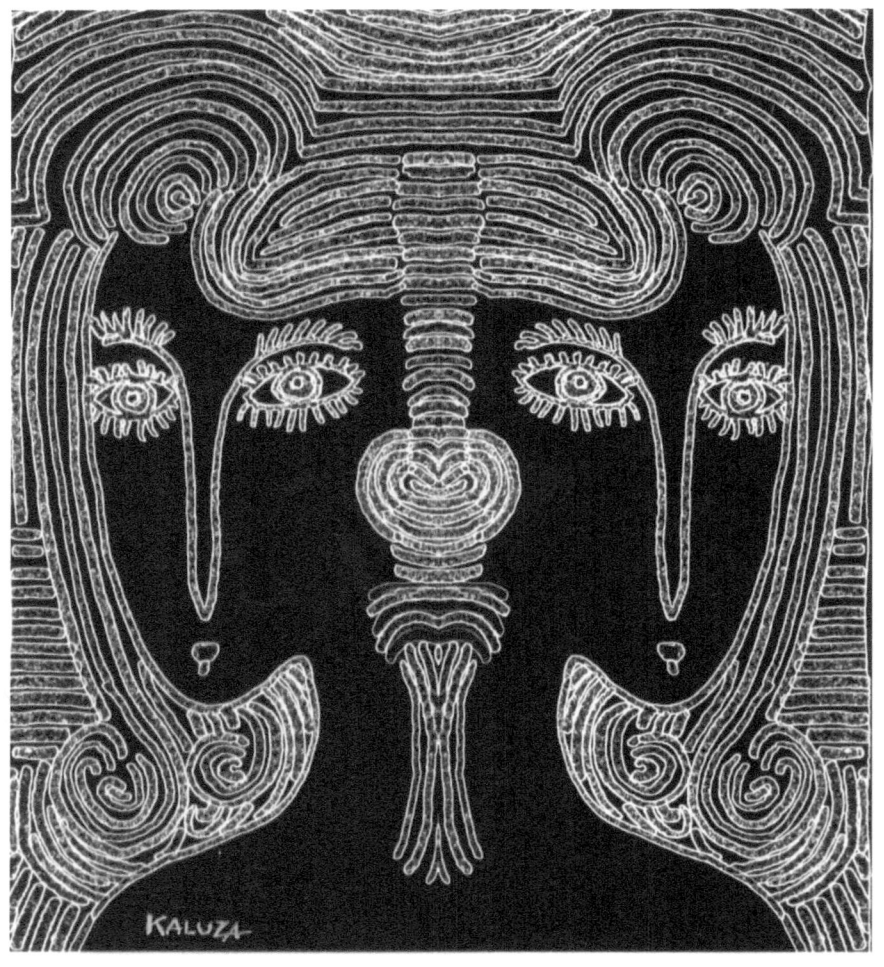

Twins

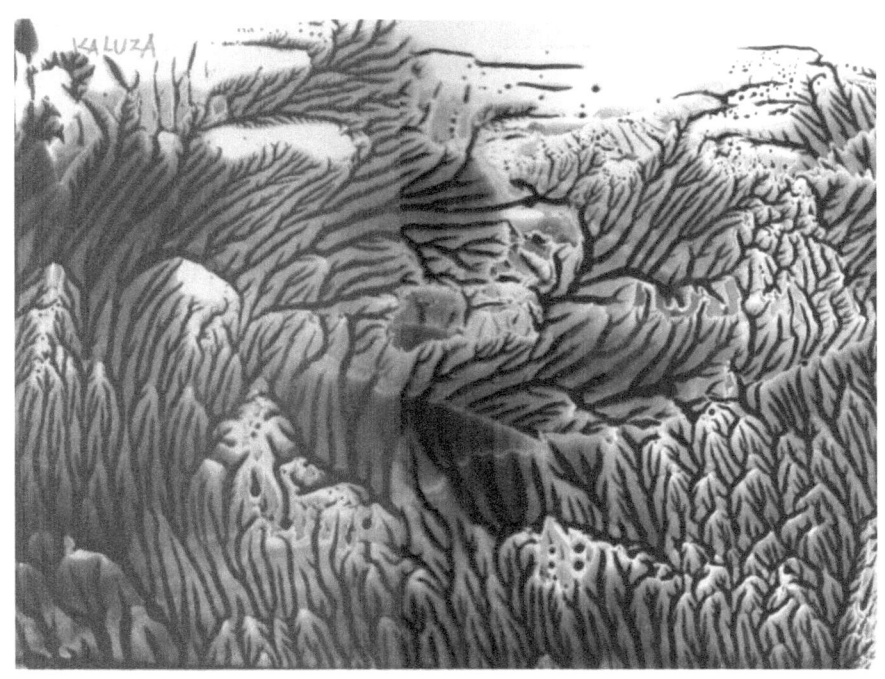

Dense Vegetation

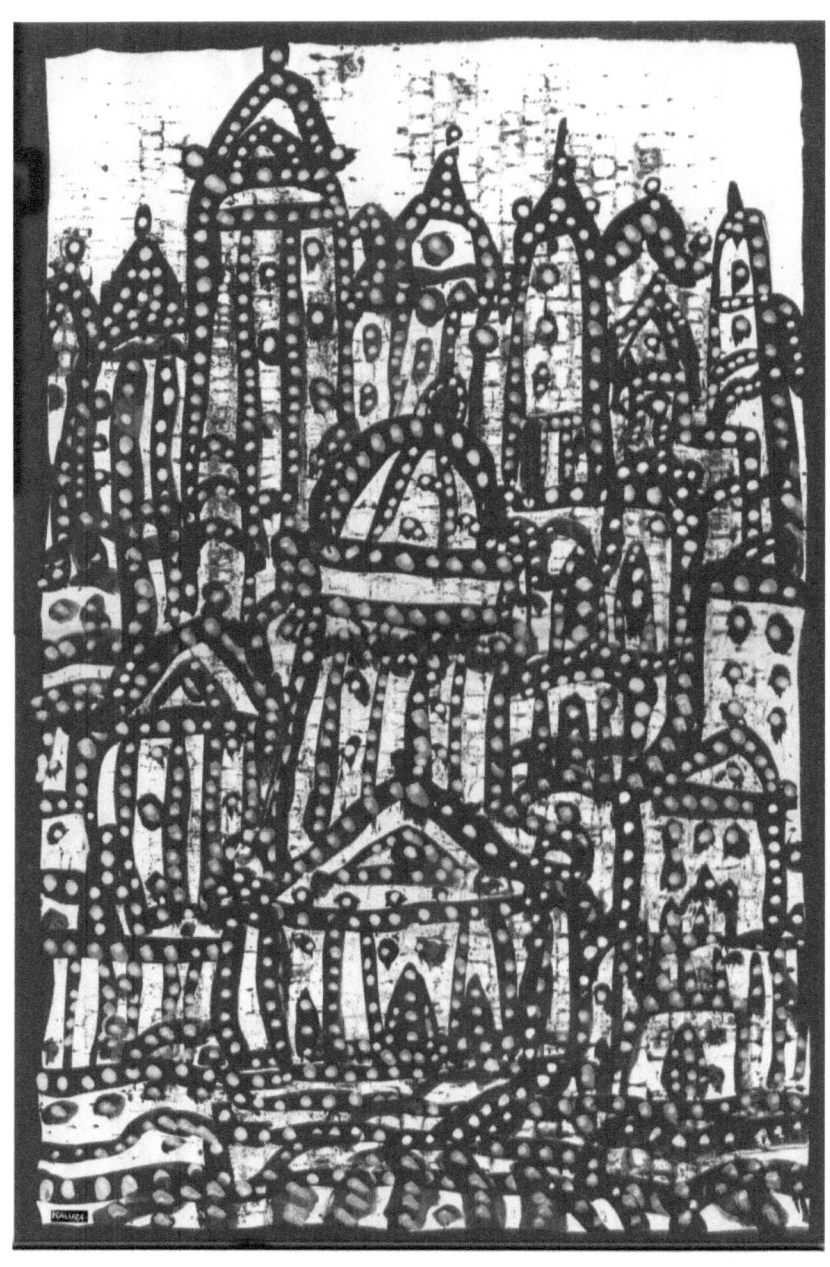

City 3

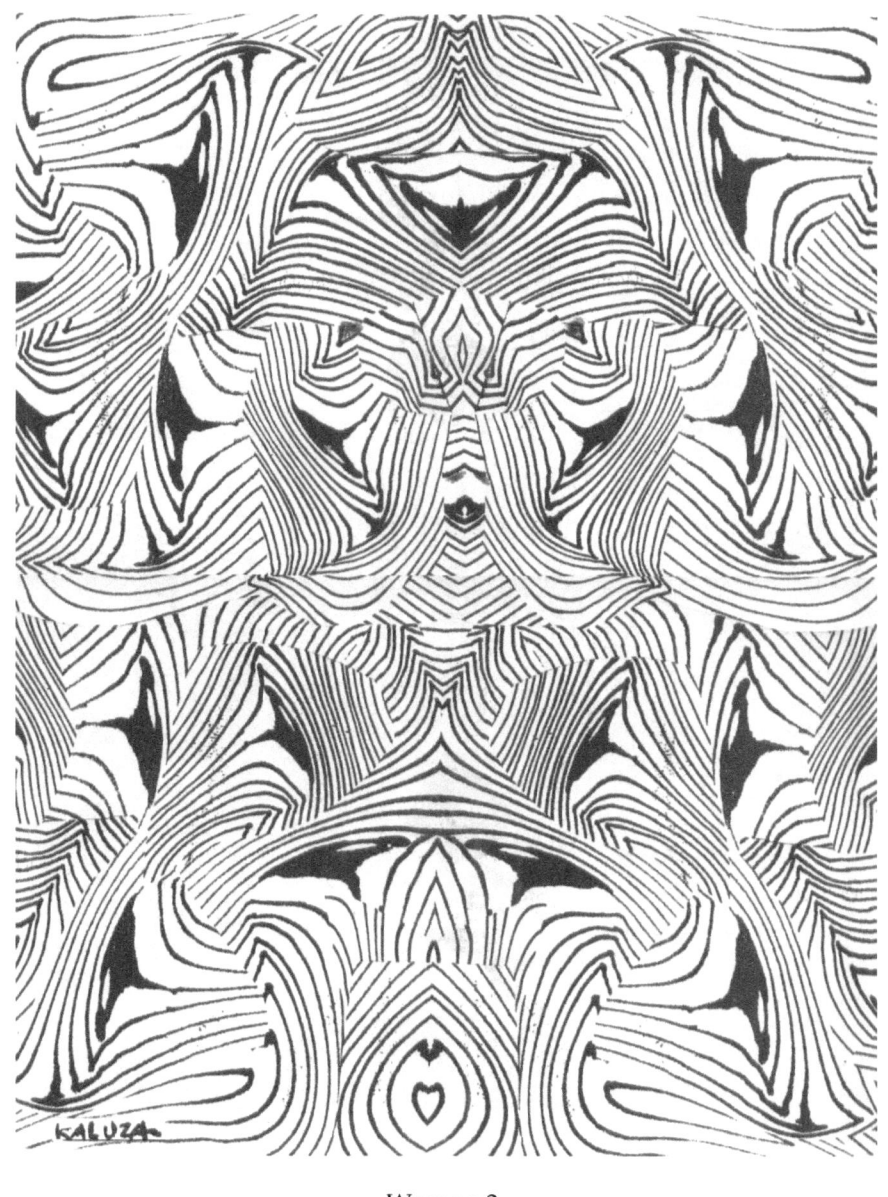

Woman 3

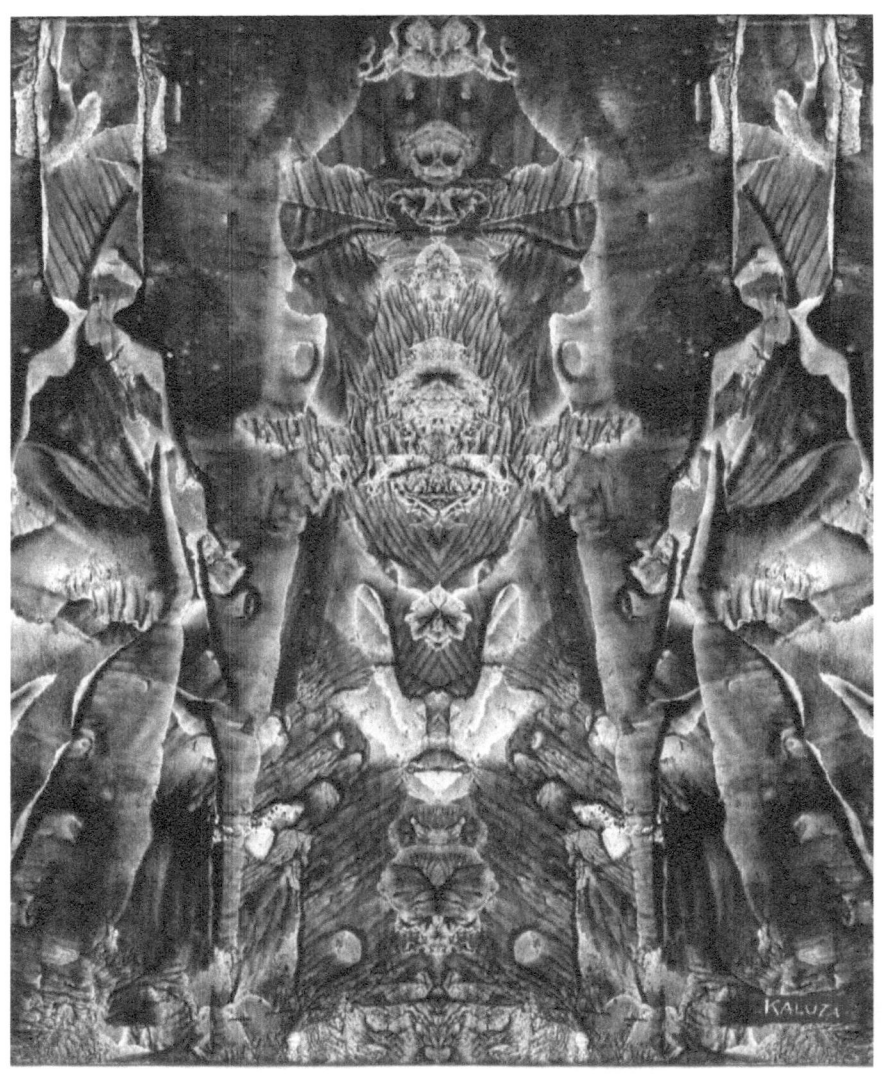

Emperess

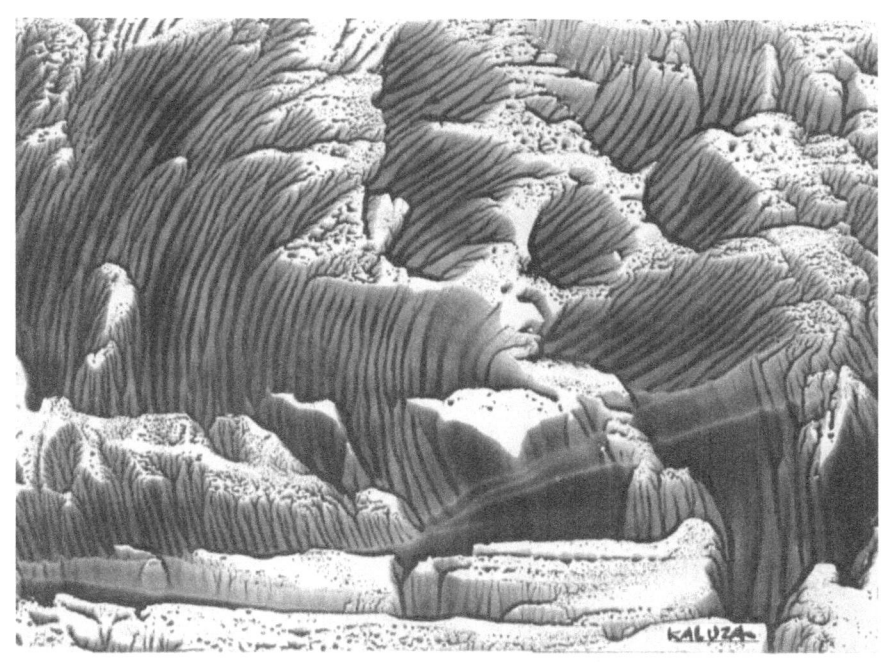

Windy Day

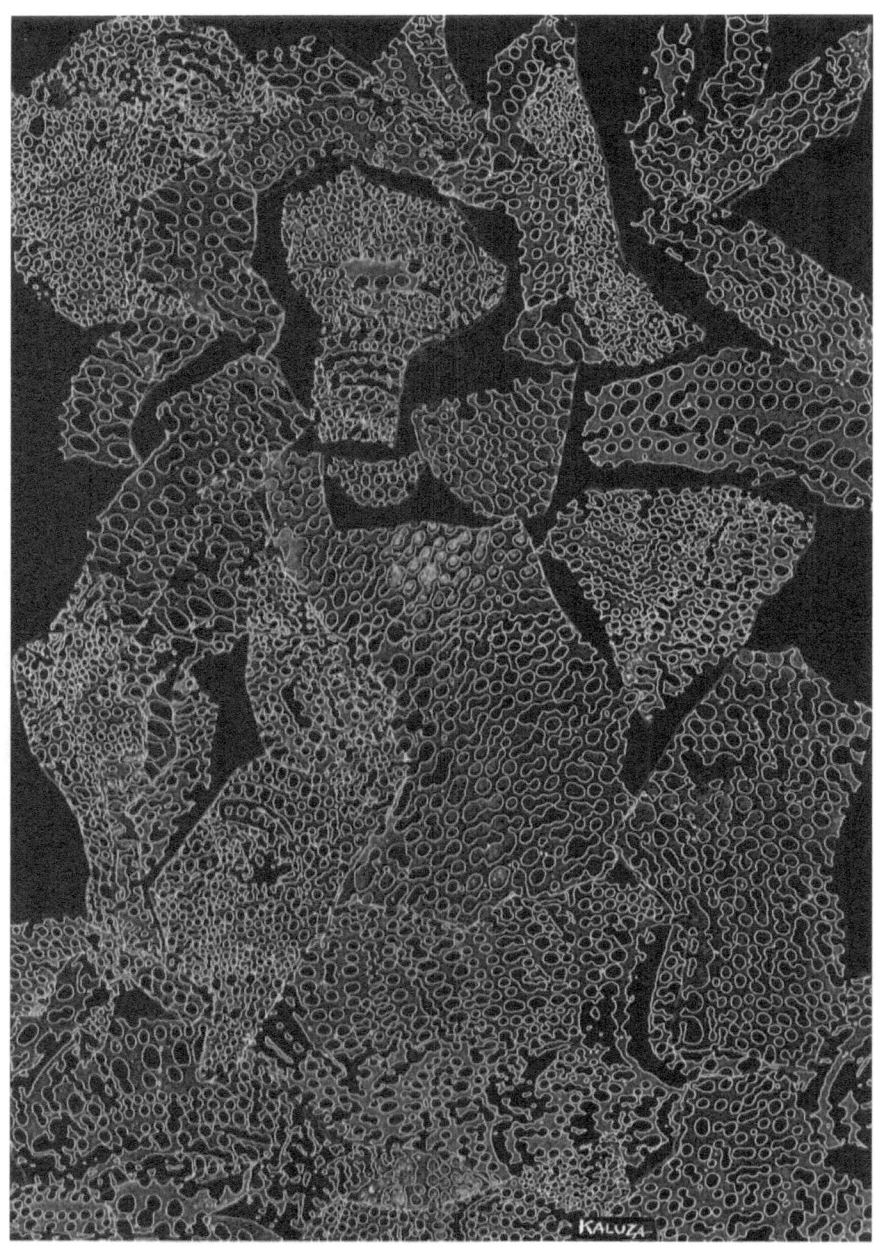

Ghastly Figure

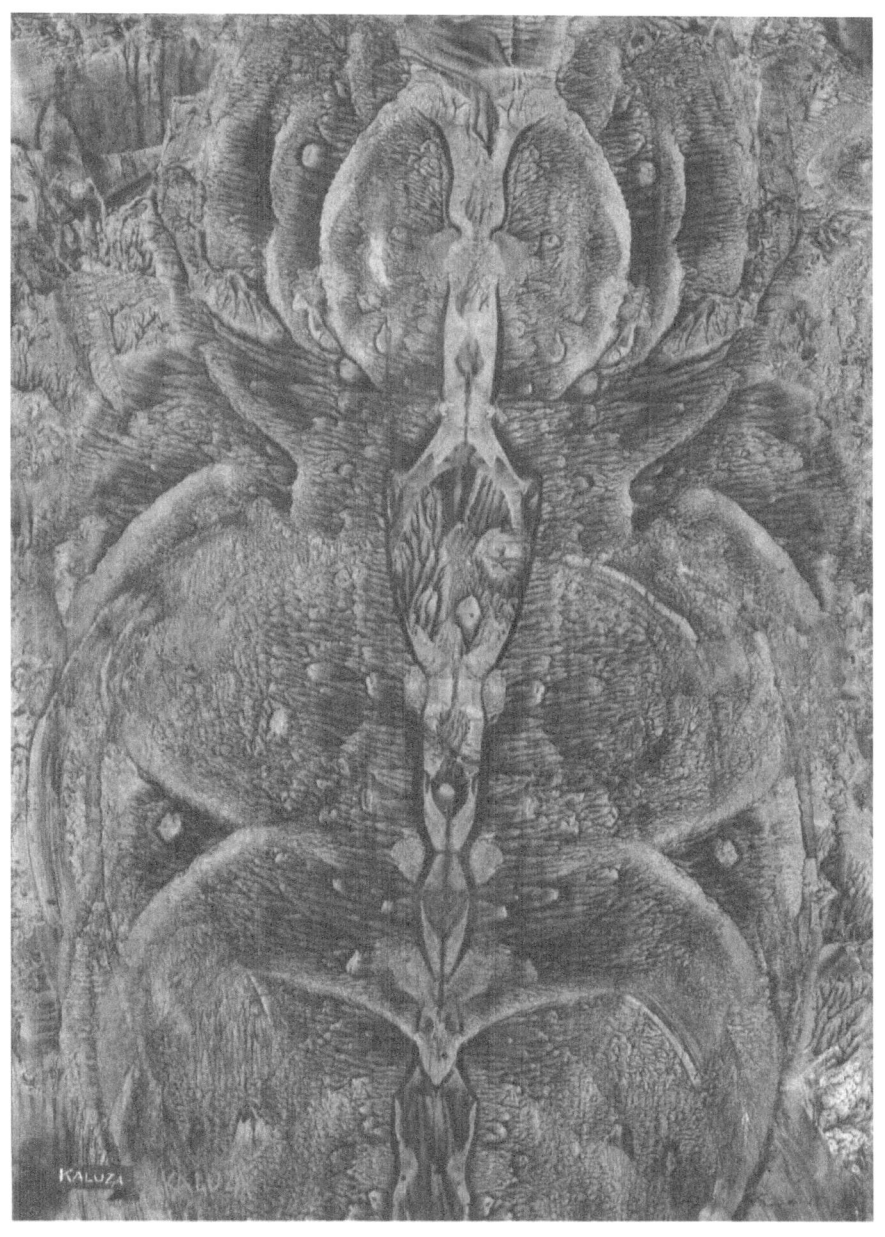

Alien Beauty

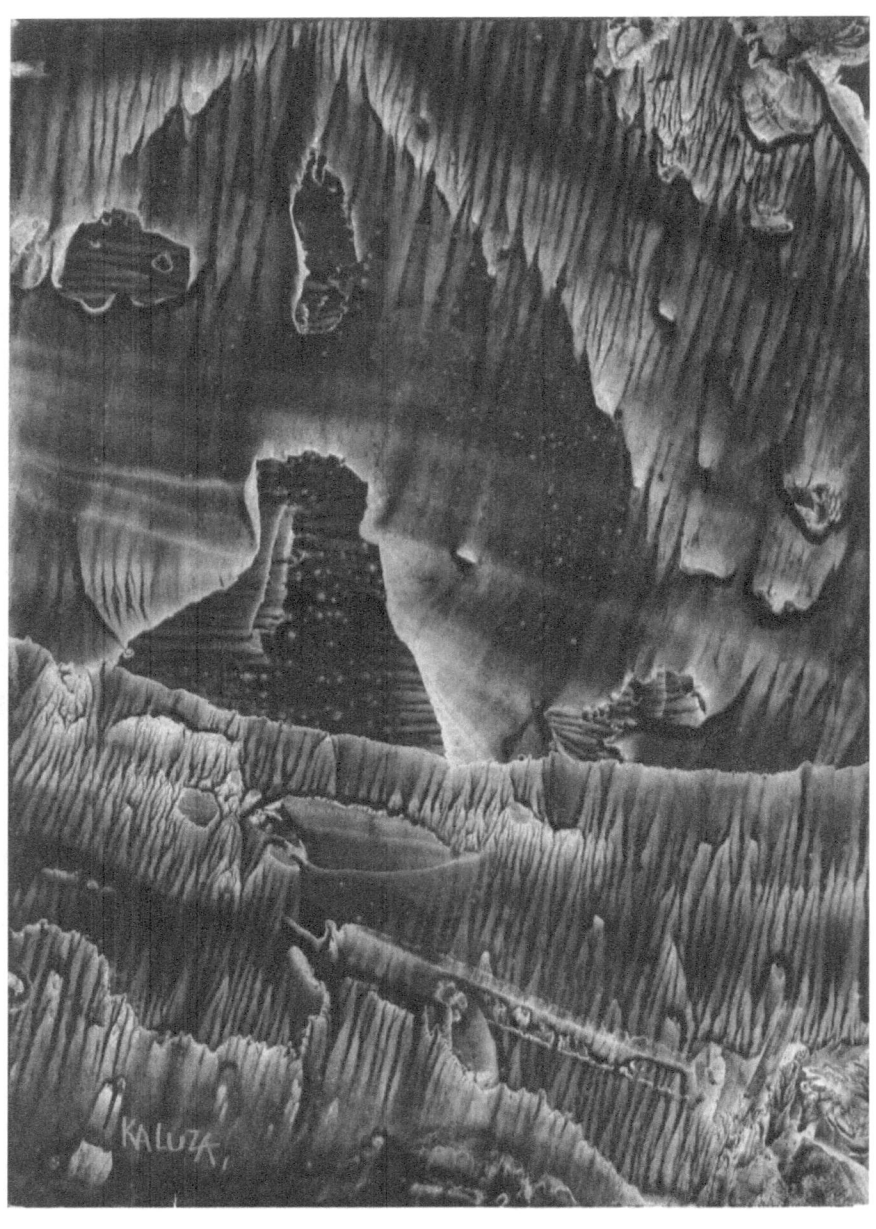

Entrance to the Netherworld

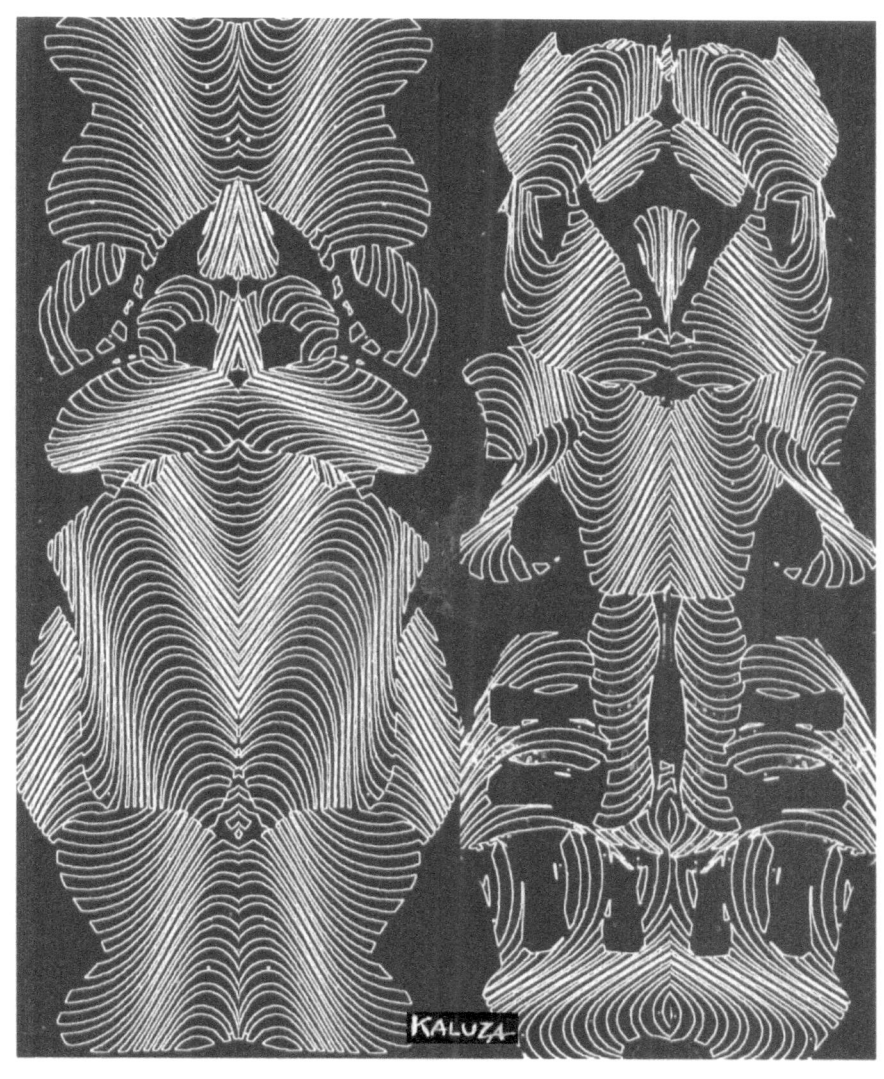

She and He

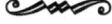